Wilmette Public Library
Wilmette, Illinois
Telephone: 256-5025

GAYLORD M

A Very Long Weekend

THE ARMY NATIONAL GUARD IN KOREA
1950~1953

WILLIAM BEREBITSKY
FOREWORD BY
LT. GENERAL HERBERT TEMPLE, JR. (RET.),
FORMER CHIEF,
NATIONAL GUARD BUREAU

 White Mane Publishing Company, Inc.

This White Mane Publishing Company, Inc. publication was printed by:
Beidel Printing House, Inc.
63 West Burd Street
Shippensburg, PA 17257 USA

In respect for the scholarship contained herein, the acid-free paper used in this book meets the guidelines for permanence and durability of the Committee on Production Guidelines for Book Longevity of the Council on Library Resources.

For a complete list of available publications please write:
White Mane Publishing Company, Inc.
P.O. Box 152
Shippensburg, PA 17257 USA

Library of Congress Cataloging-in-Publication Data

Berebitsky, William, 1939–
    A very long weekend : the Army National Guard in Korea 1950–1953 /
William Berebitsky : foreword by Herbert Temple, Jr.
        p.   cm.
    Includes bibliographical references and indexes.
    ISBN 1-57249-022-5 (alk. paper)
    1. Korean War, 1950–1953--Regimental history--United States.
    2. United States. Army National Guard--History. 3. United States.
    Army--Reserves--History.   I. Title.
    DS919.B47   1996   96-34615
    951.904'2—dc20   CIP

TO
THE MEN AND WOMEN OF THE NATIONAL GUARD
PAST, PRESENT, AND FUTURE

"Of the citizen army, the National Guard is in the first category of importance. It must be healthy and strong, ready
to take its place in the first line of defense in the first weeks
of an emergency, and not dependent upon a year or more of
training before it can be conditioned to take the field against
a trained enemy."

General of the Army
George C. Marshall
September 1, 1945

It is never too late to tell the story of what patriotic men
suffered in the defense of Constitutional liberty and the
Union of a nation. . . . It is never too late to tell the story of
man's inhumanity to man. . . . It is never too late to tell the
truth, although the truth may be sharper than a two-edged
sword. . . . It is never too late to inspire our young men to
love, and venerate, and defend the Flag of their country; to
tell them of how their fathers suffered in support of a prin-
ciple. No, it is not too late to tell this story and I have no
apologies to offer any man, living or dead, for telling it.

William W. Day I
a Private of 60, D, 10th Regiment
Wisconsin Volunteer Infantry
1889
The Running Wounded
William W. Day IV

CONTENTS

FOREWORD

Bill Berebitsky has superbly captured a little known feature of the Korean War, the role of the Army National Guard.

The story of both individual Guardsmen, and the forty-three Army Guard units that served in Korea are the focus of this accounting. The nine Guard artillery battalions that helped hold the line in April and May of 1951, and the two distinguished Guard Infantry Divisions, the 40th and 45th that joined Eighth Army in 1951 and 1952, are covered in detail.

Berebitsky records this very controversial period in U.S. foreign policy, and the internal political influences effecting the decision to mobilize citizen-soldiers to fight this country's first battle with communism. Through official records and the eyes of the Guardsmen who went to Korea the events from the local armories to the foxholes are told.

As a member of the 40th Division (there are no former members, once a member always a member) many of the names are familiar to me. They were and are magnificent examples of the modern militia. Although the 45th Division names are less well known to me, their reputations place them among our Army's finest.

Of particular interest were the accounts of professional malice, petty jealousies and prejudice Guardsmen suffered as they prepared for combat and service to their Nation. Regrettably, today's Guardsmen endure similar dispositions.

Herbert R. Temple, Jr.
Lieutenant General USA (Ret.)
Chief, National Guard Bureau
August 1986–January 1990

ACKNOWLEDGMENTS

Many men across our wonderful country helped make this book possible. They patiently answered my questions and requests for more information no matter how many times I bothered them. To list them all would take another volume. A special thanks to the following retired National Guardsmen and gentlemen. They helped me, and they served our nation well.

Brig. Gen. Don Mattson, curator; Mr. Bill Davies, librarian; Mr. Don Carmody, and the volunteers at the California Citizen Soldier Museum, Sacramento, California; Mr. Mike Gonzales, curator; Maj. Gen. Fred Daugherty, archivist; Brig. Gen. Rex Wilson, and the volunteers at the 45th Infantry Division Museum, Oklahoma City, Oklahoma; Maj. Gen. Bruce Jacobs, Historian Emeritus at the National Guard Association, Washington D.C.

Mr. Roland Baxter, Brig. Gen. George Brooks, CWO John Bushart, Mr. Bob Bryan, Mr. Thomas Cacciola, Col. Jess Carranza Jr., Mr. Bob Crews, Mr. Bill Day, Maj. Gen. James Delk, Mr. George Ellis, Mr. Ken Erckenbrack, Mr. Bob Faken, Mr. H. C. Fortenberry, Lieut. Col. George Gatliff, Mr. Jim Hester, Brig. Gen. Don McClanahan, Lieut. Col. Ralph Mueller, Col. Ezequiel Ortiz, Mr. Don Parrott, Maj. Gen. Red Pleasant, Lieut. Col. Charles Rice, Capt. Shelby Stanton, Mr. Bob Steffy, Mr. Richard Stinson, Mr. Sid Sultzbaugh, Mr. Raul Travino, Maj. Gen. Thomas Turnage, Lieut. Col. Dick Wainwright, CWO Bill Whitt, and Mr. Bert Yoder.

Also MAJ Michael Armour TNNG, SGT Don Garrison ARNG, and Ms. Renee Hylton at the National Guard Bureau, Historical Services Division.

And a special thanks to my daughter Julie Berebitsky who corrected her dad's grammar and spelling and drove him through the streets of Washington, D.C. And to my wife Beverly who could decipher the tapes when an old tanker's ears failed him.

INTRODUCTION

To the men who fought in Korea over forty years ago it is known as the forgotten war. And with that there can be no argument. Fought between the total commitment and all encompassing victory of World War II and the quagmire of Vietnam, the war in Korea rates but a line or two in today's history books.

This is regrettable because the Korean War (and make no mistake, it was a war, not a police action, civil conflict, or anything else) set in motion a number of important changes in both the foreign policy and the military forces of the United States, changes that to a large extent are still in effect today.

When President Harry Truman sent American troops to Korea in June of 1950, he did so without consulting Congress. This action set a precedent that would be followed many times in the next four decades. It has now become common place for the chief executive to send forces into action whenever he feels the nation's interests are threatened, no matter how indirectly; Lebanon, Panama, Grenada, and other little known corners of the world come quickly to mind.

Korea was the first war fought by the United States in which political considerations took precedence over military needs in the field. The decision to restrict Air Force and Navy planes from bombing Chinese bases in Manchuria cost countless American lives. Fifteen years later in Vietnam restrictions would again be placed on American air power.

Even more costly in American lives was the decision not to use the Nationalist Chinese forces on Formosa. From the opening days of the war Chiang Kai-shek had offered to send Nationalist infantrymen to Korea. The administration never took Chiang up on this offer, although General Douglas MacArthur, Commander in Chief Far East Forces, and his successors, Lieutenant General Matthew Ridgway and General Mark Clark, wanted to utilize the Nationalist troops.

After the Chinese Communists entered the war in October and November of 1950, MacArthur proposed letting the Nationalists invade mainland China, thereby diverting Communist troops from Korea. Plans to implement this operation were drawn up but never used. The British, fearing that any use of Chiang's troops might lead to a Communist move against Hong Kong and other British outposts in Asia, were aghast at the idea. Chiang's army sat out the war on Formosa, while Americans fought and died in Korea.[1]

Korea became America's first war of containment. The initial purpose of American involvement, to save the country of South Korea, was accomplished October 9, 1950, when South Korean troops crossed the 38th Parallel separating the two Koreas. By then, Truman, with the backing of the United Nations, had decided to continue on into North Korea. U.N. forces would clean out the Communists and unite the country under a democratic government.

Led by American tanks, South Korean troops captured the North Korean capital of Pyongyang, October 19. And on November 17, 7th Infantry Division patrols reached the Yalu River separating North Korea from Manchuria. The Chinese intervention and ensuing retreat back below the parallel killed the dream of a united Korea.

In June of 1951, a rebuilt Eighth Army again pushed the enemy out of all but a small corner of South Korea and advanced roughly twenty miles into North Korea on the central and eastern fronts. But this time there would be no pursuit deep into North Korea. The administration, realizing the unpopularity of the war with the American public and the amount of casualties another drive to the Yalu would incur (if indeed, it could be accomplished), stopped the advance at this point. The line stabilized and both sides dug in. For the next two years, thousands of men would die on this line while the peace talks dragged on, first at Kaesong, then at Panmunjom.

On the military side, a poorly trained, under strength, peacetime Army of slightly over half a million men quickly expanded to three times that size. The belated realization that the Communists might precipitate another Korea at anytime, anywhere in the world, led to the deployment of American troops around the globe. Only with the apparent collapse of the Communist empire in 1993 did the Army start to shrink to pre-Korean War levels.

*   *   *   *   *   *

If the Korean War has been largely neglected in the history books, the story of the part played by the Army National Guard, the nation's oldest military service, can be said to be non-existent. The crucial role played by the Army National Guard during the Korean War can be divided into six parts.

1. The sending to Korea in the first three months of 1951, thirty Guard units primarily of battalion size, of both the combat and support arms. Eight of these units, 105 and 155mm field artillery battalions (FABs) would play a decisive role in stopping the Chinese spring offensive in April 1951.

2. The sending of two partially trained National Guard infantry divisions to defend Japan in April of 1951. Thus showing the Soviets that the United States intended to defend Japan while at the same time continuing the war in Korea. For nine months these two National Guard divisions would be the only major Army units in Japan.

3. The thousands of Guardsmen rushed to Korea as replacements in the first six months of the war. These men, pulled from their Guard outfits, rushed to Korea, and assigned to the battle worn units of Eighth Army played a major part in holding the line the winter of 1950–1951.

4. The sending of two National Guard infantry divisions to Germany where they joined North Atlantic Treaty Organization (NATO) forces facing the Russians, and eastern block armies. Guard units were also sent to Alaska, Iceland, Panama, and other strategic locations.

5. The immediate mobilization of twenty National Guard antiaircraft artillery (AAA) gun battalions to defend America's major cities against Russian air attack.

6. The mobilization in late 1951 and early 1952 of four additional National Guard infantry divisions. These units would be drained of thousands of men sent to Korea as replacements. They would also train thousands of additional troops and strengthen the General Reserve.

Would the war in Korea have had the same conclusion without the existence of the National Guard? Possibly, but the greater possibility is that without the National Guard atomic bombs would have been used in Korea, or elsewhere, and the world engulfed in nuclear flames.

Today, forty-five years later, few people recall the debate over using the bomb in Korea. Both MacArthur, and General Dwight Eisenhower had advocated their use from the start of hostilities. Truman first publicly stated consideration of using atomic bombs in Korea November 30, 1950, after the Chinese almost wiped out the 2nd Infantry Division at Kunu, and forced the 1st Marine and 7th Infantry Divisions to retreat from the Chosin Reservoir.[2]

In mid-January 1951, the Communists' offensive came to a halt; Eighth Army, now under Ridgway's command, slowly started moving north again. Then, on April 11, President Truman fired Far East Commander MacArthur over policy disagreements. A Gallup poll showed that only 29 percent of the public sided with the president on this decision. MacArthur flew home and on the 19th gave his famous "old soldier" speech to Congress. Truman's popularity now hit an all time low and Republicans started talking impeachment. Truman was now more determined than ever not to lose Korea.[3]

Three days later the Chinese launched their spring offensive; the biggest battle of the Korean War. Two hundred and fifty thousand Communist troops attacked along a forty mile front. Within a week the Chinese had pushed U.N. forces back thirty-five miles, inflicting 7,000 casualties. Once again the enemy stood at the outskirts of Seoul.

How far would the Chinese have advanced without the pounding given them by the eight National Guard artillery battalions? Another twenty miles? Another thirty miles? Would they have retaken Seoul and pinned the American and U.N. forces against the unfordable Han River? How far would the Chinese have advanced before Truman pulled the nuclear trigger? What then would have been the Soviet reaction? Would the Russians, who had exploded their first atomic bomb in 1949, have retaliated or would they have left their Asian comrades to their fate?

And what effect did the arrival of the two National Guard divisions in Japan, that same April, have on Soviet thinking? With Japan defenseless would the Russians have made the twenty mile trip from their bases on Sakhalin Island to Hokkaido? And what of the reinforcing of NATO by the two National Guard divisions sent to Germany in late 1951? Did their deployment change Russian strategy?

The answer to these complex questions may never be known. What is known is that in the spring of 1951 the world stood on the brink of World War III. Without the Army National Guard it might have gone over the edge.

In any book of this type, men and units who should have been recognized are not. The thousands of Guardsmen pulled out of their units and sent to Korea as replacements receive but a few lines. Nothing is told of the six Air National Guard squadrons that served in Korea and produced four aces.

This is the story of National Guardsmen from small towns and large cities all across our country. Men who spent a night a week and a couple of weeks every summer training the best they could with what they had. Training for a ground war that in this new atomic age everyone knew would never again happen.

This is their story. The story of the infantryman and the artilleryman, the tanker and the engineer, and all those who back them up. Those weekend warriors who in the summer and fall of 1950 answered the call like the Minute Men have always done in our nation's history. They wound up in a place many of them had never heard of and they did a job. And when the job was done they came home to those towns and cities and picked up the pieces of their lives. For many of them it was back to those nights at the local armory to prepare for the next call. Their story should have been told a long time ago. For all of them it was a very long weekend.

CHAPTER 1

CALL TO ARMS

In the predawn darkness of June 25, 1950, Korean time, the North Korean People's Army (NKPA) crossed the 38th Parallel into the Republic of Korea (ROK). Less than sixty hours later President Harry Truman was contemplating the mobilization of the National Guard.

On the night of June 26, Washington time, Joint Chiefs of Staff (JCS) Chairman, General Omar Bradley, and Army Chief of Staff (COS), General J. Lawton Collins told Truman that any commitment of U.S. ground forces would necessitate a calling up of Guard and Reserve forces.[1]

At this same meeting, Truman placed General Douglas MacArthur, Commander in Chief Far East Forces, in command of all American forces in the South Korean zone of operations. The president also decided to allow Air Force and Navy planes to support the reeling ROK Army south of the 38th Parallel. The decision to commit ground troops would be delayed on the hope that with American air power the ROKs would be able to stop the North Koreans.[2]

A combination of bad weather, poor air-ground communications, and a fluid, fast moving battle line caused the air support to be of little help. The front continued to move south and the hope that the 100,000 strong, American trained ROK Army—supposedly the best for its size in Asia—could throw back the North Koreans, was fading fast.

MacArthur flew to Korea for a first hand look at the situation on the morning of the 29th. After eight hours he had seen enough. On the flight back to Japan, MacArthur told reporters that he would recommend to the president that American ground troops be sent to Korea immediately. In Washington the Joint Chiefs of Staff had come to the same conclusion, and at 5:00 A.M., June 30, 1950, President Harry Truman, the sixth former National Guardsman to sit in the White House, authorized the movement of one regimental combat team (RCT) to Korea.[3]

Still the president hesitated to mobilize the National Guard. Perhaps when the North Koreans saw American uniforms they would turn around and go back across the border. This wishful thinking quickly evaporated on the rainy morning of July 5, north of Osan. The story of the deployment of Task Force Smith and the rest of the 24th Infantry Division is well known. Joined by the 25th Infantry, and 1st Cavalry Divisions, these brave men were rushed to Korea with inadequate equipment and training. Outnumbered and outgunned, along with the battered ROK Army they slowly retreated down the Korean Peninsula. Across the country, National Guardsmen waited and wondered if the call would come.

PRIVATE WILLIAM DAY IV.
"C" BATTERY, 300TH ARMORED FIELD ARTILLERY BATTALION (WYOMING).

We had just finished our two weeks summer training at Camp Carson, Colorado, and were waiting to go home. We had our gear loaded in the baggage car, the M-7s on the flat cars, and had boarded coaches for our long train ride back to north central Wyoming. It was already hot, another in a series of scorchers with the mercury in the nineties. It wouldn't be a pleasant trip in the non-air-conditioned coaches with only C-rations for chow. Just before we pulled out someone brought the news. South Korea had been invaded! I remember thinking, where is Korea? I had never heard of it![4]

Returning from Korea, Day attended college and entered the educational profession. In 1990, Bill Day would write a moving, personal memoir of his Korean service.

SECOND LIEUTENANT EMMETT BENJAMIN.
HEADQUARTERS BATTERY, 712TH AAA GUN BATTALION (FLORIDA).

I was horrified. While in Japan I had seen the sad shape of the four occupation divisions, but even knowing that I figured we would take them without too much trouble. A few weeks later I changed my mind.

Benjamin, who had recently returned from a year's duty in Japan, would go to Korea with the 773rd AAA Gun Battalion (New York).

The waiting and wondering ended on July 19.

I have authorized the Secretary of Defense to meet the need for military manpower by calling into active Federal service as many National Guard units and as many units and individuals of the Reserve forces of the Army, Navy, and Air Forces as may be required.

With these few words President Harry Truman mobilized the National Guard. Or had he?

The question centered on "as many National Guard units." Who would be mobilized and who would not? National Guard leaders had always assumed any mobilization would encompass the entire Guard. They had not planned for a partial call-up.

For the next three years the lives of National Guardsmen and their families would be in limbo. No personal decision, big or small could be taken without first thinking, "What if we get called tomorrow?" Whether to take a new job, buy a home, or start a family, all this and more had to be put on hold. The effect on morale was devastating. Guard leaders pleaded for a complete mobilization but the Army continued with its piecemeal call-up plan right through February 15, 1952, when the last Guard units were inducted into Federal service.

General Collins later stated that a lack of modern equipment to arm Guard units precluded a complete mobilization. Collins said it was decided to put the bulk of available funds into new equipment and call up only a minimum amount of troops from the civilian components.[5]

The manner in which the Army called National Guard units to active duty during the Korean War deserves some study. As had been the case in World War II, the Guard would be mobilized in increments, or, in other words, groups of units. There were however major differences.

In late August 1940, Congress federalized the entire National Guard, and on September 16, the first units left for their training camps. On June 23, 1941, the units in the twenty-second and last increment departed their home stations. In slightly over nine months the entire National Guard of 297,754 officers and men had been mobilized. In actuality it was much quicker. By March 5, 1941, 97.34 percent of the Guard had been federalized, a time period of just over five and a half months.[6]

During the Korean War a total of nineteen increments would be called in a stop and go pattern stretching from August 14, 1950, to February 15, 1952. Not only was the time period twice as long, but whereas in World War II the increments became smaller as they progressed (the last two increments in June of 1941, totaled less than six hundred men), the last two increments of the Korean period mobilized in early 1952, each comprised a full infantry division.

After the Inchon landing on September 15, 1950, and the ensuing advance to the Yalu River it appeared the war would be over by Christmas. Subsequently, the word came out of Washington on November 10, that no more National Guard units—Army or Air—would be ordered into service and no National Guard units were likely to be sent overseas.

A week earlier MacArthur's G-2, Major General Charles Willoughby, estimated the number of Chinese "volunteers" in Korea at a maximum of 34,000 troops. In fact, the correct figure was over 300,000, and more were crossing the Yalu River every night. And at 2200 hours on November 25, the Chinese Communist Forces (CCF) struck in force. A new phase of the war had begun, and five weeks later the first National Guardsmen landed at Pusan.[7]*

This pattern of "now we need them, now we don't" would be repeated time after time as the battle line moved up and down the peninsula and then stabilized. By the time the peace talks got under way on July 15, 1951, seventeen increments had been called. Again it looked like the war would soon be over, but the talks stalled and after an eight month cessation the Army activated two more National Guard divisions. The last National Guard unit to see service in Korea would not arrive until December 10, 1952, almost two years after the first Guard troops landed at Pusan.

The problem was that no one knew if the Soviets planned to limit the war to Korea, or if Korea was just a diversion and a prelude to World War III. Lieutenant General Matthew Ridgway, who would replace Lieutenant General Walton Walker, as Eighth Army Commander in December 1950, when Walker was killed in a jeep accident and later replace MacArthur as Commander in Chief Far East, was deeply concerned about a Russian move in Europe.

In 1950, the recently formed NATO was more a political debating body than a military force. Only two American units of any

---

* The designations G-1 through G-5 refer to staff positions and sections in a unit headquarters. G-1 Personnel; G-2 Intelligence; G-3 Operations; G-4 Supply; G-5 Civil Affairs. At regimental and lower commands they are preceded by the letter "S" rather than "G".

size remained in Germany. The First Infantry Division, the "Big Red One," and the two brigade Constabulary, forever remembered as the "Circle C Cowboys." Therefore, any time Moscow made a belligerent move during the Korean War, the Pentagon rushed more troops to Europe and activated more National Guard units. Eventually two National Guard infantry divisions, the 28th (Pennsylvania), and the 43rd (Rhode Island-Connecticut-Vermont), along with supporting units would be sent to Germany to bolster NATO.[8]

Before it was over, the number of units called included eight infantry divisions, three RCTs, and 266 separate battalions, companies, and detachments. Of these, two infantry divisions and forty-one separate units would serve in Korea. One hundred and thirty-eight thousand six hundred Army Guardsmen, including those called individually, would be inducted, about thirty-seven percent of the total Army Guardsmen available. The original call-up for a twenty-one month period would be extended in mid-1951 to two years.[9]

* * * * * *

It didn't take long for Truman's July 19 proclamation to take effect. By the 29th three increments comprising 106 battalion and smaller sized units had been alerted for an August call-up. A look at the composition of the first two increments, both alerted on July 22, confirms that the JCS had mixed thoughts on where the real threat lay. Of the twenty-four battalion sized units alerted, twenty were 90 and 120mm AAA gun battalions. These battalions, situated around major cities and military installations on both coasts, constituted the final line of defense in the event of a Russian air attack.[10]

Unit strength appears not to have been a consideration in these early call-ups. Headquarters & Headquarters Detachment, 30th Ordnance Battalion (New Jersey) departed for Fort Bliss, Texas, with twenty-two officers and men. A few weeks later Pennsylvania's 32nd Quartermaster Group, Headquarters & Headquarters Company, headed for Fort Devens, Massachusetts, with forty-eight officers and men on the roster.*

With the departure of the 2nd Infantry Division for Korea on July 20, only two Regular Army divisions remained in the United

---

* The question, "What was the first unit mobilized?" cannot really be answered. In all the increments the units are listed by state in alphabetical order within the six continental armies, starting with First Army. The first increment contained thirty-four units of various sizes, all inducted on August 14, 1950.

States at anywhere near full combat strength. The 2nd Armored at Fort Hood, considered unsuitable for Korean service, and the 82nd Airborne at Fort Bragg, being held back for any emergencies that might develop elsewhere.

As late as July 25, Collins still recommended against the mobilization of full National Guard divisions. He based his reluctance to mobilize Guard divisions on several facts and assumptions; some of his reservations made sense, others were questionable at best.

1. Collins voiced concern about the impact a call-up would have upon the economy and morale of the home areas of the selected divisions.

But the divisions then under consideration were spread out over an entire state, in some instances several states. Consequently, the impact on the local economy would be negligible. With casualty figures growing higher every day and the real possibility that Korea might have to be abandoned to the enemy, this was not the time to be concerned with civilian morale.

2. Collins thought the call-up of National Guard divisions would have no bearing on the fighting in Korea since it would take months for these units to be ready for combat.

True, but why wait? By now it should have been obvious that Guard divisions were going to be needed. If not in Korea, then in Europe or elsewhere. If nothing else to replenish the depleted General Reserve.

3. Collins stated that a shortage of shipping limited the Army's ability to move troops.

This argument made no sense. There were hundreds of Liberty and other type ships in the mothball fleet. These ships were being cut-up for scrap, sold, or given to our allies every day. By the time the Guard divisions completed their training these ships could have been back in service.

4. If Communist China entered the war three to six Guard divisions would have to be mobilized immediately. Collins felt calling them now might not be wise.

Again, why wait? Back on June 28, General Dwight Eisenhower, then president of Columbia University, had gone to the Pentagon for a briefing on the Korean situation. Ike was furious with the "business as usual" attitude he found and wasted no time in ripping into Collins and the other Army staff members. Lieutenant General Ridgway, then Deputy Chief of Staff for Administration, took notes on Eisenhower's visit.

General Eisenhower dropped in . . . [and] stated in most vigorous language and with great emphasis his feelings that we ought at once to begin partial mobilization; perhaps reinforce our European forces by a division or two; publicly increase our security measures throughout the country; at once remove the limitation placed on MacArthur to operate south of the 38th Parallel; even to consider the use of one or two atomic bombs in the Korean area, if suitable targets could be found. Even after this, a month later, Collins was still against activating National Guard divisions.[11]

While the debate over mobilizing National Guard divisions continued in Washington, in Korea the men of the three American divisions continued to fall back towards Pusan. In Japan the 7th Infantry Division, already picked clean of non-commissioned officers (NCOs) for the units in Korea, was being held back for MacArthur's planned Inchon invasion. In the United States the General Reserve was down to nothing. Every unit, with the exception of the untouchable 82nd Airborne had been stripped to the bone.

Clearly the time for talk was over. On July 31, six days after he had strongly spoken against the mobilization of Guard divisions, Collins proposed to the JCS that four National Guard infantry divisions and two National Guard regimental combat teams be activated.

The Joint Chiefs concurred, and while the proposal had to be approved by the secretary of defense, Louis Johnson, and authorized by the president (done on August 10), the alert went out to the selected units the next day, August 1, 1950.[12]

On July 21, Collins had asked General Mark Clark, Chief, Army Field Forces, for his recommendations in case National Guard divisions might be needed. On July 31, after much study, consultation, and revision, Clark made his final recommendations. They were: the 28th Infantry (Pennsylvania), the 29th Infantry (Virginia-Maryland), the 31st Infantry (Mississippi-Alabama), the 37th Infantry (Ohio), the 40th Infantry (California), the 43rd Infantry (Rhode Island-Connecticut-Vermont) and the 45th Infantry (Oklahoma). The four divisions and two RCTs finally selected and making up the fourth increment inducted September 1, were the 28th, 40th, 43rd, and 45th Infantry Divisions and the 196th (South Dakota) and 278th (Tennessee) Regimental Combat Teams.[13]

These first four increments provided the bulk of the National Guard units that would serve in Korea. Out of the remaining fifteen increments, only five battalions and two smaller units would see duty on the peninsula.

The Army gave the first units mobilized three weeks to prepare for induction into Federal service. This proved impractical due to the lack of manpower to process the mountains of paperwork involved and was soon increased to a month. Converting from National Guard to Army forms constituted a major problem for all of the mobilized units.

CAPTAIN LESTER HUDGINS, SR.
HEADQUARTERS, 231ST TRANSPORTATION TRUCK
BATTALION (MARYLAND).

I was the battalion adjutant. Fortunately, I was a school teacher and wasn't working in the summer, so I went on active duty early to begin some of the administrative processing prior to the main body being called up. There was a tremendous amount of work that had to be done, and it was mass confusion.

All of our records were on the old National Guard forms, they were like a little booklet. They had to be brought up to date, then put on the Regular Army forms. Allotments, which of course we had never had to be concerned with, and other things of that sort had to be taken care of.

In 1964 Hudgins became commander of the 229th Supply and Transport Battalion, the successor unit of the 231st.

Tragedy struck on the morning of September 5, when thirty-three National Guardsmen of the 109th Field Artillery Battalion, 28th Infantry Division, died in a train wreck near Coshocton, Ohio. The unit, from the Wilkes-Barre area of Pennsylvania, was en route to its training station at Camp Atterbury, Indiana, when the accident occurred.[14]

So while most units continued their monthly training routine, other outfits, sometimes from the same city or town, headed off to training camps and an uncertain future.

CHIEF WARRANT OFFICER JOHN HOLT.
HEADQUARTERS, 231ST TRANSPORTATION TRUCK
BATTALION (MARYLAND).

We left for summer camp that year on 8 July, two weeks after the war started. While we were at camp a lot of Regular Army officers were observing us. Then General Mark Clark inspected us. If there was ever a tip off that we were going to be activated that was it. Four star generals don't inspect National Guard truck outfits unless something is being planned for them. We got home and were notified on 29 July that we would go on active duty 19 August.

Following his Korean service Holt remained on active duty for another four years before joining the Army Reserve.

CORPORAL THOMAS CACCIOLA.
"A" BATTERY, 955TH FIELD ARTILLERY BATTALION
(NEW YORK).

The trip from the old 14th Regiment Armory in Brooklyn to Fort Lewis, Washington, was indeed very different. It took approximately five days on the train but it felt more like forever.

It was August 29, 1950, and around 95 degrees when we descended into the caverns of New York's Grand Central Railway Station. I recall we were in full gear and wearing the heavy HBT [herringbone twill] fatigues. We boarded a Pullman train at 7:00 PM and finally pulled out about midnight. The windows were locked shut; not a whisper of air traversed those cars.

We were told that the train was air conditioned and I guess by the standards of 1950 it was. Huge blocks of ice, 5'x3'x9", were placed at the bottom of the cars and a tiny 5" fan then blew the ice cooled air over us. It didn't help much. Once we left the New York underground the heat and smell intensified. After a few hours the odor of sweaty bodies made you nauseous.

The train, about twelve cars long, was pulled by two coal fired steam engines. Before long everything in the train, including our food and coffee, was covered by a fine coating of black coal dust. I remember we used paper plates and cups, not our mess gear.

There wasn't much to do. I had a small checker board set and played checkers all the way across the country. Other than that I read a lot of magazines and enjoyed the scenery. We went the northern route, and I recall near Helena, Montana, seeing a sign that said 'Look out for bears.' On the morning of the fifth day, September 2nd, we finally arrived at Fort Lewis.[15]

Cacciola went to work for the Defense Department soon after returning from Korea. A pharmaceutical inspector, he worked all over the world before retiring in 1988.

PRIVATE ROBERT APPLEBY.
131ST TRANSPORTATION TRUCK COMPANY
(PENNSYLVANIA).

We were at annual training at Camp Perry, Ohio, when we got our mobilization orders. We never heard about Korea or anything else. All we knew after a few days, word came down through some of the senior NCOs that we would be mobilized and we could be going to Korea. None of the young people like myself knew anything about Korea. We just took it in stride.

They told us when we got home from annual training we'd have thirty days to get ready. We stayed at the armory for several weeks into early September. We had to prepare what vehicles we had and nail them down on flat cars. Then the troop train came in and we went down to Fort Bliss, Texas.

Appleby remained in the National Guard after his Korean service. In 1991, after forty-three years service, the one time truck driver retired as a major general.

SERGEANT AMON BAUMGARTEN.
106TH ORDNANCE COMPANY (MISSOURI).

We were associated with an ordnance company down there (Fort Hood, Texas). They kind of used us the way they wanted to. I got assigned to a dump truck hauling dirt around for some reason or other. There was a little problem between the Guard and the Regulars. I think they thought we were invading their territory or something.

Baumgarten, who had served in the Korean occupation now made the Army his career. He would serve another tour in Korea, in the sixties.

"They kind of used us the way they wanted to." With that short sentence, Sergeant Baumgarten summed up a major problem for the smaller mobilized National Guard units. Attached to large Regular Army organizations for logistical and administrative support, the Guardsmen were looked upon as a manpower pool for any fatigue detail that came along. Typical was the treatment received by the 107th Transportation Truck Company (Alabama) attached to the 12th AAA Group at Fort Bliss, Texas.

From the 107th's command report:

Normal operation and training was conducted with only two (2) Officers and fifty (50) EM (enlisted men) available. The remaining strength of the Company were utilized for practice of a parade for fourteen (14) days to honor the retirement of the commanding general of Fort Bliss, Major General Homer. The same personnel were then utilized for a period of ten (10) days to practice and conduct a parade upon the arrival of the new commanding general, Major General Lewis. With a total of sixty-six (66) EM absent from the unit on DA (detached assignment) and TDY (temporary duty) and the above mentioned personnel engaged in conducting parades, the company was able to conduct little training in vehicle driving and maintenance.[16]

PRIVATE FIRST CLASS THOMAS TILLMAN.
107TH TRANSPORTATION TRUCK COMPANY (ALABAMA).

It was hot and windy. We were in Logan Heights, Fort Bliss. I think they moved a lot of National Guard units in there that were activated, into Logan Heights. We had four man huts that we stayed in. Myself and about three others were put on temporary duty, while I guess everybody else was going through basic training. I wasn't there a lot of the time until we shipped out.

We went over and ran the infiltration course. Remember Richard Widmark in "Take the High Ground"? Remember the infiltration course they shot over? That's what we did, the little group that I was with. We put the little charges in the holes, shot the machine guns over their heads, things like that. I believe then they had to walk up a hill and we'd shoot a 105mm howitzer over them. We didn't go back to the company until the overseas alert came.

Tillman, a Guardsman at age fourteen, later attended the University of Alabama on a football scholarship.

PRIVATE JOHN FUQUA.
2998TH TREADWAY BRIDGE COMPANY (TENNESSEE).

We did not have the slightest idea we would be activated. Why would they want us? Eighty-four men out of an authorized strength of 192 and not a single piece of bridge equipment. We had no training, no equipment, no nothing. We would have been pushed to make a good ditch digging unit.

We got sent to Fort Campbell, Kentucky. We went through our basic training, but received no bridge equipment or training. We didn't even see a picture of one. On our way to Korea we were diverted to Japan. We were supposed to get our equipment and training there. But we just sat around for three weeks or so before going over to Pusan. That's when we saw our first bridge and it belonged to another outfit.[17]

Fuqua is now Director of Youth Services at the Gibson County Juvenile Court, in Trenton, Tennessee.

By August 19, forty-five days after the men of Task Force Smith fought the North Koreans near Osan, Guard units from sixteen states and the District of Columbia who would serve in Korea had been mobilized.

CAPTAIN BEDFORD BENTLEY.
COMMANDING OFFICER (C.O.), 726TH TRANSPORTATION TRUCK COMPANY (MARYLAND).

We loaded everything we had on flat cars and went up to Camp Edwards, Massachusetts. The trip from Baltimore took about two days. We had signed up some new men before we left but were still a long way from our full complement.

At Edwards we filled up to full strength fairly fast. Most of the new men were Regular Army or recalled Reservists and didn't need basic training. We did of course have to give basic to the recruits. We gave them a combination of basic and truck driving training and it worked out quite well. A commander always wants more time for training, but I thought we were in pretty good shape when we shipped out.

Bentley, who had served in World War II with the famed "Red Ball Express" transferred to the Army Reserve upon his return from Korea. He retired as a major in 1972.

SERGEANT FIRST CLASS J. BRUCE COWPER, JR.
"C" COMPANY, 101ST SIGNAL BATTALION (NEW YORK).

The only time we ever had an emergency muster was when we were called out for a snow storm or other natural disaster. So when one was called in early July we knew we were going to be mobilized. We had four weeks working seven days a week at the armory getting ready. We were allowed to go home at night. I was the supply sergeant and all of a sudden all this new equipment started to come in. I was busy just getting it all into inventory.

On August 19, 1950, we were federalized and marched down to the railroad station in Larkin Plaza, Yonkers. We were shipped to Camp Gordon, Georgia. At Camp Gordon we received some newer equipment and more men to bring us to full strength. Most of them were southern farm boys. We had some trouble training them to climb poles and string cable because they didn't want to wear boots and gaffs to climb. The farm boys became very important in Korea when we had to use donkeys.[18]

Back from Korea, Cowper became a Certified Public Accountant. Joining Bristol-Myers Corporation, he retired in 1990 as special assistant to the company vice president and comptroller.

PRIVATE ERIC HANSEN.
"A" BATTERY, 204TH FIELD ARTILLERY BATTALION (UTAH).

We ended up in Fort Lewis, Washington, in what they called the North Fort. It was a mess when we first got up there. I recall the barracks were in terrible condition. I did quite a bit of painting on the exterior of the buildings for a couple of weeks. We cleaned them from top to bottom.

Later commissioned, Hansen became Executive Officer (X.O.) of "A" Battery before moving to California.

While there is no record that Private Hansen's battalion commander, Lieutenant Colonel Joe Whitesides, painted any barracks at Fort Lewis, he was anything but happy with the situation. Whitesides, a combat veteran artilleryman, wanted nothing more than to get his cannon cockers to the nearest firing range. Unfortunately, he was bogged down in paper work. He had this to say about his outfit's first months of active duty.

At the time of our induction, our battalion was satisfactory in all phases of administration. Our supply and personnel records were complete and we had satisfactorily passed our Federal inspection. At the time, we also had our administrative personnel well trained in handling National Guard regulations and National Guard supply and administrative procedures. BUT, after induction into Federal service, it took these same trained personnel more than two months to change our records so as to conform with Regular Army procedure!

During those two months, our combat training was greatly handicapped because of the many changes involved with each individual soldier—changes that were very time-consuming. Because of this, our unit accomplished more in actual combat training during our two-weeks National Guard summer camps than we did during the first two months of training after mobilization.[19]

CHAPTER 2

WE'RE GETTING READY TO GO TO KOREA

While Joe Whitesides fought his battle with Army paperwork, one of his new neighbors at Fort Lewis had problems of a different nature.

Traveling farther than any other Guard unit would go to reach its training station, New York's 955th FAB arrived at Fort Lewis, September 2. Short of key equipment, including 155mm howitzers, high speed tractors, and ammo trucks, the unit submitted requisitions for the needed items. The requisitions failed to bring any results; this was hard to understand, as much of the equipment could be seen parked in the post motor pool. The unit would sail to Korea still short some items.[1]

Other National Guard units training at Fort Lewis took note of the equipment parked at the post motor pool.

CAPTAIN THOMAS BRINKLEY.
COMMANDING OFFICER, 138TH PONTOON BRIDGE
COMPANY (MISSISSIPPI).

I was another one of the inactive Reserve officers called up in September. I got an S-2 job in an engineer combat battalion up at Fort Lewis. Suddenly, just out of the blue, they relieved the company commander of this bridge company and assigned me the job. I took over about six weeks before we shipped out. At this time the outfit did not impress me; in fact, depress was more like it. No discipline, the unit had absolutely no discipline. And they had been poorly trained, but even with all this I could see some real good potential in the company.

I had been told it was hard, if not impossible to transfer National Guardsmen out of their unit. But I proved different. I got rid of one officer and eleven men real quick and the company began to come together and shape up.

Lot of the equipment was World War II stuff and worn out. In the post motor pool, there must have been parked 400 brand new 6x6 trucks. I'm not kidding, it looked like 400 new trucks parked there. I made some inquiries as to how we could turn in the trucks we had and get some of these new ones. By now a lot of our equipment had already been loaded aboard ship and time was getting short.

I was told none of these trucks were going to be released because the spare parts kits for them had not arrived. So a few weeks later we boarded ship and sailed for Korea with what we had. When we got to Korea we had to tow six of our trucks from Pusan to our first assembly area. We could have used those new trucks, spare parts kits or not.

Brinkley had served in Korea during the occupation, after having seen combat in Europe.

Along with equipment shortages, New York's 955th FAB also had personnel problems. After four months without a medical officer one finally reported for duty—two days before sailing. Enlisted replacements also continued to arrive. Fortunately for the 955th, a few combat veteran artillerymen were among the men reporting for duty.[2]

SERGEANT WARREN ZIMMERMAN.
"A" BATTERY, 955TH FIELD ARTILLERY BATTALION
(NEW YORK).

I first enlisted back in '39, saw combat in the Pacific with the 81st Infantry Division firing 105mm howitzers. I was working in Hayward, California, when the war broke out and heard on the radio they needed men with my MOS. They were actually advertising on the radio by MOS! I went to Oakland, signed up, and in a few days was at Fort Lewis, my first duty station back in '39.*

---

* MOS / Military Occupation Specialty. A number and designation that describes a soldier's job. Eg. 1745-Light Weapons Infantryman (Korean War era).

Got assigned to "A" Battery of the 955th FAB, a New York National Guard outfit. Sergeant Mullins was the first sergeant. He was real nice, the whole outfit was just like his own family, he had grown-up with all the kids. They had a lot of real young people. I knew they needed my knowledge as a combat artilleryman. I liked the outfit.

Zimmerman remained in the Army for another hitch before becoming an electrical contractor in California.

By October 1, forty of the forty-three National Guard units that would serve in Korea had reported to posts all across the country. They slowly filled up to TO&E strength and commenced training.*

Ranging in size from small headquarters detachments to full infantry divisions, the units were not all as lucky as the 955th in getting veterans like Sergeant Zimmerman.

PRIVATE HARRY SHOLLENBERGER.
121ST TRANSPORTATION TRUCK COMPANY (PENNSYLVANIA).

We got a few stray RAs (Regular Army personnel), they were okay. Then we got about 15 recalled Reservists, most of them were okay, too. Then we got about 30 or 40 men from units on post (Fort Eustis, Virginia). They emptied out the stockade; they were a pretty rough lot. Some of them had two or three court martials. The drivers got along good, we settled our own differences.

Shollenberger remained in the Guard, retiring after twenty-three years service as a staff sergeant.

The recalled Reservists that Shollenberger mentions constituted an important source of manpower for the under strength mobilized Guard units. When an appeal for volunteers met with little response, the Army, on August 10, involuntarily recalled 7,862 captains and lieutenants, plus 1,063 Army Medical Service officers. This was soon followed by another call-up of almost 10,000 more officers and 109,000 enlisted Reservists. The recall of these men who had fought their war five years earlier and who had virtually no contact with the Army since, led to much controversy in Congress, the media, and throughout the nation.[3]

---

* TO&E / Table of Organization and Equipment. Army manuals that list how many men each type unit has at full strength. The rank the men are authorized to hold, their jobs, and the weapons and equipment they are equipped with.

FIRST LIEUTENANT DAVE MATTESON.
"A" COMPANY, 378TH ENGINEER COMBAT BATTALION
(NORTH CAROLINA).

I was working for Pacific Telephone in San Francisco. We had just had our second daughter; she was three months old. I was in the inactive Reserves and hadn't heard a word from the Army in four years, not a word. I didn't think there was a chance I'd be called. My wife called me at work one day. We had received a big fat envelope from the Army. I told her to open it. The orders said, "On or about 1 October 1950 you will report to the 378th Engineer Combat Battalion, Fort Lewis, Washington, for seventeen months active duty."

Four of us recalled officers showed up about the same time. Captain Bill Harper, First Lieutenant Peter Dragolovich, a second lieutenant named Thompson and myself. By then the unit had pretty well filled up. We didn't do extensive engineer training, but did spend some time on the firing ranges. We spent most of the time getting the men and equipment ready for overseas shipment.

Our C.O., Lieutenant Craig, made sure we took everything we would need and if he found something extra we took that too. Everyone was very friendly and some of the wives that had come out from Carolina would have us over for dinner. My platoon needed more training, but they were hard workers, a good bunch of GIs.

Matteson, a combat veteran of the European Theater resumed his career at Pacific Telephone upon returning from Korea. He retired after thirty-six years as an assistant vice-president.

While many of the recalled officers were happy to be assigned to Guard units, this feeling was not universal. Some of them made their animosity to Guardsmen, and their dislike of the National Guard, very clear.

CORPORAL CLARK FINKS.
"L" COMPANY, 223RD INFANTRY REGIMENT,
40TH INFANTRY DIVISION (CALIFORNIA).

Our unit was fairly complete, up to strength, and the NCOs had been to at least one or more summer encampments. The officers were mainly World War II veterans. However, upon being called into active duty, about two thirds of our ranks had to be let go, seeing that they had enlisted under age. Then, one by one, our officers either got transferred out of the company, got hardship discharges, etc., leaving us by Christmas of 1950 with just a handful of National Guardsmen in the ranks and new officers called back from the Reserves.

Our new company commander openly expressed disdain, if not loathing for the NGs of whom he talked about "getting rid of" as soon as possible! He soon did, filling the weekly drafts of replacements to be sent to Korea. I discovered later that I had missed the last draft by one line on the roster. The captain had just gone down the duty roster and picked all the NGs for the drafts, but the last draft stopped just one line short of my name.[4]

Returning from Korea, Finks earned a degree in International Affairs from Georgetown University and worked for the State Department in South America.

The dislike of National Guardsmen by officers of the Regular Army and Army Reserve was of course nothing new. And while not as pronounced during the Korean War as it had been in the 1940–1941 mobilization, this irrational thinking had by no means vanished.

A case in point: Colonel Frank R. Maerdian, West Point 1928. Arriving at Camp Polk, Louisiana, Maerdian assumed command of the 279th Infantry Regiment, 45th Infantry Division (Oklahoma). Maerdian quickly made his feelings very clear. Convening a special "officers' call," he stated that he "had no respect for National Guard officers." Maerdian's ridiculous remark becomes laughable considering that the majority of officers present were veterans of the 45th of which General George Patton rated "one of, if not the best division in the history of American arms."

Maerdian, an officer of "the old school," lived by the "book," seldom asking the advice of his officers and usually ignoring their suggestions. This seems unusual given the fact that most of Maerdian's West Point classmates were now wearing stars, and he could obviously use all the help he could get. In September 1951, with the 45th Division now in Japan, Maerdian departed the 279th, still a colonel.[5]*

Officers and men continued to arrive and depart National Guard units that hectic summer and fall of 1950 as the Army fought a war in Korea and expanded worldwide.

---

* The National Guard hadn't seen the last of Maerdian. In the spring of 1952, he took command of the 160th Infantry Regiment, 40th Infantry Division (California). By then the Guardsmen of the regiment had started home and were only under Maerdian's command for a short time.

CAPTAIN JOE NADER.
HEADQUARTERS, 101ST SIGNAL BATTALION (NEW YORK).

During World War II, I started out with the 27th Infantry Division (New York). After we got to Hawaii, I came back to the States for officer candidate school. Wound up in a signal outfit attached to the British Eighth Army in Egypt, got paid in British money, ate British rations. After that it was Sicily and then Italy. After the war I was in the inactive Reserve.

Soon after the war in Korea started I was attached to the 101st Signal Battalion, a New York, National Guard outfit, as a separate signal officer assigned to the S-3 section. About a month after I joined them, we were down at Camp Gordon, Georgia, and the Army pulled fifteen or so of us out of the battalion and shipped us out to various units. I stayed at Gordon with the Signal Corps Training Replacement Center. I never did get to Korea.[6]

Nader later joined the Army Reserve, retiring as a lieutenant colonel with twenty-eight years service.

As Clark Finks of the 40th Infantry Division previously mentioned, the action National Guard leaders feared the most had already started to occur. The Army, suffering heavy casualties in Korea, began pulling individual Guardsmen out of their units and shipping them to the front as replacements. In many cases it was the man no unit can afford to lose, the combat veteran, the man who knows how to get the job done and stay alive on the battlefield.

SERGEANT FIRST CLASS RALPH MUELLER.
107TH FIELD ARTILLERY BATTALION, 28TH INFANTRY DIVISION (PENNSYLVANIA).

I joined the 16th Infantry Regiment, 1st Infantry Division as a replacement late in the Sicily campaign in 1943. Landed on Omaha Beach 6 June 1944, and was with the regiment all through the European fighting as a squad leader and platoon sergeant.

After the war I enlisted in the 107th Field Artillery Battalion, 28th Infantry Division, Pennsylvania National Guard. We were on one of the first weekend drills, 25–26 June 1950, when the war started. We were mobilized on 5 September 1950, and moved to Camp Atterbury, Indiana.

On 20 October, I received orders to FECOM (Far East Command) on a special levy to the 1st Field Artillery Observation Battalion. Instead, upon arrival in Korea, I was assigned to the 7th Cavalry Regiment, 1st Cavalry Division, as a platoon sergeant reporting for duty on 23 November. This was probably because elements of the division having been overrun several weeks prior at Unsan. I didn't get to the 1st FA Observation Battalion until 20 July 1951.[7]

Returning to Pennsylvania, Mueller rejoined the 28th Infantry Division. Transferring to the Army Reserve in 1977, he retired as a lieutenant colonel in 1982.

While Ralph Mueller and other veteran Guardsmen departed, new men continued to arrive, and slowly Guard units built up to war strength. Through October and into November, training intensified at posts around the country.

CAPTAIN RAY KOMMEL.
COMMANDING OFFICER, HEADQUARTERS BATTERY, 987TH ARMORED FIELD ARTILLERY BATTALION (OHIO).

When we first got to Camp Carson [Colorado], it was hot and windy. We got in a lot of firing practice. Colorado burns easily, so we'd fire in the morning and then spend the afternoon putting out the fires we'd set. In the morning it was nice, but in the afternoon the wind would come up and it would turn cold. On one occasion our liaison plane was up and couldn't land because of the strong wind. He finally radioed for us to grab the plane's struts as he landed and hold him down; it worked and no one got hurt.

Then it turned cold and started to snow, and of course, we didn't have any cold weather gear. They didn't have any to issue us. So most of us went into Colorado Springs to a surplus store and bought cold weather clothing so we could go out in the winter weather and continue training.*

By now we were getting a lot of lectures from people the Army had sent back from Korea. They were almost all horror stories of batteries being overrun and units wiped out. They stressed the importance of having a plan for every situation, for anything that could possibly happen, and always putting out a strong perimeter defense at night.

Kommel had been commissioned while serving with the 37th Infantry Division (Ohio) during World War II.

---

* Most of the Guardsmen that landed at Pusan in January of 1951 were still wearing summer uniforms. For an account of the Army's clothing shortages that winter, see *U.S. Army Uniforms of the Korean War*, Shelby Stanton, Stackpole Books, Harrisburg, Pa.

SERGEANT GUY WILKERSON.
"C" BATTERY, 936TH FIELD ARTILLERY BATTALION (ARKANSAS).

We had our full set of guns, all six of them when we were mobilized, and we could shoot. The rest of it, the perimeter defense stuff, the Army stuff, we didn't know nothing, no one did, but we could shoot. Rifles, carbines, howitzers, anything. We were just a bunch of country boys but we could shoot better than anyone.

When we got to Camp Carson the last of the mule pack artillery outfits was stationed there. They had these 75mm guns that they'd break down and load on these mules. It was interesting, you'd see these mules all loaded down with equipment going up and down the mountains. They retired the mules and these were the men we got—all Regulars, real good artillerymen. I don't know what happened to the mules.

The training was good at Carson but there wasn't enough ammunition, at least small arms ammo. We were supposed to fire a familiarization course on the .50 caliber machine gun and all we had was five rounds a man. Five rounds a man, that was it. The 155mm ammo seemed to be in better supply and we fired the guns a lot getting ready for the battery test which we did real good on.

One of the lieutenants that joined the battery while we were in Colorado was from West Point, if you can imagine a West Point officer with us. We were doing our job but for awhile he tried to be tougher on discipline and that sort of stuff. He soon softened up and fell right in with our group. He knew his job, and in Korea became a battery commander.

Later, when we got to Korea, we got the name of the most shootn'-non salutn' outfit in the Army. It started when a general from I Corps walked into the fire direction center (FDC) and no one stood up. They even wrote about it in the *Army Times*. All we wanted to do was shoot, shoot and be left alone.

Wilkerson remained in the National Guard working as a full time technician. Retiring in 1988 with over forty years service as a brigade command sergeant major, he was recalled for OPERATION DESERT STORM. Wilkerson was highly upset when informed he had too much rank to go with his unit to Saudi Arabia and had to remain in Arkansas assisting dependents.

As the days grew shorter and colder at Camp Carson and other posts around the country, rumors abounded. The ever changing fortunes of Eighth Army in Korea, coupled with the mixed pronouncements coming out of the Pentagon, did nothing to dispel the uncertainty. Then, in late November, the rumors turned to reality.

FIRST LIEUTENANT GEORGE BROOKS.
HEADQUARTERS, 231ST TRANSPORTATION TRUCK BATTALION (MARYLAND).

We were at Camp Edwards, Massachusetts; on the Wednesday morning prior to Thanksgiving, we were just getting in the cars to go home to Baltimore for the holiday. In those days you only had about four cars in the whole battalion. Colonel Greene, the battalion C.O., had his car and five or six of us were going to squeeze in and go home with him. Just as we were pulling away, Major Parker, the exec, came running up the road flagging us down. "Hold it colonel, hold it," he was yelling.

When he came up to the car Parker said to the colonel, "I just got a call from the Post-4, and he would like to meet with you and all your officers in his office at 1930." I looked at Colonel Greene and said, "We're getting ready to go to Korea." In definitely unmilitary language he told me to shut up.

I wasn't too surprised. Being the Battalion S-4, I had already been alerted to be prepared at any time to put in requisitions for 100 percent of our equipment. The only time you need 100 percent of your equipment is when you are getting ready to go overseas.

That night we met at Post-4's office. He pulled out a large envelope; it was stamped TOP SECRET. I'll never forget it, he opened it and started reading: "Headquarters, and Headquarters Company, 231st Transportation Truck Battalion, and the 726th Transportation Truck Company, will prepare to depart from Camp Edwards, Massachusetts, to arrive at Fort Lawton, Seattle Port of Embarkation, on or about 14 December 1950. Transportation to Pusan, Korea, will be arranged by the Commanding General, Fort Lawton, Seattle Port of Embarkation."

Now we had to sit down and decide what to do. We're all a bunch of young officers with wives and young children. In those days secret meant secret. You don't tell anybody anything. You can't even tell your wife anything. It was a long ride back to Baltimore.

Brooks remained in the Maryland National Guard. Retiring as a colonel, he was breveted to brigadier general upon becoming State Director of Civil Defense in 1979.

CHIEF WARRANT OFFICER JOHN HOLT.
HEADQUARTERS, 231ST TRANSPORTATION TRUCK BATTALION (MARYLAND).

I've been told on more than one occasion that ours was a test unit. That in the grand strategy of the Pentagon they wanted to see how soon they could send a unit from civilian status to combat readiness and then ship it out to the combat area. And everything pointed to just that. Get them ready and get them out there.

Guard units continued to receive and lose men. The Army's policy that all units would ship out for Korea at 100 percent strength meant exactly that. And if a unit needed more men what better place to get them than from a National Guard outfit, even if that unit itself was shipping out in a matter of days.

This regulation hit Wyoming's 300th Armored Field Artillery Battalion (AFAB) at Fort Lewis particularly hard. The "Cowboy Cannoneers" lost 40 percent of their enlisted personnel. Wyoming artillerymen found themselves assigned to the 819th Quartermaster Bath Company and other such exotic outfits. The loss of so many trained soldiers would delay the 300th in moving on line when it reached Korea in February 1951. To compound matters the troops assigned to the 300th a few weeks later when it shipped out included tuba players, boat operators, and men right out of basic training.[8]

Essential personnel continued to report in almost to the day the units boarded the transports.

FIRST LIEUTENANT NORMAN KING.
BATTALION SURGEON, 204TH FIELD ARTILLERY BATTALION (UTAH).

I graduated from medical school in 1948 and completed my residency to be a general practitioner in 1950. I opened up a general practice office in Roseville, California, just as the war started. If I had had any idea what was going to happen I never would have started my practice. I knew I was eligible for the physician's draft. In World War II, I had served as a pharmacist mate in the Navy, and then finished college on the GI bill. I tried to join the Navy, but for some reason they weren't taking doctors right then. I figured what the heck, I might as well get it over with, so around Christmas I went in and enlisted in the Army.

I got my papers and they sent me immediately to Fort Lewis, Washington. I thought they'd send me to Fort Sam (Fort Sam Houston, Texas, Army Medical School) for indoctrination or training. But they sent me straight up to Fort Lewis. The first thing when I got there, they gave me all the gear I would need and then I met my battalion, the 204th Field Artillery, a National Guard outfit from Utah.

We shipped out five days later on the USS *General A. E. Anderson*. On the boat I got acquainted with my men. I recall there were eight of them and we started to get things organized. My Navy training helped a lot, without it I wouldn't have known even where to begin.

Dr. Norman King is now medical director of a surgical center in Lodi, California.

At the same time Dr. King reported in at the 204th, eight other National Guard artillery battalions were in the final stages of overseas preparation.

SERGEANT WARREN ZIMMERMAN.
"A" BATTERY, 955TH FIELD ARTILLERY BATTALION
(NEW YORK).

We had built up a pretty good size battery fund. Before we went overseas we had a meeting to discuss what to buy with it. I said from my experience in combat the things I'd like to suggest were a lot of extra telephones, a lot of communications equipment. So we did. We picked up all the field telephones we could get from surplus stores and other sources. I'd learned during World War II an artillery outfit never has enough communication equipment, especially if you have a lot of outposts. When we got over to Korea we were able to run a lot of extra wire. It worked real good.

But the artillerymen would not be the first Army National Guardsmen to arrive in Korea. As Christmas 1950 approached, eight Guard transportation truck units, who four months previously had been attending drill one night a week, were closing in on Pusan.

CORPORAL CARL BOHR, SR.
HEADQUARTERS, 167TH TRANSPORTATION TRUCK
BATTALION (PENNSYLVANIA).

They put us on a train down at Fort Bliss. It took about three days to get up to Fort Lawton, near Seattle. I recall there were some other Guard outfits on the train. We stood around Fort Lawton for a few days getting shots and filling out forms. Then we boarded the troopship. It was the *Sergeant Sylvester Antolak*, an old Liberty ship. The food was good if you weren't too sick to eat it. I guess when it really got rough at least seventy-five percent of the troops were sick. Some got so sick they got put in the ship's sickbay. Most of us never took our clothes off the whole time we were on the ship.

The trip took about eighteen or nineteen days, and the closer we got to Korea the colder it got. All we had was summer gear—regular boots, the blanket type sleeping bags, no parkas or anything like that. The Navy gave us an extra blanket. I put mine in my sleeping bag and when we got off the ship I managed to keep it. It was very cold.

Back in Pennsylvania, Bohr took up the meat cutting trade before going to work for the city of Lebanon.

Once again the National Guard headed toward the battlefield.

CHAPTER 3

KEEP ON TRUCKIN'

December 31, 1950, New Year's Eve, a night for celebrating and parties; a time to reflect on the year past and a time to look ahead to the new year. As they huddled and tried to keep warm in their tents on the outskirts of Pusan, the men of the 726th Transportation Truck Company (Maryland) were not partying or celebrating. They were, however, thinking of the past five months and what the future might bring. One hundred and thirty-four days after mobilization the first Army National Guard unit had arrived in Korea.[1]

FIRST LIEUTENANT JOSEPH BRACY.
EXECUTIVE OFFICER, 726TH TRANSPORTATION TRUCK
COMPANY (MARYLAND).

> After we unloaded we went into an encampment area where there were a lot of troops. I recall that first night staying in a squad tent with some artillery officers. They were saying, "Why did you debark from those ships? We came this way expecting to get on them." They said we would not be able to go forward, that it was impossible. The Chinese had overrun their outfit and they had lost all their equipment and taken many casualties. Their whole attitude was one of defeatism. General Ridgway soon changed that. This was the situation that we walked into.*

---

* Lieutenant General Matthew Ridgway assumed command of Eighth Army on December 26. Ridgway would bring a new fighting spirit to the demoralized units of Eighth Army.

Bracy, who had received a battlefield commission in World War II, resumed his career with the Social Security Administration, becoming assistant bureau director for administration. He also remained in the Guard, retiring after 26 years service as a major.

Four more National Guard truck units came ashore the next day, January 1, 1951. Two of them, the 167th (Pennsylvania) and 231st (Maryland) Truck Battalion Headquarters Companies, had been detachment size when mobilized but were soon expanded to company strength. Their mission was to provide administrative and logistical support to truck companies assigned to them. These units might be Guard or Regular Army outfits and number anywhere from four to as many as ten companies. The two headquarters companies operated under Corps control; the 167th went to IX Corps, while the 231st joined I Corps.

By January 8, the men of the 726th had been joined by five more National Guard truck companies. The 107th and 252nd (Alabama), the 715th (District of Columbia) and the 121st and 131st (Pennsylvania).

Courtesy of Joseph Bracy

Lieutenant Joseph Bracy, X.O. of Maryland's 726th Transportation Truck Company, the first Army National Guard unit to arrive in Korea.

The 726th TTC that landed on New Year's Eve hailed from Baltimore, as did the 231st Headquarters Company. Commanded by Captain Bedford Bentley, the 726th trained at Camp Edwards, Massachusetts, before heading for Korea. There was nothing unusual about these two outfits except for one thing. Both units were manned 100 percent by African-Americans.*

---

* The 715th Transportation Truck Company (District of Columbia) landed on January 5, and became the third and last African-American National Guard unit to serve in Korea.

On July 26, 1948, President Truman issued Executive Order 9981 declaring the end of segregation in the armed forces. The Order was largely ignored by the Army and the other services. At the same time, Truman formed a committee to study equality of treatment in the armed forces. This committee ascertained that of 347,711 Guardsmen, only 6,988 were African-Americans, and while the authorized strength of the Guard was 625,000, only 15,528 positions were allotted for black Americans.

In early 1950, the Department of Defense adopted the policy of subjecting National Guard units and personnel under Federal regulations to antidiscrimination and integration during periods of Federalization. The individual states would continue to determine the status of units under their jurisdiction. What this statement meant was that the status quo would continue since at that time only a few Regular Army units had been integrated.[2]

In the first five months of the Korean War a few Eighth Army units were partially integrated out of combat necessity. But taken as a whole, when the 726th TTC came ashore that New Year's Eve of 1950, the United States Army was still very much segregated.

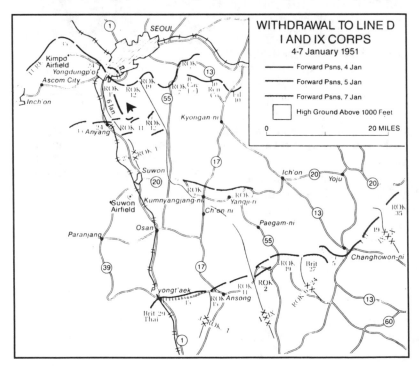

As the first National Guard units landed at Pusan, Eighth Army continued to fall back. Courtesy of the Center of Military History, United States Army, Washington, D.C.

* * * * * *

The situation as the eight National Guard truck units landed was critical. The past six weeks had seen the Army and Marines suffer their worst defeat in modern times. The loss in men and equipment had been enormous. United Nation forces that in November had sent patrols to the Yalu River had now fallen back below the 38th Parallel, setting up defensive positions along the Imjim River above Seoul.

Unable to hold on the Imjim, Eighth Army continued to fall back. Abandoning Seoul to the Communists on the morning of January 4, I and IX Corps took up new positions south of the Han River. X Corps, minus the First Marine Division regrouping at Masan, took over the central sector from the ROKs, who had a physiological fear of the Chinese.

The Marines, still short four thousand men in their infantry and artillery units after the withdrawal from the Chosin Reservoir, were held in reserve. In the seven days since the first National Guard unit arrived in Korea, Eighth Army had withdrawn another sixty air miles and the evacuation of Korea was once more being considered.[3]

Three of the truck companies had been scheduled to land on the east coast at Hungnam and join X Corps. But the situation had changed dramatically in the weeks the Guardsmen were at sea; by Christmas Day 1950, the only people at Hungnam were North Koreans and Chinese. This necessitated the rerouting of the guardsmen to Pusan.

The arrival of the three American divisions evacuated from Hungnam (1st Marine, 3rd and 7th Infantry) along with ROK and other U.N. units overwhelmed the Pusan port facilities, and several of the Guard units had to wait almost a month for their trucks to be unloaded.

PRIVATE DARCE EMERSON.
252ND TRANSPORTATION TRUCK COMPANY (ALABAMA).

We went over on an old Liberty ship, the *Sergeant Sylvester Antolak*. The weather was terrible the whole way; the captain of the ship said we were dodging a typhoon or something. I think we went through the middle of it.

Just after we landed, our C.O., Captain Troy Brumley, got us all together for a talk. He was a leader; he'd go all out for you. He said, "I didn't bring you guys over here to get killed. I never want you to do anything stupid. I'm going to take care of you, but if I catch one guy out of line he's had it. One guy can cost a lot of lives. I've got a job to do and you guys have a job to do, and I don't want any of you guys getting killed." He was fantastic.

We waited about a month for our trucks and equipment. I and everybody else was upset. We were there and we wanted to get going, instead we were put to work guarding POWs. There were thousands of them and we guarded them on the docks before they got shipped out to Koje Island. Our first sergeant was a World War II veteran, a very sharp soldier. He said, "Don't trust anyone but Americans. Stay alert at all times." He told us that two GIs had been stabbed to death on that very dock the night before. We stayed alert.

After the war Emerson went to work for Libby Owens Ford Glass Company, in Illinois. In 1960 he transferred to their California plant where he is still employed.

Equipped with fifty-two, $2^1/_2$ ton trucks and capable of transporting an entire infantry battalion, the Guardsmen went to work as soon as their trucks were off loaded.

CORPORAL ROBERT APPLEBY.
131ST TRANSPORTATION TRUCK COMPANY (PENNSYLVANIA).

We were scheduled to go into Hungnam up on the east coast. This is what we were told on the ship. We didn't know an evacuation had taken place; we knew there was a problem because we were kept off the coast for a few days. Then we were told that the reason we weren't unloading was that the troops that had been pulled out of Hungnam were being unloaded at Pusan and we had to wait.

We got off at night and they moved us up to the top of a hill looking over the city. They put us in squad tents with no heaters in them. It was muddy, sloppy, slushy cold. We still were wearing all our summer gear we had been issued at Fort Bliss. In a few days the ship with the equipment arrived. As soon as everything was unloaded we moved out.

We had some guys that had never driven, or barely ever driven a $2^1/_2$ ton truck because we didn't have enough of them to train with back at Bliss. It didn't matter; we just got in the trucks and headed up to Taegu.

Alabama's 107th TTC didn't have the luxury, if it can be called that, of staying in Pusan even a full day. The Haleyville unit's trucks had arrived on a different ship and had already been serviced and loaded when the men debarked on January 7. The 107th headed north that night.

PRIVATE THOMAS TILLMAN.
107TH TRANSPORTATION TRUCK COMPANY (ALABAMA).

We docked in the morning, I believe, and of course the military is always so efficient. We were all ready to debark and get off that damn ship but it seemed like it took forever. They had a Korean band down on the dock playing for us, welcoming us to Korea I suppose, but it seems to me like we were waiting forever before we got off.

The thing I remember of Pusan, it was wintertime and it was wet and the mud had to be nearly knee deep. The first thing they did was tell my platoon to go eat, then we were going to have a meeting and that we would move out that night. I remember getting in a long chow line and this guy in front of me had all this winter stuff on. All we had was summer gear. We had no winter sleeping bags, no snow pac shoes; we had combat boots and all summer clothing.

I remember standing in this line, and this second lieutenant walked over and tapped me on the shoulder and said, "Hey soldier, do you know where the officer's mess is?" Of course I didn't know anything; I had just got over there with a load of turkeys. But this guy in front of me turns around, and he's a full bird colonel and he says, "Right at the end of this line, Lieutenant."

That night we moved out. I'm driving the next to last truck in the column. I recall we were hauling gas or diesel in 55 gallon drums and 155mm howitzer ammunition. They told us that along our route we would have to ford a stream and if we were going to be ambushed that's where it would happen. Supposedly some outfit had been wiped out at that spot sometime before. I remember we were driving along with just our night lights on and all of a sudden the column stops. I had no earthly idea what was going on.

My assistant driver went up to the head of the column to see what was happening. I climbed into my summer sleeping bag and waited, I was almost freezing to death. All of a sudden I heard the door on the other side opening. I opened my eyes and it was a Korean. I started screaming and trying to get out of that sleeping bag, but the quick release wouldn't open the way they're supposed to. I thought I was going to have to cut my way out of it.

I guess my screaming and hollering scared him as much as he'd scared me. He slammed the door shut and disappeared.

When the guys came back to the trucks the one in back of mine was gone, it had been stolen. Evidently it was a gang of South Korean thieves. If it had been a North Korean or Chinese soldier I wouldn't be here.

FIRST LIEUTENANT JOSEPH BRACY.
EXECUTIVE OFFICER, 726TH TRANSPORTATION TRUCK COMPANY (MARYLAND).

We finally got unloaded and began drawing equipment. We had to mount the .50 caliber machine guns and we weren't that familiar with their operation, but we got them on the mounts and then tested them. We went up to Taegu and then on our first mission, moving elements of the 1st Cav at night.

I hadn't become familiar with the division's code names yet; I went with the lead platoon and I saw this road sign that said 'Danger Forward.' I thought, "Oh God, are they trying to tell us something!" Later I learned this was the code name of the 24th Infantry Division's forward command post (CP). Those first weeks things were pretty disorganized.

As Bracy, and the other National Guard truckers headed north, one outfit, the 121st TTC went south. Assigned the mission of truck support at the POW compounds on the island of Koje, the Pennsylvania unit spent its entire Korean tour in this capacity. The POWs, now numbering over 40,000, had been held in the Inchon area as late as mid December. When it became apparent that the Communists would soon recapture Inchon, they were moved to Pusan, and then to Koje, a small island off the southern Korean coast.[4]

PRIVATE FIRST CLASS EUGENE WOLFE.
121ST TRANSPORTATION TRUCK COMPANY (PENNSYLVANIA).

When we first got to Hialeah Compound we put up our tents in the former rice paddies. We had no heat, no lights; we huddled in the tents like dogs. We took a number 10 can, put some stones in the bottom and any kind of fuel we could get and lit it. That was our heat. I recall that went on for a week and a half or so. We unloaded all of our equipment off the ship, then we waited.

They had decided they were going to move all the POWs to Koje Island. So we stayed at Hialeah about a month, loaded everything back on a ship, sent an advance party out, and went to Koje Island. We moved everything that came on that island, no matter what it was, with a $2^1/2$ ton truck.

Lumber, rice, clothing, we moved everything for the POWs plus our own troops twenty-four hours a day for the next twelve months.

Wolfe remained in the Guard retiring after thirty-six years as a chief warrant officer.

SERGEANT FIRST CLASS BERT YODER. 121ST TRANSPORTATION TRUCK COMPANY (PENNSYLVANIA).

I was detached to the engineers. They had seen on my service record that I was a plumber before I went in and they had a job for me. With that many POWs on the island it wasn't long before they ran out of wood to cook their rice. So we made oil burners for them and for about three months all I did was put oil burners in the POW compounds.

Courtesy of Bert Yoder

Sergeant First Class Bert Yoder, of Pennsylvania's 121st Transportation Truck Company. The 121st spent its entire Korean tour on Koje Island.

I had a jeep and a trailer and a couple tanks of gas. They'd open the gates and send me in there, all alone with 10,000 of them. The Chinese were not bad; they told me that their Government had told them if they went to Korea and helped the North Koreans their families would be well taken care of. All the fanatical Communists were kept in a separate compound. The North Koreans were the worst.

Yoder, a World War II veteran, returned to Pine Grove, Pennsylvania, and resumed his trade as a plumber.

While the truckers hit the road, the two Guard truck battalion headquarters companies also went to work.

CORPORAL THOMAS TOBIAS. HEADQUARTERS, 167TH TRANSPORTATION TRUCK BATTALION (PENNSYLVANIA).

We didn't stay at Pusan more than a day or two before we moved up the coast about twenty miles to Haeundae. We set up camp about half a mile from the beach in an abandoned Korean school. It was cold, but nothing like it was farther north. I think being close to the sea had something to do with that. We stayed at this location the entire eighteen months we were in Korea.

Our job was to give support to four Regular Army truck companies. These four outfits hauled ammunition. The ammo would be unloaded from cargo ships out in the bay and brought to shore in landing craft and then loaded on the trucks. The trucks would go up to the ammo storage point about four miles back in the hills, but sometimes they'd go right from the beach all the way up to the front lines.

I was the mail clerk. Twice a day I would go to Pusan, and pick up and drop off the mail. The round trip took about two and a half hours. I had to take someone with me to watch the jeep. If you left a jeep unguarded for thirty seconds it was gone. At first I took another GI, but then we found a dependable Korean and he went with me.

We went on alert a few times for guerrillas, but nothing happened. They were active back in the hills near the ammo point, and I believe they had a little action up there. We were told they were led by a Russian.

Tobias also returned to Pine Grove, and went to work for ALCOA where he remained for forty years.

By mid January, Eighth Army was once again driving north. Wonju was retaken on the 20th and Suwon on the 26th. The advance was uneven, with some units meeting little resistance while a few miles in either direction the Chinese fought furiously. By now the National Guard truck units were working all along the 155 mile front.

CAPTAIN BEDFORD BENTLEY.
COMMANDING OFFICER, 726TH TRANSPORTATION TRUCK COMPANY (MARYLAND).

We moved up to Taegu and went to work. We were assigned to a truck battalion but I can't recall which one. Every morning I'd tell battalion how many trucks I had available then they'd give me the day's mission. Generally the three platoons would go out on separate assignments, we rarely worked together as a company. As a rule the trucks would be back in by nightfall although occasionally they would be gone twenty-four hours or longer.

North of Taegu the roads were in terrible condition, really more like one lane trails. The engineers worked on them constantly. That, along with the cold weather, lack of spare parts, and the fact that most of the trucks were World War II leftovers caused twenty, to as much as fifty percent of the trucks to be on deadline at any given time.

At this time the front was fluid and we moved around quite a bit. All in all it was quite an experience.

CORPORAL ROBERT APPLEBY.
131ST TRANSPORTATION TRUCK COMPANY (PENNSYLVANIA).

Our initial mission at Taegu was to support units above Angdong and to move troops from Pusan up to the line. The "red diamond route" south to Pusan was extremely dangerous because of all the guerrillas that were bypassed and roaming the mountains. Several events come to mind while at Taegu.

Several nights after arriving I was Corporal of the Guard. Around 0100 I heard a shot and a call for "Corporal of the Guard." I ran out and found one of our sentinels had been shot in the leg. He was down and bleeding. Obviously there was some panic and scrambling but nothing was found.

On the 23rd of January we received fire into the compound. Everyone started shooting. No one was hit and we eventually captured a North Korean. Several nights later on the 28th, I was on a patrol outside the compound with about six others when we were fired on. I put my carbine on automatic and fired. I saw a man go down. We worked our way to where the firing had came from, but found nothing. It was much too dark to pursue anyone, and we never found out who had fired on us.

Around noon on 1 February, my 20th birthday, Chuck May and I were dispatched for a single truck run. As we were crossing the compound we heard firing from what sounded like a burp gun. Dirt was kicking up about ten feet in front of us. Chuck and I unslung our carbines and fired towards the wall that surrounded the compound and the woods beyond. We then worked our way to where the firing had come from. All we found were expended casings from an automatic weapon. They were somewhat smaller than our .30 caliber casings. Everyone was alerted, we departed, and things eventually went back to normal.

On March 15, ROK troops entered Seoul and the South Korean capital was once more in U.N. hands. Eighth Army continued moving north meeting stiffening resistance and at times localized counter attacks.

CAPTAIN SIMON PORTER.
HEADQUARTERS, 231ST TRANSPORTATION TRUCK BATTALION (MARYLAND).

After we landed at Pusan we headed north, moving several times before settling in at Uijongbu, above Seoul. We were with I Corps at this time and had five truck companies attached to us for logistical support. Sometimes we had more, sometimes less, but it was usually four or five companies. I was battalion maintenance officer and had a crew of about twenty or so mechanics; about half American and half Korean, to keep the trucks running.

One afternoon I noticed a lot of activity in the hills to the north of us about 3,000 yards away. It looked like the hills were covered with ants, all moving. I told Colonel Greene, the C.O., "I think I see some gooks up in the hills." He said, "No, Tony, I don't think so." I was sure and replied, "The hell it isn't!"

An hour and a half or so later the word came from I Corps, "Withdraw and quickly!" We had a number of vehicles on deadline waiting for parts, I didn't want to leave them for the Chinese or destroy them. We hooked up a bunch of cables and moved out, each running truck pushing one and pulling two others. I don't recall how far back we went or how long it was before we went back to Uijongbu.

Porter, who had served in Italy during World War II, remained in the National Guard. He retired as a major with over thirty years service.

On May 16, 120,000 Chinese attacked the 2nd Infantry Division near Hangye. Attached to the Indian Head Division was Alabama's 252nd Transportation Truck Company. For their service over the next six days the Hamilton unit received a Presidential Unit Citation.

PRIVATE DARCE EMERSON.
252ND TRANSPORTATION TRUCK COMPANY (ALABAMA).

I just don't remember much of what happened during this time. I remember we hauled ammo right up to the front and came under sniper fire. I'd fire the .50 caliber machine gun in the general direction of the snipers but could never see exactly where they were. I remember we carried the wounded and dead back off the line; they didn't have enough ambulances. I remember a medic calling me over and saying, "Look at this." He pulled back a sheet covering a body and the man's face and front of his head was gone, all that was left was his hair. It made me very mad.

I recall driving around a corner and there was a burned out tank with a six inch hole in the side of the turret. There were dead Chinese or Koreans all around it. They had taken a lot of Gooks before they got it. Back in Alabama, before we were a truck outfit we had been a tank company. I thanked God we had been changed.

The amount of miles driven and the tons of supplies hauled by the National Guard truck companies reached astronomical proportions. Typical was the work of the 715th TTC (District of Columbia). The "Capitol Truck Company," as Captain Maurice J. Burke's outfit was known, landed at Pusan, January 5, and joined General Almond's X Corps. By August 14, one year after its mobilization, the unit had logged 439,717 miles over the rugged Korean roads. In their first seven months in Korea, the 715th hauled 35,724 tons of supplies and transported 11,435 troops.

Their finest hour came in mid-May when the Chinese hit the 2nd Infantry Division above Hangye. When, as so often happened, ROK units on their flanks collapsed, the 2nd was in danger of being destroyed. The only help available, the 3rd Infantry Division, was in Eighth Army reserve at Ichon, over a hundred and fifty miles away.

The 715th along with other Guard and Regular Army truck outfits began moving elements of the 3rd on the night of the 17th. Going without sleep or food, drivers of the 715th, and the other truck companies pulled off the "miracle of the 3rd." "The Reds couldn't believe it could be done," said Captain Burke. "They knew the 3rd couldn't be in the mountains–but they were there nevertheless. After that the tide in the 'Battle of the Soyang River' turned radically."[5]

By July the main line of resistance (MLR) had stabilized. There would be two more advances to secure better defensive positions, but the war of movement was over. The job of the National Guard truckers did not ease, for now it was an artillery war and thousands of tons of ammo had to be hauled twenty-four hours a day. The Guardsmen also continued hauling supplies and troops, working with every American and U.N. front line unit in Korea.

PRIVATE DARCE EMERSON.
252ND TRANSPORTATION TRUCK COMPANY (ALABAMA).

We hauled the Turkish Brigade for about a week or so from the rear up to the front. They were the meanest men in Korea. They carried bayonets and long sabers that looked like they came from the Civil War; they must have been three foot long. They were there to fight and they didn't particularly care who they fought. They were great people, but people you didn't want to upset.

The Turks loved coffee. I had a bunch of the little packets of freeze dried coffee that came in the "C" rations in my truck. I couldn't stand the stuff, didn't like it at all. I gave it to the Turks. They poured it in their canteens, shook it a bit and drank it down cold.

One of their officers rode in the cab with me. He spoke some English, and all he talked about was wanting to get at the enemy. I told him I was here to fight for my Country, get rid of the damn Commies and go home. He said when his men got done with the Chinks they'd want to go home.

One or more of the Guard truck outfits seemed to be continually attached to the 1st Marine Division. Much larger than an Army division, with its attached ROK troops the Marine unit numbered around 25,000 men. Having little organic trucking, the division depended on the Army for the movement of supplies and personnel.

CORPORAL ROBERT APPLEBY.
131ST TRANSPORTATION TRUCK COMPANY (PENNSYLVANIA).

Around mid-August of 1951 we were in direct support of the 1st Marine Division, north of Inje. Late at night we had just completed dropping off artillery ammunition at a forward ammunition point. After we were unloaded we were instructed to pull our vehicles into a holding area. Just after midnight the guns began to fire and shells seemed to whistle overhead all night. We suspected something big was going to happen. Around 0500, just before day light, we observed a lot of activity; Marines were coming from everywhere and eventually were loaded onto our trucks.

We moved out, probably about 30 trucks in our convoy, thru riverbeds and trails, over ridges, and eventually winding down into the "Infamous Punchbowl." Evidently the North Korean observers could see us from the ridges surrounding the valley because the artillery started to fall. They were obviously trying to target the arrival of the troops. The Marines unloaded quickly and moved out.

Coming out of the valley and up the ridge I bent the left tie-rod on my truck. I now had to move forward and back up to make every left turn. The trail was narrow and I was holding up the trucks behind me and they were bunching up. About half way up the ridge on a sharp left turn a Marine general was observing the move and giving orders. When he saw my difficulty he verbally insulted my ability to drive.

No explanation mattered, and it was no time for a 20 year old corporal to debate the problem. Anyway, he ordered me to pull off the trail and let the other trucks get by. He accused me of bunching up the vehicles and drawing fire from the North Korean forward observers. In retrospect I guess I did cause a lot of incoming artillery to fall in the valley.

Corporal Robert Eichensehr, another squad leader, pulled alongside and offered to help. I explained my predicament, but he was ordered to move out as the general assailed him too. He moved out immediately and after all the trucks had been recovered I worked my way out. Eichensehr still reminds me of our run in with the Marine Corps.

Winter came and the truckers' time in Korea grew short. The last major mission of the 107th TTC, before the Guardsmen returned to Alabama in February 1952, involved the movement of the 40th Infantry Division (California). The Californians, who had spent the previous nine months in Japan training and guarding the island of Honshu, replaced the veteran 24th Infantry Division in January.

The two divisions exchanged equipment in place, the men taking only their individual weapons. The 107th moved both outfits. The 40th from Inchon to the front, and the 24th back to Inchon, a total of over 35,000 men. One of the first National Guard units to arrive in Korea had transported one of the last.[6]

On February 2, 1952, the first Guard truckers started home. They didn't all leave. Because of the point system in effect it would be midsummer before the men of the 167th TTB Headquarters Company, still on the beach at Haeundae, departed. By then forty-one National Guard units were in Korea. But the men of 167th and the other seven Guard truck outfits could say "We led the way."

CHAPTER 4

DISPLACE FORWARD THE GUNS

In the fifteen day period February 2–17, 1951, nine National Guard artillery battalions landed at Pusan. After a short period of training these nine battalions moved to the front where they joined one of the three corps making up Eighth Army.*

Eight of these battalions would go on line in the period March 30–April 15. They would play a decisive role in stopping the Chinese offensives in April and May. The ninth unit, the 300th AFAB (Wyoming), arrived at the front May 15, and joined the 2nd Infantry Division near Chaun-ni. Within hours the "Cowboy Cannoneers" would be in the middle of some of the heaviest fighting of the war, the Battle of the Soyang River. For their part in this action elements of the 300th would receive a Presidential Unit Citation.

Mobilized in the first three increments, the units, listed below, trained at Fort Lewis, Washington, Fort Hood, Texas, or Camp Carson, Colorado.

UNIT	STATE	GUN	KOREA	CORPS
176TH AFAB	PA	105 HOW SP**	2/17/51	I
196TH FAB	TN	155 HOW TOWED	2/09/51	X
204TH FAB	UT	155 GUN SP	2/02/51	I

---

* The 780th FAB, an Army Reserve unit from Virginia, armed with 8 inch howitzers also arrived at this time.
** SP/ self-propelled: an artillery piece mounted on a tank chassis capable of rapid movement with light armor giving the crew a minimum of protection.

213TH AFAB	UT	105 HOW SP	2/16/51	IX
300TH AFAB	WY	105 HOW SP	2/16/51	I
936TH FAB	AR	155 HOW TOWED	2/10/51	I
937TH FAB	AR	155 GUN SP	2/10/51	IX
955TH FAB	NY	155 HOW TOWED	2/02/51	I
987TH AFAB	OH	105 HOW SP	2/16/51	IX

The corps assignments listed are the unit's initial assignments. As the Chinese attacks in April and May tore holes in the U.N. line, Eighth Army rushed the National Guard battalions from one sector to another as the situation dictated. In May, Arkansas' 937th FAB would be assigned to all three corps at various times, and on occasion fire in support of two corps simultaneously. In the months ahead National Guard artillerymen would fire in support of every American, South Korean, and U.N. infantry unit in Korea.

The Army planned for the Guard units to go to Japan for a period of training before heading for Korea. Unfortunately, in six months of combat American and ROK forces had lost 238 artillery pieces including twenty-seven 155mm howitzers, and one 8 inch howitzer. Desperately short of artillery Eighth Army Commander, Lieutenant General Matthew Ridgway, cabled Chief of Staff General Joe Collins, and requested that the battalions be shipped directly to Korea and that "all necessary action" be taken to "speed" and "advance" the arrival date.[1]

At Pusan the battalions were given their corps assignments. The corps artillery officers were astounded at the lack of actual training the Guardsmen had received in the States. At first they failed to understand, or discounted, the handicaps the battalions had operated under the previous five months and the havoc the wholesale transfer of men had wreaked on the cohesion of the units. It soon became obvious that to send these green troops into battle would be unproductive and possibly suicidal.

It was therefore decided to send the Guardsmen to training areas where they would receive a concentrated three to four weeks training under the watchful eye of veteran corps artillerymen. These training areas were located thirty or forty miles north of Pusan in small valleys that had seen heavy fighting the previous summer during the Pusan Perimeter battles. Evidence of this fierce fighting still littered the Korean countryside. While the units had varying experiences during this period, those noted in the command report of the 176th AFAB (Pennsylvania) were typical:

Arrived Pusan Korea 17 February, bivouacked at Pusan assembly area until 28 February. During this period unloaded cargo

Three of the National Guard artillery battalions that landed in February 1951 were armed with the reliable M1A1 155mm howitzer. New York's Battery "A" 955th FAB in action, May 1951.

ships, ten–fourteen men on duty around the clock to make sure the right equipment unloaded.

On 1 March moved to Kumhae for further training. [This plan is satisfactory since the organization had only limited training in the States due to lack of equipment and personnel, and never had the opportunity to function in the field.] Up to almost full strength upon arrival at Pusan, 645 officers and men.

Spent all of March at Kumhae training and testing. I Corps provided expert artillerymen to assist in training. Also received a copy of a captured document that explained how the CCF (Chinese Communist Forces) has special units to attack artillery positions. They are light and travel fast. Perimeter security training was emphasized.

On 1 April, I Corps informed the battalion they had passed its test and that "the battalion knowledge of F.A. technique is sound and its experience is sufficient enough to permit its commitment to combat."

The next day the 176th boarded three LSTs for the quick trip up the western coast of Korea. Debarking at Inchon the 176th headed north. On April 7, the battalion went into action firing in support of the 25th Infantry Division.[2]

The units had been warned to be alert for North Korean guerrillas while in these training areas. These warnings were not always taken seriously.

MASTER SERGEANT BOB STEFFY.
HEADQUARTERS, 987TH AFAB (OHIO).

Leaving Pusan, we moved north near the village of Yangsan on the Yangsan River for more training. At this time I was the Battalion S-2 Sergeant. Each night a perimeter guard was posted with walking posts on the village side and a machine gun from each battery on the river side.

On the fateful night—it must have been nine or ten or so— I was in the operations tent typing away. The Officer of the Day (O.D.) was zonked out in the back of the tent. Suddenly from down along the river a burst of machine gun fire was heard. The O.D. was on his feet before he was awake. "What the hell was that?" "Sounded like a .50-caliber, Lieutenant," I replied.

The O.D. pulled out his .45 and charged out into the darkness. I turned out the light. Not long afterward the lieutenant was back in the tent. "What was it?" I asked. "'A' and 'B' thought they heard somebody coming across the river, nobody answered their challenge, so they fired." This happened two or three more times during the night.

Months later one of "C" Battery's Reservists came to say good-bye; he was leaving the next day. (I'd finally got back to a firing battery where I belonged.) We smoked and talked and he reminded me of the incident at Yangsan. The kid asked me if I knew what had happened that night and I told him what the O.D. had said. "That wasn't it at all," he said. "Our .50 was the farthest upstream and we got bored. Somebody had brought some beer. (I believe we'd had a PX ration that day or the day before.) We sat there and listened, we couldn't see a thing, and whoever was on watch would have a beer and throw the empty can in the river."

This is a good time to point out that the Yangsan was maybe a hundred yards wide, but shallow enough to be wadeable. Korea, being a mass of broken stones, had some pretty rough stream bottoms and some of those rocks were big. The empty beer cans went tumbling downstream, hitting rocks at random. "A" and "B", hearing the rattling of the empty beer cans, assumed there was an infiltration, and since there was no countersign they fired. I never did hear if there were any casualties among the cans.[3]

Steffy, a veteran of the 37th Infantry Division (Ohio) had seen action on Luzon during World War II.

Other incidences were not this frivolous. At these training areas many of the young National Guardsmen first saw the horrors of war.

SERGEANT WILLIAM DAY IV.
"C" BATTERY, 300TH AFAB (WYOMING).

We moved to a site near the village of Sodong-ni on the north side of the Naktong River. Our camp at Sodong-ni was along a road and we were continually covered with dust. On the other side of the road was the river and the women would strip down to shorts and wade in the icy water searching for clams and whatever else they could find. We watched and shivered in our field jackets. The Koreans were very hardy people.

One day we worked on a "simulated perimeter of defense problem." We would move in, dig foxholes and machine gun pits, then fill them in, and move out. We were always digging foxholes and then filling them in. This was an area which only months before had been a part of the Pusan

Perimeter. We heard an explosion nearby and there was concern whether anyone was hurt. As it turned out, a group of six or seven children playing along the river where we were dug in found a 81mm mortar shell that had not exploded when it hit the soft mud. It was still armed and went off while the children were playing with it. One boy was blown to bits and several others seriously wounded—the so-called "fortunes of war." (In July of 1987, I was told by Captain Robinson, the Battalion S-4, that the shell had been a 3.5" bazooka round from our firing rather than what we had previously believed.)[4]

By late March eight of the nine Guard battalions had completed their training and passed the tests administered by the various corps artillery sections. They then headed north for their initial combat assignments. Most of the units followed the trail of the 176th AFAB and returned to Pusan where they boarded Navy LSTs and sailed to Inchon.

Courtesy of Bob Steffy

Four of the Guard artillery battalions were armored and equipped with the 105mm M-7. This one, belonging to Ohio's 987th AFAB, was in action near the Iron Triangle, September 22, 1951.

FIRST LIEUTENANT NORMAN KING.
BATTALION SURGEON, 204TH FAB (UTAH).

I don't remember how long it took to get to Inchon; it didn't take too long. I know the officers were able to go up into the LST and have better conditions and food and things like that. It was kind of a vacation for us. The Navy always had things a little better.

We arrived in Inchon and we were loading our stuff on a train when a railroad car tipped over and one of the boys was pinned under there with his leg caught. It was terrible. I had to crawl under the train and give him morphine just to alleviate his pain. I couldn't stay with him because we had to move on. I never really found out what happened to him, but I think he died. It was things like that that you kind of remember.

The honor of being the first National Guard artillery battalion to fire on the enemy went to Arkansas' 936th FAB. I Corps placed the battalion in general support of the 3rd Infantry Division, then on the offensive thirty miles north of Seoul.

Going into action on March 30, the 155mm gunners from the Fayetteville area knocked out a machine gun nest and destroyed a battery of Chinese 75mm artillery. Called on continually, the battalion expended 1,199 rounds its first two days at the front.[5]

A Regular Army man who had served in Korea before the war describes his first days with the 936th FAB.

CORPORAL RICHARD STINSON.
"A" BATTERY, 936TH FAB (ARKANSAS).

This artillery unit was from Berryville, Arkansas, a National Guard outfit. Most of the officers and men were related. But don't let this fool you, it was a pretty well trained outfit. A bunch of us Regular Army personnel met up with the 936th at Camp Carson. The one thing I couldn't really hack was that everyone called each other by their relative (cousin, uncle, brother) name. Us RA men were the only ones that called the officers, "Sir."

Most of the gunnery jobs were already taken by the Guardsmen, so I got put in the wire section. Being a cannoneer and gunner most of my Army career, I was kind of happy for the change. I learned how to string wire, set up telephones, etc. The 936th had 155mm howitzers; I had always been in 105mm outfits, so I spent a lot of time around the gun sections learning what I could. There wasn't too much difference in preparing the guns for action, the main thing being the size of the projectiles. Anyway, we packed the guns and equipment, got on a train and went to Camp Stoneman, California, where we boarded ship.

After we got to Pusan we trained a bit and then headed north over the winding road. We got to our position and got the guns ready for action. Our wire section was busy laying wire and setting up phones to the guns and to the various sections. The brass said that we were supporting the 65th Infantry Regiment, 3rd Infantry Division.

In our area there was a dead Chinese lying on the ground by the mess hall tent. We all had to look at him while we ate our chow. Yuk! He didn't look so good with maggots crawling all over him; after awhile a truck came by and picked up the body. We asked if the enemy ever came back this far and were told, "Hey, ask some of the artillery battalions in the 3rd about that."

It seemed that the North Koreans and the Chinese had a habit of ambushing the artillery outfits. We had to set up a perimeter defense with machine gun posts around the battery. This took away a couple of men from each section. We moved around a lot and supported other divisions including a ROK division. It seems like when you supported a ROK outfit, you always caught hell; the Chinese liked to push them around.

In May I got an emergency leave and went home. In my view "A" Battery, 936th FAB, was very well trained and did its job well. Arkansas should be very proud of this unit from Berryville.[6]

After his leave, Stinson returned to Korea and joined the 196th FAB (Tennessee). Now retired, Stinson resides in Detroit.

Two of the Guard battalions, the 204th (Utah) and the 937th (Arkansas), were equipped with the M-40, 155mm self propelled gun. Mounted on a M-4 tank chassis and weighing 42 ton, the gun could be used in a direct fire role, as well as operating as conventional artillery. The 204th and 937th were the first units to arrive in Korea with this potent weapon, and Eighth Army wasted no time in seeing what they could do.

General Ridgway visited the 937th on April 5. He was extremely impressed with the M-40's firepower and immediately laid forth a plan to exploit the long-range capability of the weapon. He stated that plans would be formulated to have the 937th fire on the vital enemy troop and supply concentration at Chorwon.

Ridgway delegated the planning of the mission to Brigadier General Bittman Barth, artillery commander of the 25th Infantry Division. Barth was also impressed with the Guardsmen, stating that the 937th was *"an excellent unit [that] had its feet on the ground from the start."*

The mission, set for the night of April 8, called for a battery to move up directly behind the infantrymen of the 25th Division on the south bank of the heavily defended Hantan River. It was thought that a surprise artillery attack would pin down and disrupt the Chinese long enough for the engineers to bridge the river. The 937th's "Long Toms," as the M-40s were known, were the only weapons that could reach the Chinese assembly areas in and around Chorwon almost fifteen miles away.

A composite battery, with guns from all three firing batteries under the command of Captain Aloysius Zeiler, commander of "B" Battery, was formed for the mission. Under the cover of darkness, supported by a company of Rangers and an AAA battery, the force moved out. Occupying previously dug in positions Captain Zeiler's men fired 120 rounds at a range of 25,715 yards. After thirty minutes the unit ceased firing and moved back to their original positions. Through aerial photographs and actual observations it was reported that the target was destroyed.

The successful mission had not been without cost. On the afternoon of the 8th, a survey team from Headquarters Battery hit a mine, killing one man and seriously wounding two others.[7]

CORPORAL GEORGE GATLIFF.
"A" BATTERY, 937TH FAB (ARKANSAS).

On 2 April, we moved into position near Uijongbu and the next day headed toward Kumhwa, stopping near Changgori. On that day, 3 April, we fired our first combat round at the Chinese. The next day we moved to near Changgpbu to support the 25th Infantry Division. On 5 April, General Ridgway visited us to tell us of a special mission he had planned for us. It had been kept a secret that our guns had a far greater range (about 18 miles) than anything in Korea at that time.

The mission was for us to move out after dark to a forward position and fire on Chorwon where there was a concentration of Chinese soldiers and supplies. It was hoped if the Chinese saw us they would think we were a new, strange looking tank. We started preparing and training for that mission and on 7 April we moved to a position astride the 38th Parallel. On the night of 8 April one gun from each battery moved forward and successfully completed our special mission.[8]

Courtesy of the U.S. Army Military History Institute, Carlisle Barracks, Pa.

Two of the Guard artillery battalions arrived with the versatile 155mm M-40 gun. Arkansas' 937th FAB lights up the Korean night with their "Long Toms."

Gatliff remained in the National Guard. Commissioned, he became Arkansas state assistant inspector general, before retiring after forty years service as a lieutenant colonel.

The 937th was popular with the brass that April. On the 11th, Ridgway returned in the company of Secretary of the Army Frank Pace, Jr. And on that day the 937th FAB earned a footnote in American military history.

*   *   *   *   *   *

The relief of General Douglas MacArthur as Commander in Chief Far East and commander of U.N. forces in Korea, along with the myriad of other commands and titles he held, had all the elements of a situation comedy. To say it was handled poorly would be a gross understatement.

After much deliberation, President Truman, on April 9, announced to his top advisors his decision to sack MacArthur. He could no longer tolerate MacArthur's vocal opposition to the administration's Korean policy. General Ridgway would replace MacArthur as commander in chief, and Lieutenant General James Van Fleet would take over Eighth Army.

It was decided that Army Secretary Frank Pace, Jr., then en route to Japan and Korea for an inspection tour, would have the dubious honor of giving MacArthur the news. Fearing a leak if Pace's instructions were sent over Army communications, Truman and his advisors decided to send them over the State Department network to American Ambassador John Muccio in Pusan. Muccio would then inform Pace who would fly back to Tokyo and do the deed.

By this time, Pace, unaware of the situation, had arrived in Japan where he attended a luncheon given by MacArthur and the General Headquarters (GHQ) Staff. That evening Pace received a puzzling cable from Secretary of Defense George Marshall, who had replaced Louis Johnson the previous September. As Pace recalled it, it said: "This is explicit, repeat, explicit. You will proceed to Korea and remain there until you hear from me." Pace, who was leaving for Korea the next day, had no inkling as to what this message pertained and did not alter his plans.

Pace arrived at Taegu on the evening of the 10th. After meeting with Ridgway he turned in for the night. In Washington, it was now the early morning of the 10th and the plan to fire MacArthur was coming up to speed. The cable to Muccio would go out that afternoon. He would decode it and pass it to Pace, who would return to Tokyo and present it to MacArthur at 1000 hours, Japan time, April 12.

Washington in 1951 was no different than today. By now rumors of MacArthur's impending dismissal were rampant, and hard questions were being asked by the media. Fearful that MacArthur might create a crisis, either militarily or politically, if he got wind of the news, Truman had Joint Chiefs Chairman, General Omar Bradley, cable MacArthur at noon on the 11th, relieving him of his command. A press conference was quickly called and within minutes the news flashed around the world. Unfortunately, Bradley's cable had been delayed and MacArthur learned of his dismissal from an aide who heard the news on the radio.

And where was Arkansas native Pace while these momentous events transpired? Where else, but along with Ridgway at the 937th FAB visiting his fellow Razorbacks where he pulled a lanyard and sent a 155mm shell heading north. As Ridgway later recalled, a reporter who had heard the news on the radio asked "whether I was not due congratulations." Finally, at 1645 hours that afternoon, an astounded Pace got the word and informed Ridgway he was the new Supreme Commander of the Pacific.[9]

On April 6, Utah's 204th FAB became the third National Guard artillery battalion to go into action. Initially assigned to I Corps, the battalion was placed in support of the ill-fated Gloucester Battalion of the British Brigade. On April 19, a battalion of the 45th British Field Artillery Regiment took over support of the Gloucesters. The 204th then moved to new positions to the east, in support of the 3rd Infantry Division.

Eighteen hours later the main thrust of the Chinese Spring Offensive hit the Gloucesters. Four days later the 800 man British unit mustered thirty-eight officers and men. Had the Utah battalion not moved when they did, they undoubtedly would have been wiped out.[10]

Four of the National Guard artillery battalions were armored and equipped with the M-7, self propelled 105mm howitzer. First produced in 1942, over 3,500 of these dependable weapons were manufactured during World War II and saw action around the world. While at Fort Lewis, one Guardsman working on his newly acquired M-7 found a maintenance form that had been filled out in North Africa! First of the AFABs to go into action was the aforementioned 176th.

FIRST LIEUTENANT JAMES KERCHEVAL. "C" BATTERY, 176TH AFAB (PENNSYLVANIA).

Our first mission was to fire in support of the 25th Infantry Division near Yongpyong. We set up an outpost (OP) forward of the unit and swept the approach to it with mine detectors; we then marked the swept trail with toilet paper.

The first men to man the outpost were National Guardsmen; they carefully walked between the two lines of toilet
paper and up to the OP without any problems.

Later that day two Regular Army men were assigned to replace the Guardsmen. These were two of the men that had
been assigned to us at Camp Carson, to bring the unit up
to full strength. They didn't like us and didn't think we knew
what we were doing. We showed them the path and told
them to stay within the area that had been swept. Before
they had gone a short distance we heard an explosion; they
had moved off the path and set off a bouncing betty mine.
Both men were severely wounded from the waist down and
immediately evacuated.[11]

Kercheval had served as a B-24 and B-17 navigator during
World War II. He flew on thirty-five combat missions over Europe
and received the Purple Heart.

On April 8, two National Guard 155mm battalions added their
combined thirty-six howitzers firepower to Eighth Army. The 196th
(TENNESSEE) and the 955th (NEW YORK) were both armed with
the M-2 tractor towed howitzer, another weapon that had seen considerable World War II service. The 196th went to X Corps on the
east coast, while the 955th joined I Corps and went into action at
Suim-Ni in support of the 24th Infantry Division.

A week after the two 155mm outfits began pounding the Chinese, the 987th AFAB from Ohio came on line. Assigned to IX Corps
on the central front, the Buckeyes were placed in support of the
1st Marine Division.

Utah's 213th AFAB became the eighth National Guard artillery battalion to go into action when "B" Battery commenced firing
at 1833 hours on the 22nd, also in support of the Marines. The
213th had landed at Inchon on the sixth and spent the next two
weeks being shuttled from one end of IX Corps to the other, never
going into action, their orders being changed every few days.

This period saw the unit attached or planning operations with
the 92nd AFAB, the 27th ROK FAB, and the 16th Royal New Zealand
Artillery Regiment. Then, at 0645 hours on the morning of the 22nd,
orders came to join the Marines at Hwachon, sixty-five miles
northeast of the unit's position near Kapyong. Service Battery remained at Kapyong, IX Corps having requisitioned their trucks to
haul ammo for other units. Three and a half hours after "B" Battery
fired its first round the Chinese struck.[12]

The National Guardsmen of the eight artillery battalions remember the next week in a dim haze. A week of going without

sleep or food, a week of firing and falling back and firing again. The Guardsmen would not only fight the Chinese with their 105s and 155s, they would fight them with machine guns, rifles, and hand grenades. And when the week was over, these eight battalions would have written another page in the long and illustrious history of the National Guard.

CHAPTER 5

WE GOT THE FLOCK OUT OF THERE

The brunt of the Chinese attack fell on I Corps in front of Seoul. This was not unexpected as the Chinese had made no secret of their plan to retake the South Korean capital by May 1, the Communist holiday. At this time five of the Guard artillery battalions were attached to I Corps. From east to west were the 955th, 176th, 936th, 937th and 204th.

Courtesy of Thomas Cacciola

Corporal Tom Cacciola, of New York's Battery "A" 955th FAB.

At the eastern end of I Corps sector, New York's 955th FAB was firing in support of the 19th Infantry Regiment, 24th Infantry Division, when the Chinese attacked. The enemy quickly drove between the 19th and the 5th RCT on the 19th's right and by daylight had penetrated almost three miles.[1]

CORPORAL THOMAS CACCIOLA. "A" BATTERY, 955TH FAB (NEW YORK).

Between the 8th and 21st of April we moved northward, firing all night long and then

54

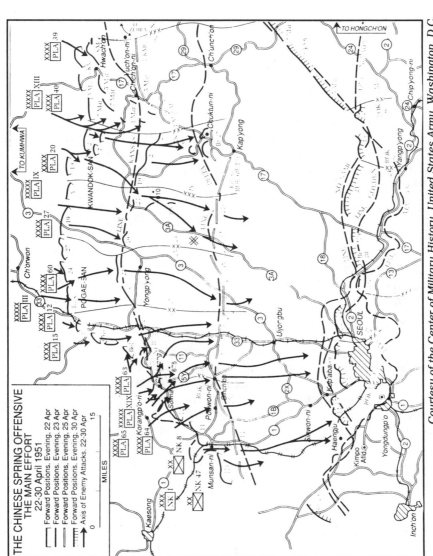

Courtesy of the Center of Military History, United States Army, Washington, D.C.

The Chinese offensive April 22, 1951, I and IX Corps sector. Seven Guard artillery battalions helped hold the line in this sector. The enemy reached the outskirts of Seoul but was held there.

returning back to a base position. We were firing in support of the 19th Infantry of the 24th Division and had advanced about ten miles north of the Hantan River.

It was rumored that a big Chink attack was on the way. No one ever worried about the North Koreans, they were really not on anyone's mind. It was always the Chinese we worried about.

On the night of the 22nd all hell broke loose. I remember it well. There was a full moon and the guns and men were clearly visible in the moonlight. The 955th joined up with the 555th FAB (we called them the triple nickels), part of the 5th RCT. The 555th FAB had 105s; my buddies and I called them pea-shooters compared to our big 155mm guns. We covered each other's withdrawal. Each time we moved south the 555th would fire, and then we would fire and they would retreat.

And then, and this must have been around 0200 or maybe 0300, I could see infantrymen stumble by. Then I remember men of the 555th running through our positions to the rear while we were firing. I distinctly remember one officer coming in between our guns and asking in what direction did his men go. The Chinks had broken through and the 555th overrun. I don't know what happened but many of them were killed.

Now there was no one between us and the Chinks. "A" Battery was put to the test. We were firing like crazy, like a .50 caliber machine gun at point blank range. We were firing to the front and to both sides. The battery officers were screaming at the men to keep firing. Every man was working at his best. Our only problem was if we had enough powder bags and shells. In the short lulls between the firing I could clearly hear the Chink's bugles blowing.

With all the chaos that was going on, my good friend and buddy, Jack Gallagher, and I talked briefly and joked about how Kim Il Sung wanted to have dinner at a restaurant in Seoul tonight and hence we were going to retreat all the way to Seoul. Quite a sense of humor I would say!

We retreated four times that night, about ten miles, in order to reach the Hantan River. At daybreak I could see thousands of Koreans trying desperately to get into small flat bottom boats and cross the river. They had all their belongings and some had small children on their backs. I wondered how many Chink soldiers were side by side with the

Koreans and would cross the river, reassemble and attack us from the rear. What a chilling thought![2]

The Pennsylvanians of the 176th AFAB were supporting the 2nd Battalion, 27th Regiment of the 25th Division, which had closed to within five and a half miles of Chorwon. At this position the 176th was now the northern most FAB in all of Korea. In the first hours of the attack, 50,000 Chinese hit this area. Backed by massive artillery fire and tanks, they quickly overran the Turkish Brigade on the division's left flank. This in turn caused the 24th Infantry Regiment on the 27th's left to withdraw south across the Hantan River.

In the early morning hours of the 23rd, the Chinese hit the Wolfhounds, and the 176th AFAB went to work. At daybreak the 2/27 reported that the 105 gunners had killed 768 Chinese, plus many more that could not be counted. The 25th Division artillery commander, Bittman Barth, recalled:

It was a machine gunner's and artilleryman's dream. The Reds came swarming across the rice paddies in front of the waiting doughboys in mass formation. Eight batteries of artillery, all the machine guns available, and several tanks poured in rapid fire. After about thirty minutes the Reds had had enough. The remnants retreated, carrying what wounded they could and leaving nearly a thousand dead and wounded behind. The Wolfhounds were not bothered anymore that day.[3]

Just to the west of the 176th, Arkansas' 936th FAB, minus "C" Battery, was supporting the Turkish Brigade then attached to the 25th Division. "C" Battery, detached on the 20th, was in support of the 65th Infantry Regiment, 3rd Infantry Division, to the Turk's left.

At 2330 hours the Chinese hit the Turks and the 65th Infantry Regiment with an estimated 50,000 men. Due to the exposed position of the Turkish artillery, they were soon ordered to withdraw and the 936th became the Turk's sole artillery support. Around 0200 hours on the morning of the 23rd a Turkish liaison officer arrived at the battalion FDC and reported that two units of his brigade were surrounded and that communications had been lost. The 936th continued to fire in support of the Turks until 0600 when they also lost communications. At 1000 orders came to displace to a new position twelve miles distant near Ch'udong-ni. The battalion had fired ninety-one missions expending 1,912 rounds since the attack began.[4]

The "Long Toms" of Arkansas' 937th FAB were also in support of the 25th Infantry Division when the Chinese struck. The preceding week had seen the unit move eight miles north of the 38th Parallel firing at enemy positions dug in on the mountain ridges. As early as the 16th increased reports of troops and pack animals to the battalion's immediate front indicated that the Chinese were planning a major attack. Mist, fog, and increasing amounts of low hanging smoke caused much of the firing to be unobserved during this period.

For the 937th the battle started on the night of the 21st when large contingents of enemy personnel were reported in the battalion sector. The next 24 hours saw the 937th fire at everything the Chinese had. Vehicles, artillery pieces, dug in troops, pack animals, convoys, reported camouflaged tank positions, road blocks and enemy emplacements were all under constant fire. At 0430 hours on the morning of April 23, verbal orders were received for all guns to withdraw from their positions. As the enemy drew near, small arms fire was heard in the valley on the battalion's left flank and an air alert was given as a lone enemy bomber harassed an adjacent division CP.

The guns retreated about four miles on the main supply road (MSR) and took up new positions, firing harassing missions as directed by I Corps. Later that morning, at approximately 1045 hours, under verbal orders of the 25th Division Artillery, the 937th displaced another ten miles south of the Imjin River and set up near Changgo-ri. Due to increased enemy pressure the battalion was alerted for full withdrawal once more and the guns again fell back, this time to the vicinity of Uijongbu.

Higher headquarters issued orders that future firing positions and battery placements were to be of a temporary nature due to the enemy's rapid advance. The battalion continued to fire and fall back. By now the battlefield was covered by dense smoke and the results of the firing were almost impossible to determine.

At one point communications with I Corps were lost and for a time the 937th was on its own. Battalion Commander, Lieutenant Colonel Thomas Douglas, finally got clearance from the 3rd Infantry Division, into whose sector the unit had moved, to fall back.[5]

CORPORAL GEORGE GATLIFF.
"A" BATTERY, 937TH FAB (ARKANSAS).

On the night of 22 April the Chinese hit us hard. We were on a hill on the south side of a valley and could see the tracers on the mountain that was north of us. We could see that the battle line was moving towards us and knew we were in trouble. I had been up late watching the "firefight" on the mountain, then went to bed to read a new book I had just received. Not long after I finally went to sleep we were alerted to prepare to move. It was several days before I had the opportunity to sleep again.

Some weeks before, I had found a farmer's "A-Frame" and had made me a bamboo walking stick. The first sergeant, Gene Reeves, never liked for me to have them, but had no reason to make me discard them. While preparing to move, we were burning some documents. I went out to add more to the fire and found what was left of my walking stick in the fire. I asked who had done that, and someone told me the first sergeant had did it and had thrown my "A-Frame" down the side of the hill.

About 3:00 A.M. we received the word to move south, after the Chinese got so close that we could no longer fire on them with our big guns. We moved about four miles, still on the Uijongbu-Kumhwa road, and set up and started firing again. Later that morning we moved south again, setting up near Changgo-ri. We sent all of our soldiers and equipment, except the gun sections, on south to Seoul. We moved the guns to a position one mile northeast of Uijongbu.

Our type battalion had three firing batteries and each battery had four guns. Normally, each battery is assigned a sector of direction. In this case, however, we were covering such a wide sector that each gun in the battery was aimed in a different direction. During the first night we ran out of ammunition and since the main Chinese assault was headed for our battery, the other batteries brought all their ammunition to us. We took several prisoners here, this was on 24 April.

On 25 April we found out we had been forgotten—or abandoned—by the 25th Infantry Division, the unit we were supporting. We loaded up and moved out. We were told later, by our air observers, that the Chinese moved into our positions shortly after we had moved out. They also told us that a medical unit that was near us did not make it out and was destroyed.[6]

To the west of the 936th and 937th, the 204th FAB was now in support of the 3rd Infantry Division. Late in the afternoon of the 22nd, battalion air observers reported thousands of enemy troops moving south. They made no effort at concealment and seemed unconcerned with the artillery and air strikes raining down on them. That night the battalion air observers kept flying, adjusting fire by flares and moonlight. By now the 204th was in range of Chinese artillery and 300 rounds fell in the battalion area, but caused no casualties.

The next morning the battalion was ordered to fall back 10,000 yards, setting up near 3rd Division headquarters. By now the Chinese offensive was in full force; it was impossible for the 204th to register their guns, simply because there were too many targets. For the next seventy-two hours the guns would fire continually, expending over 1,600 rounds during the night of the 24th alone. The choice target was a gathering of 2,000 troops and 600 pack animals congregated in a small village. The 204th fired 240 rounds onto the target using time on target fire methods. Observers reported the target almost completely wiped out.

On the morning of the 25th the battalion once more retreated, this time falling back 8,000 yards. A heavy fog had settled in covering the move from the Chinese who now occupied the hills on both sides of the battalion. Within fifteen minutes of "B" Battery clearing their former position it was overrun by the Chinese.[7]

**PRIVATE FIRST CLASS RONALD RANSOM.
"B" BATTERY, 204TH FAB (UTAH).**

I had been the battery commander's jeep driver, but when we got to Inchon, I transferred to the mess section. I wanted to get a promotion and couldn't get it driving a jeep. About midnight or 0100 on the night of the 22nd, the C.O., Captain Bishop, came around and woke everybody up. He said, "Bring your weapons, ammo and everything you've got because something's happening."

He took us out to the perimeter—cooks, everybody—and placed us in foxholes. The forward section of the perimeter was a hundred yards or so in front of the guns and went all the way around the battery. I don't recall, but I think he kept us separated, one man to a hole, so we could cover a wider area.

I had my carbine, a .45 caliber pistol, an old .45 caliber "grease gun," a few hand grenades and lots of ammo. It was a scary night. There was no activity, no one came at us at all, but planes were dropping flares; the little parachutes drifting down, and the guns were firing away. We were out there all night.

Then at daybreak the mess section got called back to cook breakfast. We were just starting to serve the first man when we got a march order. It was difficult because in the kitchen you had hot things going and you had to get them out and get them out in a hurry. Nobody got breakfast. We loaded everything, pancakes that were cooked, scrambled eggs that were cooking. We loaded everything on the trucks and proceeded to get the hell out of there.

The thing I recall, as we were going down the road, the Chinese or North Koreans were coming down the mountain. There were lots of them and you could see them easily. They were shooting at us, but they were a bit too far away for them to be effective with their weapons. We were just out of range, but you could see them coming and even hear them.

The mess section and the supply section went back into Seoul and set up in a bombed out school.We didn't rejoin the gun sections for a week or so, and the gun crews had to eat "C" rations during this period.

Later moving to California, Ransom is now Chief, Customer Support Branch (computers), for the California National Guard in Sacramento.

On the central front the Chinese hit IX Corps with 90,000 men. At this time two National Guard artillery battalions were on line supporting IX Corps operations. Ohio's 987th AFAB, backing up the 6th ROK Division on the corps' left flank had just moved into position the afternoon of the 22nd. The ROKs collapsed within minutes, falling back without the slightest resistance.

Major General William M. Hoge, IX Corps commander, stated in his official report: "The rout and dissolution of the [ROK 6th Division] was [sic] entirely uncalled for and disgraceful in all aspects." Eighth Army Commander, Lieutenant General James Van Fleet, remembered: "Everywhere—in the nearby battle lines and at headquarters all the way back to Seoul—our soldiers were damning the South Koreans. At the first sign of trouble they had collapsed; they had threatened our whole army with extinction." The first American unit threatened with extinction was the 987th AFAB.[8]

MASTER SERGEANT BOB STEFFY.
HEADQUARTERS, 987TH AFAB (OHIO).

What we derisively called Second Bull Run was an embarrassment. I was always shaky about using the term, but I understood its origin and meaning. Our battalion had for its symbol a charging red bull on a yellow triangle. It connoted power and speed and the triangle said it was armor. It was a great logo.

We had encountered little resistance and were moving forward at a pretty good clip. Then on Sunday, the 22nd, we were ordered into a new firing position. To get to this spot we had to traverse a road that was a narrow shelf on the side of a mountain and the other side was a sheer cliff overlooking a stream that was a hundred or more feet below us. In my opinion it took a real Phi Beta Kappa to send armor over that road. Later I was told that Lieutenant Colonel Denison, 987th skipper, objected to this position but was overruled by Regular Army brass.

By evening we had gotten all of "A" Battery and half of "B" Battery into position and firing. I don't recall how much we fired, but the cannoneers were busy. I was in the operations tent and was keeping track of the action on a situation map. A feature of this map was a no fire line, a line plotted far enough ahead to prevent our shelling our own troops.

Suddenly I was told to move the no fire line back 3,000 yards. A little later I was told to move it back again and then once more. Finally, when the no fire line was almost to the guns, Major James Snedeker, the S-3, gave the FDC, break station-march order (BSMO). To quote the sheep-herder, "We got the flock out of there."

I gathered up my map and equipment and headed for my M-39. This was a full tracked personnel carrier and a royal pain; they were later turned in for half-tracks. Anyway, the driver, a kid of maybe eighteen or nineteen years was nervous and scared and he couldn't get that abomination to start. A lieutenant came by in a jeep and shouted to get that vehicle out of there. I said it wouldn't start. He screamed to leave it. I asked if I should burn it, and he said, "No, just get the hell out of there."

A stream of angry and frustrated soldiers started back to the rest of the battalion over that impassable road. I remember it was a bright moonlit night. I had my carbine and a Browning automatic rifle (BAR) that someone had given to the colonel, who gave it to me, with ONE magazine of ammo.

The 6th ROK Division was running over us in their eagerness to leave. I recall they were carrying their clothes and dragging their women, and that they had loads of onions or something equally pungent.

There was one spot where we held up to fix the road enough to get what equipment we could out, and I decided the BAR was too heavy so I threw away the bipod. As we worked, the Koreans were urinating on anything in front of, or under them, and the stones were pretty wet. The Koreans kept bringing that damned bipod back to me and I kept throwing it away.

I don't know what it was with our tank retriever, but it was blocking that sheep path called a road. Nor do I remember how we rolled it over the side and down into the canyon where it caught fire. I do recall helping to push a 6 x 6 truck over the side and I remember the alarm when the retriever's ammo started to explode. One memory is how thirsty I was. I came upon an abandoned jeep and I relieved it of the five-gallon water can strapped to the fender. Now I was moving down the road with a carbine, an 18-lb. BAR, and a five-gallon can of water. Nope, I can't explain it.

Now things get confused; forty-two years later I'm not sure of the order of events. Someplace along the line I found myself alone in the bright moonlight. In my mind's eye I could see people in the wrong colored uniforms lying in ambush above me and watching me. I decided that I could be in danger of capture, so I pulled my stripes off and threw them away. It was no secret that Oriental interrogators leaned pretty heavily on anyone who had access to important information and an intelligence NCO might be a ripe candidate for questioning.

I know that somewhere I met Captain Dale McMannus, SFC Fred Adams, and SFC Charley Morgenstern. They were going back in after the guns and invited me along. We only got so far when we met a Headquarters Battery jeep coming out. The sergeant in charge told us they had gotten close enough to see the guns and that the enemy was swarming all over them. Our little quartet about-faced and headed back to where the remaining nine guns of the battalion were set up.

The first person I saw was Lieutenant Paul Burns, and I leaned against him and poured out my frustration. God, I was mad and frustrated. Later we learned that the gun crews had been able to disable their guns before abandoning them. That was half of the battalion's 105mm howitzers.[9]

Bob Steffy and Headquarters Battery Commander Ray Kommel were, and still are, the best of friends. They had served together in the Philippines with the 37th Infantry Division (Ohio) during World War II. Kommel recalls the night of "Second Bull Run."

CAPTAIN RAY KOMMEL.
COMMANDING OFFICER, HEADQUARTERS BATTERY, 987TH AFAB (OHIO).

After we landed at Inchon, we immediately went into support of the 1st Marine Division; also in this sector we were supporting a ROK battalion. That's when we went down in the canyon. Headquarters Battery got all the way in and got set up, but the firing batteries had trouble. Every time they'd get one gun in, they'd have to stop and build up the road.

The guns that made it in started firing early in the evening. We started to fire at maximum range and in a couple of hours we were down to minimum range. Then we got a call from the liaison officer. He said, "I don't know about you, but if it was me, I'd get the hell out of there."

And that's the order we got; BSMO, get the hell out of here. And, of course, it was chaos. The self propelled guns were the first ones on the road and the first one out collapsed the road and then the wheeled vehicles couldn't get out. I had a wheeled vehicle and I lost all my equipment. About everybody that was down there lost their equipment because they couldn't get out.

When we got blocked down there we kept getting messages over the radio. "Do not destroy equipment. Help is on the way!" All we could do there was just wait and wait and wait, and finally about daybreak we decided that no help was coming, so we started walking out. I got beyond the block a ways, and there was a half-track that had worked its way down there, so I got on it and rode the rest of the way out.

After we got out of the valley and started to regroup we set up a perimeter defense. We began to take some fire from the ridges and the men on the perimeter started to run. I remembered from World War II, when I was a forward observer [FO] with the infantry, the same thing happened and this one sergeant had just stood up and yelled at them, "Okay, you yellow bastards get back here" and they turned around and went back to their positions. So I did the same thing and it worked this time, too. It was automatic, people just don't like to be called that.

Photos courtesy of Bob Steffy

Korea was the second war Ohio Guardsmen Bob Steffy (left) and Ray Kommel (right) fought in together.

That morning, Major Lentz, the battalion exec took a jeep
and some people back down to see if the equipment could
be saved. They got ambushed going around a corner and
one man got killed, so they came back. Then the Marines
went down there and they couldn't get the equipment out.
So we went back to a staging area a few miles back and
reorganized. It was a pretty bad feeling. I'd never had to
suffer defeat before. I was ashamed that I had to leave the
guns and equipment and the way we had to get out of there.

The failure of the ROK 6th Division left a ten-mile gap between
I Corps 24th Infantry Division and IX Corps 1st Marine Division,
causing both units to fall back. The key position in the IX Corps area
was the town of Kapyong, a vital road and rail junction. The loss of
Kapyong would allow the Chinese the opportunity of attacking Seoul
from the east and encircling the battered units of I Corps.

General Hoge entrusted the defense of Kapyong to the 27th
British Commonwealth Brigade. The 16th New Zealand Artillery
Regiment, which along with the 987th AFAB had been supporting
the ROKs, rejoined the brigade. To reinforce the New Zealanders,
Hoge ordered the 213th AFAB (Utah) to Kapyong.[10]

The 213th, operating with the 1st Marine Division, had barely
got their 105s warmed up when the Chinese attacked on the night
of the 22nd. The next day the battalion moved back to Sindang-ni
and went into support of the panic stricken ROKs above Kapyong.
The ROKs continued their speedy withdrawal, moving south in a
ragged formation, eight men abreast and on the double. At 1730
hours the battalion was assured by the ROKs that the troops now
visible in the surrounding hills were friendly. At 2000 this information was corrected: the oncoming troops were Chinese.

At 2050 IX Corps ordered the 213th to move to Sakchang-ni,
300 yards in back of an Australian infantry battalion. During this
move one M-7 howitzer, a half track, and a trailer were lost—the
howitzer when it ran off the road avoiding a group of South Koreans. Then, at 0140 hours the orders came attaching the 213th to
the New Zealanders. Leaving "A" Battery to cover the Aussies, the
battalion moved out at 0300.[11]

FIRST LIEUTENANT THOMAS CHRISTENSEN.
EXECUTIVE OFFICER, "A" BATTERY, 213TH AFAB (UTAH).

These were some tough moves. Nobody knew for sure where
the CCF were and how far they had penetrated. We traveled
in blackout conditions over narrow roads also occupied by
the bugging out ROK soldiers. When the word came to withdraw to Kapyong, "A" Battery was left behind as the rear
guard. We fired on the rest of the night at road junctions

and mountain passes and at the same time defended the perimeter of the battery.

Just as it got dawn we withdrew amid bugle calls, small arms fire and with mortar rounds following us back to Kapyong. Welcome to the shooting war. We managed to hold there although our supply line was cut for a period of time.

The 26th in particular was a memorable day. We moved up a road about four miles above Kapyong and took up positions on a hill overlooking a small valley. The guns were placed to the right of the road and we had to stagger them to get them all in position. One of our concerns in this position was a big tree that was a little to the right of number three gun. When the gun traversed in that direction the tree interfered with its line of fire. If the battery was given a mission in that direction the gun would not be able to fire.

A small squad of combat engineers were moving by us and we enlisted their help. They proceeded to wrap primer cord around the trunk of the tree to blow it apart. As they got ready to fire the charge they yelled "Fire in the hole." Our men moved away and everybody stopped what they were doing to watch. When the blast went off they started cheering and yelling. It really shook that tree but it remained standing.

Over in Headquarters Battery, about two hundred yards away, they heard the blast and naturally thought enemy fire was incoming. They jumped into their foxholes only to hear my men cheering and yelling. I very soon got a phone call from the battalion exec chewing me out for not informing them in advance of the blast. We still had to cut the tree down with axes to clear our field of fire.

Our Battery C.O., Captain Ray Cox, sent out patrols each afternoon, mainly to check our flanks, to see what was out there. They usually went out a mile or so. For some reason that afternoon he decided to lead the patrol himself, probably because of our unstable position. I don't need to point out that captains rarely lead these types of patrols. He did and found the Chinese on a hill to the right and above us two miles or so out. They got into a small skirmish and inflicted some casualties on the enemy before returning to the battery.

Upon his return we beefed up our perimeter defense on that side. At this time we were supporting the 19th ROK Infantry. Early the next morning the Chinese tried to break through and there was a vigorous firefight. It was good that the extra defensive positions had been established.[12]

A farmer, Christensen served twelve years as a state representative in the Utah State Legislature.

Only one National Guard artillery battalion had been assigned to X Corps on the eastern sector of the front. The 196th FAB (Tennessee) fired its first shot on April 8 in support of the 7th Infantry Division. When the Chinese attacked on the 22nd, the Memphis unit was still with the 7th near Hadumu'dong and also firing in support of the 5th ROK Division on the 7th's right flank.

Falling back to Umyong'ni on the 23rd, the 196th hooked up with the Army Reservists of the 780th FAB. Firing continually, the 196th expended 9,114 rounds during the week of April 22–29. The North Koreans did not press their attack in this area as hard as the Chinese did in the central and western sectors and X Corps was able to hold along the Soyang River.[13]

On the 29th the Chinese made one last effort to take the South Korean capital. Once again heavy artillery fire and air attacks broke up the attacking force. In the eight day period 22–30 April, the U.N. Command estimated the enemy had suffered 80,000 casualties, the vast majority (over 70,000), in front of Seoul in the I Corps sector.

Casualties in the six American Divisions totaled 314 killed and 1,600 wounded; total U.N. casualties numbered about 7,000, the bulk of these in the ROK units. A staggering defeat had been inflicted on the enemy. But on May 1, Eighth Army Commander Van Fleet warned his command that the Communists had the manpower to strike again "as hard as before or harder."[14]

CHAPTER 6

THEY'LL NEVER GET OVER THAT HILL

Van Fleet was correct. Even as Eighth Army units started moving forward, the Chinese were planning another major attack. When it was over two National Guard units and elements of two others would have earned Presidential Unit Citations.*

By May 11, intelligence reports and aerial sightings suggested that the attack would come in the next few days. The largest concentration of enemy troops appeared to be west of the Pukhan River in the west central sector near the boundary of IX Corps and X Corps. Van Fleet instructed IX Corps Commander Hoge to place his corps artillery on that flank. All units were directed to make maximum use of artillery. No limitation was to be placed on the expenditure of ammunition; Van Fleet wanted five times the normal amount of fire available when the attack came. And so was born the "Van Fleet day of fire."**[1]

* * * * * *

---

* 196th Field Artillery Battalion (Tennessee); 252nd Transportation Truck Company (Alabama); 300th Armored Field Artillery Battalion, less Battery "B" (Wyoming); Headquarters Battery and "C" Battery, 937th Field Artillery Battalion (Arkansas).
** Van Fleet day of fire per tube.

105mm howitzer	300 rounds.
155mm howitzer	250 rounds.
155mm gun	200 rounds.
8 inch howitzer	200 rounds.
75mm howitzer	250 rounds.

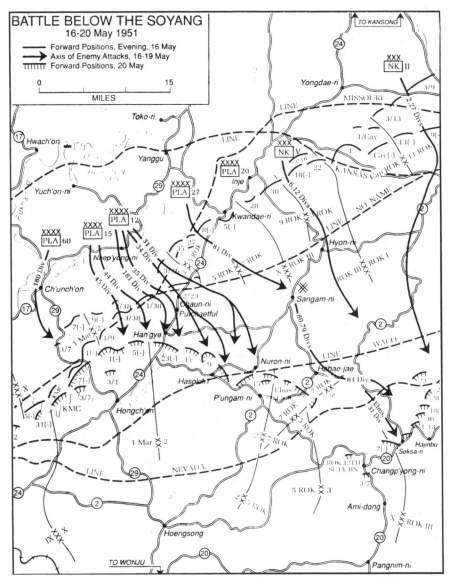

Courtesy of the Center of Military History, United States Army, Washington, D.C.

Two National Guard units and elements of two others were awarded Presidential Unit Citations after the Soyang River battle.

Wyoming's 300th Armored Field Artillery Battalion failed its test. Less than four months after being judged the best artillery battalion in the entire Sixth Army area, the men from the Big Horn Mountains of Northern Wyoming failed the readiness test administered by I Corps Artillery. This failure can be attributed to one thing: the Army's policy that all units depart for Korea at full strength. (See chapter 2.)

So while the other eight Guard artillery outfits moved to the front in April, the 300th remained near Kumhae working out the kinks that had shown up on the test. After several more weeks of training, the battalion was retested on May 9, and passed with a score of 84. Reassigned to X Corps, an advance party headed to the front the next day.

The balance of the unit arrived at Wonju on the 14th, and X Corps attached the unit less "B" Battery to the 2nd Infantry Division. "B" Battery was detached and assigned to the 1st Marine Division; they would not rejoin the 300th until May 25. During their ten day absence "B" Battery would fire 4,822 rounds in support of the Marines.[2]

The trip north was unique in that the 300th moved by rail instead of going by ship to Inchon as the other National Guard artillery battalions had done. The threat that the port of Inchon could still be taken by the Chinese was undoubtedly the reason for this change.

PRIVATE FIRST CLASS EARL HUMMELL. "A" BATTERY, 300TH AFAB (WYOMING).

We went up by train. Each M-7 gun and crew had a flat car. We had to live, eat, bathe, and everything else on that flat car and hope we didn't roll off at night

Courtesy of Earl Hummell

Private First Class Earl Hummell of Wyoming's 300th AFAB standing next to a M-7. Hummell is wearing the rubberized coveralls issued to M-7 crewmen.

when we tried to sleep. We went through seventy-seven tunnels; one of those tunnels was something like fourteen miles
long. It went in the side of a mountain, made a three hundred and sixty degree turn in there, and came out the other
side at a lower elevation. We were right in back of the engine and you could hardly breathe. We tied scarves over
our faces to filter out the soot. It was quite an experience.
The trip took about three days, and we were very, very happy
to get off that train.

Unaware that the enemy had temporarily abandoned their effort to capture Seoul, and that twelve Chinese divisions had moved
in front of X Corps poised to strike, the men of the 300th were
astounded at the peaceful routine they found at the front.

PFC Hummell continues:
It was about twenty miles from the railhead to our position
in a valley. We pulled in and there was a tank battalion in
front of us and another one in back of us. They had a baseball diamond set up and were playing softball; we couldn't
wait for the next day to get organized and challenge them to
a softball game. We had a real good team. Another outfit
had a volleyball court set up. We thought if this is combat,
it beats training all to hell.

One thing bothered me. I said to Jack Toth, our section
chief, "There's one problem here, we fired these guns about
eight hours a day during training, then went to bed. The
infantry is going to want us to fire twenty-four hours a day.
How are we going to do that?" They didn't have a sleep plan,
no one had thought of that. By the way, when we got home
Jack stayed in the Guard, he wound up a colonel. Another
thing, we hadn't fired the guns at night, not a round, and
no one really knew if we could fire them at night.

We thought we were as safe as could be. The tankers said,
"It's real quiet, nothing's happening. Don't worry, you've
got plenty of infantry in front of you. See that big hill on the
left, it's manned by infantry and the top is mined. They'll
never get over that hill."

Hummell later became an orthodontist in Sacramento,
California.

The 300th registered their guns that afternoon, the 16th, and
settled in for their first night at the front. Things were quiet. Then,
sometime after 2300 hours, machine gun fire could be heard coming from the front increasing in volume in the next hour. At 0030 a

star shell burst over the valley. The scene it illuminated shocked the men who were on watch.*[3]

SERGEANT WILLIAM DAY IV.
"C" BATTERY, 300TH AFAB (WYOMING).

A parachute flare goes up and the whole area is bathed in the eerie white-silver intense light of burning magnesium. We can see the whole valley and are stunned to discover the MSR is clogged with trucks full of men, and other men are walking down the highway—all to the rear. The 5th and 7th ROK Divisions are in full retreat.

Then all hell breaks loose. Fire Mission! Fire Mission! The gun crews spring into action. "C" Battery, with its six 105mm howitzers, fires mission after mission. By 0800 we can see the Chinese coming across the rice paddies and down the road at Chaun-ni.

The guns are hot and ammunition can't be uncrated fast enough. The motor pool uses every truck available to haul ammo. The cooks, clerks and everyone available prepares ammo while the gun crews stay at their posts and continue to pour a withering fire on the enemy. The forward observers are being overrun—their last words are "Just keep shooting, you can't miss."

The cannon barrels are too hot to touch. Ammunition is very low. The enemy is closing. One Sherman tank is burning on the road in front of us; five others pull up on two knolls behind us and start firing direct fire.

Close station-march order (CSMO) is given. We are moving to the rear. It is 1000 hours, May 17, 1951, and the battle of the Soyang River is under way.[4]

PRIVATE FIRST CLASS EARL HUMMELL.
"A" BATTERY, 300TH AFAB (WYOMING).

After the first night the whole thing went into a blur and I can't remember the sequence of what happened. It's amazing to find out how long you can go without sleep. I didn't

---

* Various military histories show different dates for the events of the next two weeks. Eg.: The above on the 15th. This deviance is undoubtedly because so many of the events occurred around midnight and the fact that the men involved were too busy to worry about the date. The dates used are from Mr. Day's book, "The Running Wounded," and the command reports of the 300th AFAB.

know, I'd never been put to that test before. I found out in the next four or five days.

One interesting incident I do remember and maybe it was the second night. A Navy F7F twin engine Tigercat came over right down the side of us. He lowered his landing gear and flaps (I guess to lower his air speed) and started firing his cannon in short bursts. We stopped firing and wondered "What in the world is that crazy guy doing?" If we hadn't stopped firing we would have knocked him down. He made three passes then wagged his wings and left.

About five minutes later we got the order CSBO. This was different than the usual CSMO. It meant close station, bug out. You don't load up your ammunition, you don't pull your telephone wires or anything. You start your engines, turn 180 degrees and go.

I didn't find out till about ten years later what that guy in that plane was doing. All the time he was flying around our position he was trying to get our attention and he was radioing: "Get that artillery out of there, there's a whole division of Chinese coming up on their left rear flank." Of course we couldn't see them and we didn't have a radio to hear him. But someone at corps heard him and got the message to us to get out of there. He saved us. We would have been dead or POWs in fifteen minutes.

I'm not sure how many times we fell back, maybe three or four times a day for five or six days or so. We'd fall back maybe two or three miles then set up and start firing again. We got real good at setting up, then falling back.

The 300th wasn't the only National Guard artillery unit attached to the 2nd Infantry Division. Tennessee's 196th FAB had joined the "Indian Head" division on May 1, after being attached to the 7th Infantry Division during April. At 0900 hours on the 17th the unit was notified that the enemy had penetrated the 23rd Infantry Regiment's sector and that they should be prepared to withdraw on short notice.

That night the battalion received eighty rounds of 76mm fire in their positions but luckily suffered no casualties. After firing 2,650 rounds in twenty-four hours the 196th was ordered to fall back 5,000 yards south of the NO NAME Line where they went in support of the 3rd Infantry Division's 15th Infantry. The 196th would fire a total of 23,329 rounds during the month of May.[5]

By May 20, the Chinese Sixth Offensive had been stopped, and by the 23rd, Eighth Army was back on the attack all along the front.

On the eastern front X Corps Commander, Lieutenant General Edward Almond, perceived a chance to trap large numbers of the retreating Communists. Almond hastily mounted OPERATION CHOPPER (also known as Task Force Baker, or Task Force Gerhardt) one of, if not, the most ill-conceived operation of the entire Korean War.[6]

Almond's plan called for a task force to travel fifteen miles into enemy territory to Inge, and then on to Kansong another fifty-two miles distance on the east coast. Once there they would set up a perimeter and deny the retreating forces the use of the road net that went through the town. At Kansong the task force would be supplied by sea and supported by naval gun fire. Tanks from the 2nd and 3rd Infantry Divisions were to lead the way but it would be hours—if not a day—before more than a few tanks could arrive.

In the early morning hours of May 25 the 300th AFAB received an urgent radio message from X Corps artillery operations center. "Load your vehicles with all the ammunition and fuel they can carry. You are going on a special mission." By daybreak the unit had arrived at the assembly area just south of Chaun-ni where they joined up with the 187th Airborne Regiment and other elements of the task force.[7]

As the units formed up, Almond landed in a helicopter at the 187th command post. He was in a rage that the task force had not yet moved out. Almond ordered that the 187th send whatever troops were available on the road to Inge immediately; the other units could catch up with them. Intelligence had reported four or more Chinese divisions covering the road, and the 187th staff regarded Almond's plan as suicidal. Fearing he would be relieved of his command if he argued with Almond, 187th Commander, Brigadier General Frank Bowen, ordered his first battalion to move out.[8]

Now under heavy pressure from Bowen, the force commander, Colonel George Gerhardt, informed 300th Commander, Lieutenant Colonel John F. Raper, Jr., that his outfit would lead the assault. Raper was shocked. He protested that this was an inappropriate role for artillery. Gerhardt replied, "You're armored, aren't you?"[9]

"A" Battery took the point and the rest of the battalion followed. With "A" Battery leading, the task force headed north towards the first day's objective, the Soyang River. Meeting increasing opposition, the force covered twelve miles and reached the river after dark. That night some tanks arrived and the next day took over the point. Just before dawn on May 27, the advance guard, including "A" Battery, moved out towards Inge. The balance of the 300th remained at the river. The entire route went through a defile with the Soyang on the right and high hills on the left. Within minutes the column came under heavy fire; the enemy raked the advance guard with machine guns, mortars, and bazookas from their entrenched positions.

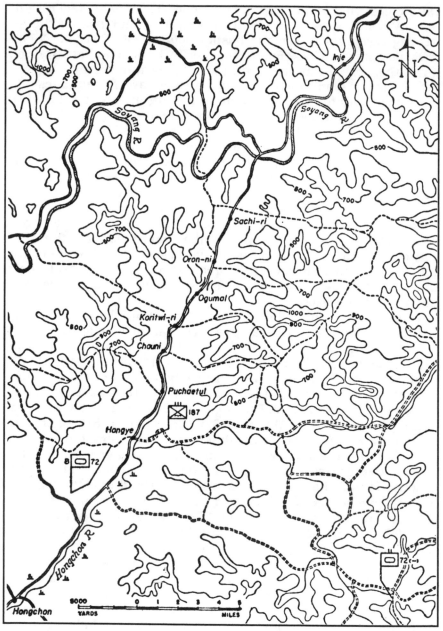

Courtesy of the Center of Military History, United States Army, Washington, D.C.

The road to Inge. Note the flags designating the command posts of the 187th Airborne, and elements of the 72nd Tank Battalion. Guardsmen will not be surprised that Wyoming's 300th AFAB is not shown.

Reaching Inge about noon on the 27th, the advance guard fought its way into the town, three tanks and a handful of infantrymen preceding "A" Battery. Colonel Gerhardt now ordered the rest of his command to move forward from the north bank of the Soyang to Inge. Leaving late in the afternoon the balance of the 300th spent the entire night on the road arriving at dawn to support the advance.

Moving out the next morning the advance guard ran into withering fire and managed to progress only 3,000 yards. The task force operations section then ordered the advance guard to disengage and return to Inge. By now "A" Battery was in a tight spot. Pinned down in their open topped M-7s, and on a narrow road, the withdrawal order necessitated that each vehicle turn around individually. Directing the guns in the withdrawal, "A" Battery Executive Officer, Lieutenant Richard Friedlund, was killed. Before "A" Battery could disengage, another man was dead and eighteen wounded. OPERATION CHOPPER was over.[10]

PRIVATE FIRST CLASS EARL HUMMELL.
"A" BATTERY, 300TH AFAB (WYOMING).

We went forward to an assembly area through the battlefield that we had been shooting into. The engineers were already there and they were using bulldozers to stack the bodies into piles. They had five or six piles as big as haystacks and the ground was still covered with bodies everywhere you looked as far as you could see.

We went through this area for a while then came to a halt and lined up our guns. I remember nothing happened that day. Evening came and we all went to sleep. Next morning we woke up and a column of tanks had come in and were parked right next to us; we'd been so tired we hadn't heard them pull in. I guess the paratroopers also arrived about that time. This was the task force forming up of OPERATION CHOPPER. I don't recall if we took off that day or the next day.

I don't recall taking much fire on the way to the river; it got worse the next day when we took off for Inge which I think was two or three miles away. The tanks were leading, then some engineers, then us. The paratroopers were riding on the tanks. We went into a canyon and most of the tanks and engineers got knocked out.

We had to run through a series of roadblocks; there must have been ten of them. We were firing our guns into the hills surrounding the road the whole time. The next morning we left Inge, but didn't get very far. The column came to a stop at a big bend in the road. Word came down that there was a bridge around the bend and two GIs were laying on it. They were probably dead, but no one knew for sure.

Our commanding officer came up and said we had to get those two men off the bridge. He wanted one volunteer from each gun to go out and get them. No one volunteered. That bridge was zeroed in by at least four enemy machine guns and it was going to be impossible to get those men off. We drew straws and I got the short straw from my gun. I knew it was a suicide mission. I peeked around the corner and could see the machine gun bullets hitting on the bridge. No way were we going to be able to go out there and get them off that bridge. But orders are orders and we had to do it.

I'll never forget, we finally got the six guys together and I was put in charge of the detail. It was six PFCs and privates and I was going to lead the six of us to slaughter because there was no way we were going to get on that bridge and back off it. Less than a minute before we were heading around the corner to the bridge, a lieutenant colonel walked up. He was the tank battalion commander.

He said to my C.O., "What's going on here, why is this column stopped?" My C.O. said, "We can't go any further because there's some GIs on the bridge around the corner." The colonel asked, "What are you going to do about it?" And my C.O. said, "I'm sending a detail of six men out there to get them off that bridge." And the colonel said, "Like hell you are! Who's in charge of the detail?" I said, "I am, sir." And he said, "Discharge your detail. Tell them to get back on their guns and tell them to tell the drivers to crank up their engines. We're coming around this corner and I want every gun you've got blazing." My C.O. said, "What about the GIs on the bridge?" The colonel said, "We're going to run over them. We're not going to risk six men to get two off that bridge."

So we took off and ran over the two guys. They were probably dead, and I think the colonel made the right decision. It certainly saved my life. The colonel got killed later that day. We never did reach our objective; we turned around and came back.

The failure of OPERATION CHOPPER was Eighth Army's only setback the last week in May. Elsewhere, all across the front, U.N. forces were again advancing north.

In the X Corps sector Utah's 213th AFAB was in support of the 24th Division's, 21st Infantry, near Hahongjong-ni. At 0200 hours on the 27th a force of 4,000 enemy troops which the infantry had encircled attempted a breakout. Their only escape route led them directly through the valley occupied by Headquarters Battery and "A" Battery. Men from both units rushed to their positions and engaged the oncoming Chinese with their rifles, and other small arms, killing a hundred of them. At one point the Chinese got within twenty feet of "A" Battery's switchboard.

At daybreak the attack abated. "A" Battery Commander, Captain Ray Cox, then organized a counterattack. Taking one M-7 and a combined force of about forty men from both batteries, Cox progressed up a side canyon three-fourths of a mile from where the attack had originated. At a cost of four men wounded, Cox and his men killed 105 of the enemy, plus another 200 estimated killed. Eight hundred and thirty-one Chinese had had enough and surrendered to the small force. For this action the two batteries were awarded a Presidential Unit Citation.[11]

The last major Eighth Army offensive of the Korean War, OPERATION PILEDRIVER, commenced on June 3. The operation called for I Corps, supported by IX Corps, to advance to Line WYOMING, twelve miles north of the MLR. On the eastern front X Corps would drive towards the Punchbowl, also approximately twelve miles distant.

Due to a number of factors including incessant rain, stiffening enemy resistance, and troop exhaustion due to the fact that Eighth Army had been in continual fighting since May 21, the advance slowed to a crawl. Led by ROK Marines in a night attack on June 11, the 1st Marine Division reached Line KANSAS overlooking the Punchbowl, and by June 14, I and IX Corps units had secured Line WYOMING.[12]

The peace talks opened at Kaesong July 10, 1951, only to be abruptly broken off August 23, when the Communists claimed that an American plane had bombed the neutral zone that surrounded the ancient city. An investigation failed to turn up any evidence to back the Communist claim. Lieutenant General Matthew Ridgway, now U.N. commander, became angry. He felt the enemy was stalling and building up forces in the Kaesong area under cover of the neutral zone. To counter the suspected buildup Ridgway proposed to capture the city which was just inside North Korean territory three miles south of the 38th Parallel.

Because of the political implications involved, Ridgway requested permission to mount the operation from the Joint Chiefs of Staff on September 11. That same day an Air Force plane accidentally strafed Kaesong, and Ridgway had to apologize to the Reds. Due to the strafing incident and the fact that Ridgway had been forced to apologize, the JCS denied his request to attack Kaesong.

Ridgway exploded. He vowed never to resume the talks at Kaesong even if given a direct order. This outburst put President Truman and the Joint Chiefs in a tight spot. To fire Ridgway, the man who saved Korea, was unthinkable. The old Army adage, "Never give an order that isn't going to be obeyed," had never been tested at this level. A solution had to be found and quickly. It was the Communists who saved the president from a very tough decision.

During this "recess" liaison officers from both sides had been meeting at Panmunjom, a village five miles east of Kaesong, discussing the issues and charging each other with more violations of the neutral zone. On October 7, the Communists gave in on the Kaesong issue and on October 25, the senior delegates sat down at Panmunjom and the talks resumed.[13]

The incident involving the Air Force at Kaesong deeply concerned the Army. Stringent measures were now taken to insure that no Army unit would accidentally fire into the new neutral zone around Panmunjom.

FIRST LIEUTENANT JAMES KERCHEVAL.
HEADQUARTERS, 176TH AFAB (PENNSYLVANIA).

In October, I transferred to battalion headquarters as assistant S-3. We were located just south of the Imjin River, six or seven miles from Panmunjom, supporting the 1st ROK Division. One day several officers from I Corps showed up. They looked over our positions very carefully, then started to pound stakes into the ground. They were laying out "no fire" zones. We were ordered not to fire inside these stakes, nothing, no howitzer fire, no machine gun fire, no rifle fire, nothing. Any weapon that could fire into Panmunjom was given a field of "no fire" zone.

These "no fire" zones led up to the neutral zone at Panmunjon. We asked what we were expected to do if enemy troops appeared in these areas. We were told to use hand grenades and bayonets. Hell, we were an artillery outfit, we didn't have any hand grenades.[14]

The Guard artillery units continued to fire in support of Eighth Army operations through the summer and into the fall. With the front static the hectic days of April and May now settled into almost a routine. Most of the units dug in and remained in the same location for weeks or even months.

The 204th and 937th were not afforded this luxury. Armed with their flat shooting 155mm Long Toms, the men from Utah and Arkansas, continually went right up to the MLR to take bunkers and other well dug in positions under direct fire.

CORPORAL GEORGE GATLIFF.
"A" BATTERY, 937TH FAB (ARKANSAS).

I don't remember much about this time except in late September we were told to take one of our guns forward as we did when we fired on Chorwon. This time however we would be firing directly into the enemy dug into the side of a mountain. We were with the Marines and would slip forward after dark with some of the Marine tanks. My gun was selected. I was the driver and we departed before dark because we had to cross a big mountain on the way.

We waited on the south side of the mountain for the southbound traffic to clear the narrow road. After the road cleared, we moved out. It was a slow climb to the top so we were running late. When I finally got to the top I started driving as fast as I could to make up for the lost time.

The road was very steep and very crooked. As I was coming up on one of the curves, I saw I was going too fast so I started slowing down. About the time I got the gun under control, it hit some large rocks in the road and slid off and damaged the tracks on one side. We were stranded there and were unable to go on to complete our mission.

The firing battery chief, Master Sergeant Junior Hensley, who was with us in a jeep, left us there and went back to get mechanics to come and repair the tracks. While we were waiting they started hauling dead Marines from the area we were supposed to go to. We found out later that they had been overrun by the enemy and almost wiped out.

There has never been any doubt that God was watching over me. I also worry though. If I had not wrecked the gun would I have been killed with the Marines, or, if I had not wrecked the gun and had completed our mission, perhaps the Marines would not have been overrun? I will never know. [15]

New York's 955th FAB also went on a special mission about this time. As had happened so many times in the past to the Guardsmen, someone didn't get the word.

CORPORAL THOMAS CACCIOLA.
"A" BATTERY, 955TH FAB (NEW YORK).

We were in the Chorwon area and got a march order to move into the Chorwon Valley, quietly and in the dead of night. This was in October, and we had never done this before. It was a moonless night, probably about ten or eleven, when we moved out on the five or six mile trip to the valley. I remember no one was allowed to use a flashlight or light a cigarette. The drivers of our prime-movers, the tractors that towed the guns, had to keep their lights off.

I recall the mess section was making coffee and soup as we prepared to move out. It was pitch dark and the road was full of dust. When the mess sergeant yelled, "Coffee and soup ready," guys were stumbling over each other in the dark to get to it. It was so dark and there was so much road dust, I got a cup full of mud! The cook said, "Just skim the dirt off the top." It tasted terrible.

Anyway, the Chinks were going to get a surprise from "A" Battery of the 955th. I'm not sure if "B" and "C" Batteries were along. We went deep into the valley and were all set to fire when all of a sudden the entire valley lit up. An Army search-light outfit at the rear of the valley had turned their lights directly on our position. It was light enough to play a game of baseball.

We went berserk. What happened? Who did this to us? I looked down the valley and saw four of these huge lights shining right at us. I could hear our officers screaming on the radios trying to get the lights turned off. We were per-fect targets for the Chinese artillery and mortars. Worse, maybe the searchlight unit thought we were Chinks!! We were petrified!

I think in about one or two minutes the lights went out and everything went pitch black again. Thank God! We went ahead and fired the mission and then pulled out of the valley just at daybreak.[16]

As the line remained stable in the fall of 1951, there was time to once again rebuild the shattered ROK Army. The Korean Military Advisory Group (KMAG), the organization formed to train the South Korean Army in 1949 when the United States' occupation ended, numbered 470 officers and men at the start of the war. It eventually grew to 1,308 American advisors. To supplement the KMAG instructors officers and men would be detached from their units for short periods of time to assist in the training.[17]

FIRST LIEUTENANT JAMES KERCHEVAL.
HEADQUARTERS, 176TH AFAB (PENNSYLVANIA).

In September I was sent to Camp Jecelin to help train the 30th Field Artillery, 9th ROK Division. This was located northeast of Seoul about twenty miles from our unit's location. I was the only American artillery officer with the unit.

The first thing I noticed during my initial inspection was that there were no latrines, and that human waste was on top of the ground everywhere. The flies, and there were a million of them, would go from the solid waste and onto the piles of rice waiting to be served. I got some field manuals and went to the Korean general in charge of the camp and explained how this could cause dysentery, and how to dig latrines. The next morning there were latrines all over the place and the ground was clean.

My job was to observe the Koreans and then tell them what they were doing wrong. They were green, but they worked hard and caught on pretty fast. Their main problem was adjusting fire. They liked to shoot and just keep firing till they hit the target; even if it took a hundred rounds. I taught them how to bracket the target and not waste ammunition. I also instructed them on target selection and priority and how to determine whether to fire or not fire.

Every Sunday there would be a big feast and we would sit around and discuss the week's training. The main course was kimchee, which is rotten cabbage. I tried it, but I'm a meat and potatoes man and kimchee wasn't my dish.[18]

The second Korean winter arrived and the nine National Guard artillery battalions continued to fire in support of U.N. forces. By now it was an artillery war and tremendous amounts of ammunition were expended by both sides. By January 31, 1952, Wyoming's 300th AFAB had fired 303,932 rounds, over 5,000 tons of steel. The other National Guard artillery battalions fired comparable amounts. As the war came to an end in the summer of 1953, the amount of ammunition fired made even these figures appear insignificant. In both June and July of 1953, U.N. artillery units fired over 2,000,000 rounds.[19]

December 1951 saw the first National Guard artillerymen start home. Few Americans would ever know what they had accomplished, but they knew. For the rest of their lives they could say that when the chips were down they had stopped the Communists and saved the city of Seoul.

CHAPTER 7

BRIDGES & ROADS

Soon after their arrival in Japan, in April of 1951, the men of the 578th Engineer Combat Battalion (ECB), 40th Infantry Division (California), were visited by Lieutenant General Matthew Ridgway. Ridgway had just returned from the Korean front and in attempting to impress the seriousness of the situation to the troops, he said, "The overriding factor in the Korean combat has been the engineers, and that brings it right down to you." While some infantrymen and artillerymen may have disagreed with Ridgway's assessment, the men of the ten National Guard engineer units already in Korea would have given him no argument.[1]

The National Guard's substantial contribution to Eighth Army's non-divisional engineer force consisted of six engineer combat battalions, three bridge companies, and an engineer group headquarters. The units, listed below, trained at Fort Lewis, Washington; Fort Belvoir, Virginia; or Fort Campbell, Kentucky, before heading for the Far East.

UNIT	STATE	KOREA	CORPS
116TH ENGINEER (C) BN.	ID	2/28/51	X
151ST ENGINEER (C) BN.	AL	2/09/51	I
194TH ENGINEER (C) BN.	TN	2/16/51	IX
378TH ENGINEER (C) BN.	NC	2/24/51	IX
1092ND ENGINEER (C) BN.	WV	3/03/51	I
1343RD ENGINEER (C) BN.	AL	2/09/51	X

138TH PONTOON BRIDGE CO.	MS	2/16/51	I
1437TH TREADWAY BRIDGE CO.	MI	3/02/51	IX
2998TH TREADWAY BRIDGE CO.	TN	2/27/51	X
1169TH ENGR. GROUP HQ. & HQ. CO.	AL	2/28/51	I

Like their comrades in the artillery the Guard engineers began arriving in February of 1951, and by March 3, all ten units had landed at Pusan. The six engineer battalions stayed in the Pusan area for a short time awaiting their heavy equipment which in most instances was on a separate ship from the men. In contrast, Mississippi's 138th Pontoon Bridge Company had their equipment waiting for them and headed north as soon as it was off loaded.

SERGEANT WILLIAM SHEFFIELD, JR.
138TH PONTOON BRIDGE COMPANY (MISSISSIPPI).

About sixty percent of our equipment came from storage in Japan. Someone had put it on a ship and it was waiting to be unloaded when we arrived at Pusan. But we still had our old Bay City crane; we'd brought it all the way from Picayune. Somehow we got another Bay City from a Michigan National Guard outfit. That gave us a total of five cranes.

As soon as we got everything unloaded we left Pusan in three convoys and headed toward Seoul. Most of the men and equipment went in the first two convoys. I went in the last one with the maintenance section and the last two cranes. At this time I was a crane operator. It didn't take long for the company to go into action; they built two small bridges over a tributary of the Han River, even before all of the convoys arrived and set up.

Then we built our first big one, over the Han River just south of Seoul, a 1,000 foot long pontoon bridge. It took about two days from start to finish. The aluminum bridge sets we had were only 660 feet long, so we had to finish it with rubber pontoons. They didn't really fit, but we made them work. A tank outfit, part of the 3rd Infantry Division, started across. We had been told to only let three tanks on at a time, but you can't hold up a war and we let five go on at once. That's about 250 ton. The bridge held up fine, no problems at all.[2]

Later commissioned, Sheffield became commander of "A" Company, 890th Engineer Battalion, the successor unit to the 138th Pontoon Bridge Company in Picayune, Mississippi.

The next bridge company to arrive, Tennessee's 2998th Treadway Bridge Company, landed on February 27. It would be five weeks before their equipment caught up with them.

SECOND LIEUTENANT JOHN FUQUA.
2998TH TREADWAY BRIDGE COMPANY (TENNESSEE).

We worked on the docks and various other jobs while waiting for our equipment. While we were waiting we finally got to see a bridge that another outfit picked up. Our bridge was still en route to Pusan. We still hadn't had any bridge training, but once we got the equipment it wasn't too bad. Many of the men were farm boys and had been building things all their lives. We picked it up pretty quick.

The equipment finally arrived and we headed north. Our convoy had been on the road a couple of days when we stopped at a school building to spend the night. About 3:00 AM there was a death in the small village nearby and the mourners began wailing and beating gongs. Naturally, we thought we were being attacked until our interpreter explained their custom. Needless to say, no one slept any more that night.

Once we got up north the three platoons were separated along the Han River. Each platoon built and maintained a bridge in their sector of the river; some were big, some small. I learned quite a bit during this time and they gave me a battlefield commission.

One time, Corporal Sam Caldwell and I were sent along with several trucks loaded with bridge trusses to help supervise a dry stream crossing. A combat engineer battalion was to erect the bridge for a tank convoy on their way up the road. We reported to the officers in charge. They told us we were not needed as they would construct the bridge themselves.

Several hours later no progress had been made. The sergeant in charge came over and asked if we knew how to build this type of bridge. While Sam worked the dry ground sections, I worked the stream area and we had the bridge erected in short order.

Later, I took a platoon to dismantle a bridge over the Pukhan River, below the Hwachon Reservoir Dam. This was the dam the Chinese were always opening to flood the river and knock out our supply lines. The Navy finally blasted it with torpedoes. Anyway, we were out there four days and under fire at times; actually I think it came from some South Koreans. I received the Bronze Star for this operation.

One funny thing I recall. Our C.O. was Regular Army and always saying how dumb the Guardsmen were. One night we got into quite an argument over this and I said, "You get two or three of the RA men's records and I'll get a couple of the Guardsmen's records and we'll see who's dumb." I'd set him up because I knew my men's test scores. The first one I laid out had an IQ of 148, the second one, 136. The argument ended pretty quick.[3]

The lack of specialized training the units received prior to shipping out that Lieutenant Fuqua mentions above and also in chapter 1, made a tough job even tougher. From the command report of the 151st ECB (Alabama) April 1951:

Lack of heavy equipment during training, denying the opportunity of developing the required number of heavy machinery operators imposed undue hardships and heavy responsibility upon the few [operators]. Without tending to be critical in any respect, and with full and sincere appreciation for the military emergency which exists, it is the genuine and authentic opinion of the Commander and staff, that inadequate training for units with such diversified responsibilities as the Combat Engineer Battalion cannot possibly be in the best interest of the Service. In order to become versatile in organic missions it is imperative that unit training and operational equipment be made available.[4]

Both the bridge companies and the engineer battalions had a layer of command between themselves and their corps headquarters. This was the engineer group, one of which, the 1169th, was a National Guard unit from Alabama. These units operated in much the same manner as the truck battalion headquarters companies only on a larger scale.

Besides giving administrative and logistical support, these units would estimate how many men and how much equipment were required to complete a specific job. They would then attach troops and equipment from units under their control to the outfit doing the job. Under this command structure, it was not unusual for one battalion to control the bulldozers and other heavy equipment of five or six other battalions for varying periods of time.

FIRST LIEUTENANT DAVE MATTESON.
HEADQUARTERS, 378TH ENGINEER COMBAT BATTALION (NORTH CAROLINA).

In 1951, we were assigned to build a high level road about 15 to 20 miles long, from a main north-south road, to the east, more or less paralleling the front, toward a lake or reservoir in the north-east sector of the central front. The units north and east of the reservoir were being supplied by rafts, mules, and backpacked "A" frames, and a good road was needed to get the ammo and supplies up to the front in that area.

At that time each battalion had four bulldozers (one in each of three line companies and one in HQ. Company), but for this operation group headquarters loaned us about everything they had available. It must have been 16–20 dozers and extra operators. The job was urgent and the plan called for the equipment to be operating twenty-four hours a day. It's a "sitting duck" job and takes a lot of guts to operate a dozer at night with lights on in a forward area, way out on a long limb subject to infiltration and or a breakthrough.

One time, well along on the project, we got a report of an enemy breakthrough and were ordered to pull out. The only way out was back over the lateral road that we were hacking out of the rocky slopes. We had withdrawn several miles back along the road when word came that everything was under control and to go back in. I was the motor officer and had the job of getting the long line of dozers turned around and headed back several miles east over the road that we had cut to the current work site.

Understandably some of the dozer operators were reluctant to turn around and it took me awhile to convince them that we had to believe the report and were indeed going to go back. I believe it was daylight at the time, as I have a very clear mental picture of the line of dozers and the looks of doubt, and in some cases anger, on the operators' faces as they turned around and went back.[5]

Upon arriving at the front the engineers were augmented by the hiring of Korean laborers. As many as 5,000 of these unskilled men would be assigned to a battalion. Even with this additional help the amount of work assigned to the Guard engineer units was staggering.

In late April and early May 1951, Idaho's 116th CEB worked on twelve bridges simultaneously. At the same time the unit reconstructed the Wonju-Hoengsong MSR to a full twenty-two foot roadway and was also responsible for sixty miles of road maintenance in the battalion area. During this period the unit worked three eight hour shifts with all its equipment, plus additional equipment provided by other units.[6]

Courtesy of the U.S. Army Military History Institute, Carlisle Barracks, Pa.

The Guard engineer units constructed hundreds of bridges. This treadway bridge by North Carolina's 378th Engineer Combat Battalion spanned the Pukhan River in the 6th ROK Division sector, November 1951.

CAPTAIN RICHARD OLIVER.
S-2, 116TH ENGINEER COMBAT BATTALION (IDAHO).

As far as I was concerned we were better equipped for the engineer tasks than the active Army engineer units. We hadn't had as much infantry training as the Army units. If we had had to go on line somewhere as infantry we would have had to do on the job training.

But the engineering part of it—we were good. Our staff officers and most of the line officers were either engineers or had road construction jobs, or been in some other construction trade. The men running the equipment were mostly heavy equipment operators or farm boys that had run heavy equipment all their lives. We had more skilled people to start with than the Regular Army had.

Headquarters supplied each company with 500 Korean laborers. They were very good at building retaining walls out of rock. They also performed general labor on the road jobs. The Koreans were paid in won and I'm sure it amounted to a dollar a day or less. We supplied them with rice and shelter.

When the Chinese attacked in May we were supporting the
1st Marine Division and the 2nd Infantry Division. We were
almost at the junction where the two units came together.
Parts of both divisions were overrun; we were lucky they
didn't get back to where we were. After a week or so we
regrouped and started to move back up.

Group sent down an order to check out a bridge site maybe
ten miles from where we were bivouacked. So I took a recon
sergeant and four or five men in a couple of jeeps and went
to look it over. We went up this road five or six miles and
passed a group of infantrymen sitting along the road eating
"C" rations. They looked at us kind of weird, but no one
flagged us down and we kept on going. Another one or two
miles along, the road went up then made a sweeping turn
and descended into a small valley. My map showed the
bridge site another mile and a half or so.

The next thing I knew there were six tanks off on our right,
about a hundred yards away firing at something. I looked
up and a mile or so across the valley were some enemy
tanks firing back. Shells were falling all around our tanks.
We didn't wait to see the outcome, we turned around and
got the hell out of there.

On the way back we stopped and talked to the infantrymen,
I don't know if they were Army or Marines. They said, "Captain, what the hell's going on? Didn't you know you were
going out in front of the front?"

Another thing I recall, when we moved back up there was a
Chinese body lying in the middle of an intersection and
everybody's trucks kept going over, and over, and over it.
Nobody paid any more attention to it than you would a dead
dog in the road. The body had just flattened out as big as a
living room and you could barely discern that it might have
been a man at one time.

Oliver later served in the National Guard Bureau as Chief of
Supply and Logistics before retiring as a colonel.

Assigned to X Corps, Alabama's 1343rd Engineer "C" Battalion also played a vital role in stopping the Chinese May offensive.
Tens of thousands of tons of artillery ammunition moved to the
front in the Soyang River area over roads and bridges built and
maintained by the 1343rd. Shortly after the Communists were
stopped, "B" Company built a 200 foot "double-single" bridge over
the Soyang near Inge. Fighting the flooded river and torrential rain,

"B" Company completed the bridge in ten days, earning the praise of X Corps Commander, General Edward Almond, who said, "Alabama can well be proud of its National Guard."[7]

While the primary job of engineer battalions is building roads and bridges, the "C" in their designation stands for combat. Only one National Guard engineer unit, West Virginia's 1092nd Engineer (C) Battalion, fought as infantry in Korea. Attached to the 3rd Infantry Division on April 24, the battalion moved on line northwest of Uijongbu. Contact with the enemy was light and no casualties were suffered. On the 27th the crisis was over and the 1092nd went back to maintaining fifty miles of road and rebuilding seven hi-level bridges in the I Corps sector.[8]

A shortage of equipment, and the resupply of engineer parts was a major problem for the National Guard engineer outfits. At times extreme measures were necessary to keep the units operating.

CAPTAIN THOMAS BRINKLEY.
COMMANDING OFFICER, 138TH PONTOON BRIDGE COMPANY (MISSISSIPPI).

After we successfully put the big floating bridge across the Han River, we set up bivouac on the south side of the river in a big apple orchard where we could camouflage all of our equipment. This became our permanent base.

Getting replacement equipment and parts of any type—forget it. If you blew an engine on a truck or piece of equipment and tried to get it through ordinary channels they'd laugh at you. I soon became a non-com: Supply Sergeant Tom Brinkley. Brinkley, Captain? Never heard of him! When they had light colonels and full birds fighting over equipment I didn't stand a chance. I had to develop something, and that was stealing.

I stole stuff off the docks in Pusan. I'd take a truck and a sergeant. We'd go down there and casually walk around and find what we needed and then write the numbers off the crates. Then we'd type us up a requisition and put those numbers in; then we'd go back and walk around like we didn't know where anything was, get the paper work cleared, load up and leave. I recall we got a welding machine once, and another time even some clothing for the men.

When you've got a platoon of men thirty miles out working on a bridge you can't haul food out to them, you need another kitchen, so that's another thing we got off the docks. When you're a captain with a bastard outfit not assigned to a division you've got no clout. Captains were a dime a dozen.

All of the National Guard units mobilized the summer of 1950 lost men soon after going on active duty. Many Guardsmen were under age while others failed their physical or mental tests. Dependent status also cut into the ranks.

Going on active duty August 19, 1950, Tennessee's 194th Engineer Combat Battalion left some troops behind for a completely different reason. Headquartered in Oak Ridge, many of the unit's men were employed at the Atomic Energy Commission (AEC) plant located there. The AEC requested that seventy-one members of the unit be given deferments. Later this figure was reduced to fifty-eight. The AEC not only wanted these individuals working at Oak Ridge, but the chance, however slight, that at some point they might be captured could not be risked. This did not worry the soldiers of the 194th; thirty-six of the fifty-eight officers and enlisted men offered deferments refused to accept them and expressed a desire to go with their outfit.

Joining IX Corps on March 21, the battalion commenced road maintenance on the roads forming the triangle Ichon-Chonso-ri-Yoju, some of the worst roads in Korea. The battalion, working two ten hour shifts, continued this road work until the Chinese offensive in April. At this time elements of the battalion withdrew, while others furnished trucks to front line units to evacuate equipment.

The Chinese advance continued and on April 29, the battalion was ordered to prepare plans to remove a 700 foot floating steel bridge spanning the Han River. The line held at this time and after a few days the unit resumed road work. May saw the 194th enter the bridge construction business in a major way. First came the construction of a 744 foot M-2 Treadway bridge across the Pukhan River. This was followed by a 232 foot I-beam bridge near Ichon. The maintaining of four other bridges also kept the 194th busy that month.[9]

As with the other National Guard engineer units, the 194th suffered a shortage of parts and equipment. It was a never-ending problem.

CAPTAIN GEORGE WARNE.
S-4, 194TH ENGINEER COMBAT BATTALION (TENNESSEE).

I'd been C.O. of "C" Company, but when we were mobilized I took over as S-4. The man I replaced was one of the key men in the handling and storage of nuclear weapons at Oak Ridge. The AEC wasn't about to let him go to Korea.

The usual supply lines that provided food, clothing, tents, that type of material came through fairly well. These lines had been pretty well established by the time we got to the combat zone. The problem was in the supply and resupply of ordnance equipment and parts; trucks, trailers, heavy equipment, and their parts, that sort of thing. I recall a jeep was stolen from our motor pool. It took weeks to get a replacement. It took us the better part of a year to get a new ten ton wrecker. Our $2^1/2$ ton dump trucks would break down and parts were in very short supply. The same scenario applied to the heavy engineer equipment—dozers, engineer trailers, cranes, construction equipment. It was very hard for the maintenance people to keep that stuff on the road. We would rob a broken truck to fix up two others.

The replacement equipment had to come from depots located in Japan. There were two grades of equipment available: new from Stateside and rebuilt in Japan. When new equipment arrived we made every effort to latch onto the new Stateside equipment. The material from Japan, dubbed "Yokohama Rebuilts," was a poor second choice and had a very short life span in the tactical areas. Korea was very rough on vehicles and equipment.

Remember, most of our equipment was World War II stuff built in 1943, or 1944. We didn't have the luxury of the post-war stuff that was available in the States. We knew if we busted up any of our equipment we were going to be without it for a long time.[10]

Warne, a B-26 pilot in World War II, later returned to Korea for visits, when his son, an Army colonel, was stationed there.

The final National Guard bridge outfit to serve in Korea, Michigan's 1437th Engineer Treadway Bridge Company, landed at Pusan March 2, 1951.

CORPORAL ERNEST PERRON.
1437TH ENGINEER TREADWAY BRIDGE COMPANY
(MICHIGAN).

After we were mobilized we went out to Fort Lewis. There the unit filled up with recalled Reservists. They were from all branches of the Army and the finest people I ever served with. We shipped out of Fort Lawton in January; the trucks and equipment went ahead on different ships and some of it we never saw again. The first stop was Camp Schimmelpfennig near Sendai, in Japan. We stayed there thirty days or so training, then headed for Pusan. It took about ten days to get our equipment, then we headed up to Taegu.

It was bitter cold and snowing, and we were damn ill equipped. All we had was a piss poor vest under our field jackets. We had no parkas, and the only winter underwear we had we'd brought from home. I remember leather boots and the blanket type sleeping bags. We damn near froze to death.

I can't remember where our first bridge went in, but I recall we put it in at night and it took all the bridging material we had. We had it operational by daybreak. Our company was really not supposed to build bridges; our job was to transport the material and supervise the construction. What a joke! We did 95 percent of the construction ourselves.

There was a Regular Army outfit we worked with, the 11th Engineer Battalion. They got credit for most of our work. Hell, we called them the 11th Engineer Sign Painting Battalion. We'd put the bridge in and they'd have their sign up before we were through.

I'm retired now so I can say what I think and that outfit sure didn't do what they were given credit for. I'm still mad about that damn battalion taking credit for our work. But we were a bastard company and they had the rank; they even got a citation and we got shit.

On April 9, the Chinese opened the sluice gates of the Hwachon Dam. The water rushed down the Pukhan River, wiping out one bridge. Only the quick work of the 1437th Bridge Company saved the next bridge from tearing loose and floating down river. The men were finishing breakfast when a soldier stopped by and mentioned that the river seemed to be rising. Within ten minutes the men from Saulte Ste Marie, Michigan, had loosened the south end of the bridge allowing it to swing to the north bank. A small detachment, now stranded on the north shore, quickly attached cables all along the structure and then anchored the cables to trucks, thereby saving the bridge from destruction.[11]

Corporal Perron continues:

When the bridge went out, myself and maybe ten others were stranded on the north side. We did have the power boats. They were nineteen foot inboards, but Sergeants Lynn McDonald, and Frank Smith had to secure them as the river rose twenty-five feet in a matter of minutes.

About an hour later a Marine colonel came up and informed us he had two companies of Marines on the north shore (where we were), and that was all that stood between the river and the whole damn Chinese army. He offered to let us have any heavy weapons and grenades he could spare. This sure as hell did not help morale any. You never saw guys dig fighting positions so fast. Hell, we beat the Marines. All this while we were still trying to rescue our bridge.

One of the trucks holding the bridge was under ten feet of water in a matter of minutes, that's a lot of water! In a day or so the water receded and we were able to secure the bridge.

Later on that spring the Chinese broke through near Chunchon; I had a detail working on a bridge just south of there. A platoon of Marines came up and set TNT charges all over it, and the lieutenant in charge told me he was going to blow the bridge. I told him we were there for bridge maintenance and didn't have any orders about blowing the bridge. After checking this out he gave me the charging handle and told me to blow it at the first sign of trouble.

We waited for a day and a half, and not a man or vehicle crossed that bridge. About then the small arms fire was getting too close for comfort and I decided to blow it. Just about that time we saw a mobile crane pull up on the far side and it was one of ours. There were forty men hanging on to it, some tied on with ropes. They had tied themselves to the boom and anywhere else they could get on.

These men were all that was left of a British company that had been caught in their sacks a couple nights before. Corporal Keith Ewing, and PFC Pete Myers had picked them up on the road. I had no idea that we had a crane on the far side. To this day we can't figure out how Keith and Pete got through because the MSR had been cut for two days. That night the MSR got reopened and we were busy on the bridge again.

That was the big problem in Korea, the lack of command and control. We were spread out all over and never were told anything. I took people out on bridging jobs and be gone as long as seventeen days and not a damned soul checked on us to see if we had rations or were even alive. Hell, one time I took a group of trucks to Yongdungpo and ended up under the command of I Corps, and we were a IX Corps unit, and nobody informed the company. I don't know how in the hell we all got back as well as we did.[12]

Perron, who first joined the Guard in 1948, remained with the 1437th. He retired in 1989 as the unit's first sergeant after forty-one years service, all with the same outfit.

The flooding of rivers by the Chinese caused problems for another National Guard outfit.

SERGEANT FIRST CLASS WILLIAM SHEFFIELD, JR.
138TH PONTOON BRIDGE COMPANY (MISSISSIPPI).

During the summer of 1951 the enemy started blowing up the reservoirs and turning loose lots of water, causing everything to flood. We had a bridge across the Han River at this time and so much debris was coming down the river that I Corps ordered us to cut the bridge loose on both sides and let it ride out the high water.

When I pulled the last pin on the far side, it had terrific pressure on it and some of the cables began to break. It sounded a lot like guitar strings popping. I ran off the bridge and drove back to the company to get a roll of cable to tie to the far side. I would then have a bulldozer pull it to the near shore.

I got the cable, but just as I got back to the bridge it broke loose and started floating down the Han. That was the last float bridge to go, so the only thing into Seoul was a wooden bridge built on the Yongdungpo to Seoul side. We now had to get our float bridge either sunk or beached before it went down river and crashed into the wooden one and destroyed it. I don't recall how far down river the wooden bridge was, but it was a ways.

Well, a group of men got on the bridge and started knocking holes in it to sink it, but they weren't having much luck. Then the bridge went around a wide curve in the river. It washed up close to the bank and some men jumped off and with the broken cables and some rope tied it to a rock crusher that was there. That held it and we saved the bridge.

The most amazing thing about this story is that we started taking the bridge apart right then and worked on it until dark. In two days' time we took the bridge apart, hauled it out, reassembled it and had it back in service. I have never seen a more dedicated group of men than the ones I was with at that time in Korea.[13]

On July 21, 1951, Alabama's 151st ECB had the unique experience of destroying a Communist bridge with axes. The incident occurred when a 50-foot wooden bridge the Reds had constructed broke loose and swept down the flooded Imjin River. Careening down river the bridge headed for a pontoon bridge the Huntsville unit had constructed connecting the peace talk site at Kaesong with the U.N. advance base.

The Chinese bridge hit an amphibious DUWK, sinking it and then smashed into the Alabamans' pontoon bridge. The bridge bounced up and down, swung back and forth, but held. The engineers then "counter-attacked" the floating bridge with axes, dismembering it and it floated away. "Proving one thing," PFC Thomas Ledbetter said, "the 151st Engineers are the best damn bridge builders in Korea."[14]

The American soldier is known for many things. Courage under fire, devotion to duty, and compassion for children come to mind. And, when time allows, the never ending search for a beer. Preferably cold.

SERGEANT FIRST CLASS ROBERT MCKEE. "A" COMPANY, 151ST ENGINEER COMBAT BATTALION (ALABAMA).

We were assigned a company of Korean men to be utilized as laborers on road maintenance and other pick and shovel type projects. One project took a squad of our company and a number of the Koreans to the northern outskirts of Seoul. On the way back to our base at Anyang one of the laborers told our men where a brewery was located. Naturally the truck detoured to the location of the hoped for treasure. And there it was, damaged but still standing, protecting the full vats of beer inside.

All canteens and water cans were quickly emptied and filled with the beer which was sampled and found to be quite tasty. Quite a bit of tasting went on during the return trip to Anyang and upon arrival most of the people aboard the truck, American and Korean, were drunk. Two of the Koreans had fell off the truck somewhere in route and were never heard from again.

The company greeted the returning men with open arms, applause and handshakes. Beer, or any type alcohol was a very scarce commodity. Local home made beer was available but we had been warned of its possible detrimental effects; but this was different, here we had a full legitimate brewery.

Needless to say, word circulated around and the brewery quickly became a rendezvous for trucks from throughout the area. At least one of our trucks was dispatched daily. Following such extensive use even the great vats of beer began to draw down. And therein lay a problem, or should I say two. Because two bodies were discovered in one of the vats. We had often questioned and wondered what the shreds and lumps in the beer might be.[15]

Receiving a direct commission, McKee served thirty-three years before retiring as a colonel in the Alabama National Guard.

As the war entered its static phase in the late summer of 1951, the engineer battalions worked on a variety of assignments. Construction of camps for rear echelon units and the installation of aerial tramways to supply units on distant mountain peaks kept units busy. The removal of hundreds of minefields laid in the first year of the war was a never ending task. Another important job handled by the engineers was the establishment of water supply points.

CAPTAIN RICHARD OLIVER.
HEADQUARTERS, 116TH ENGINEER COMBAT BATTALION (IDAHO).

A group of men were trained in purifying water. They had big tanks and chemicals and so on. We'd set up wherever there was water and supply pure water for maybe ten thousand men. I don't recall exactly how many gallons a day, but it was thousands of gallons. Units came with anything from big water tankers to small trailers to pick up their water.

We rigged up a shower point next to the water point and also made a bath tub out of one of the big rice cooking pots our Korean laborers used. It was three or four foot across and three foot deep. We put it in a tent and one of our warrant officers rigged up fifty gallon drums with coils running around them to heat the water. It was great.

We were supporting one of the Mobile Army Surgical Hospitals (M.A.S.H.). They tried to stay pretty close to us because we'd use our road graders to cut them out a flat area to erect their camp. So they usually set up within a mile or two of us. The nurses and doctors would come over and use the shower and tub.

The static front also allowed the engineers to construct more or less permanent camps for themselves.

CORPORAL MACK VINSON.
HEADQUARTERS & SERVICE COMPANY, 1343RD ENGINEER COMBAT BATTALION (ALABAMA).

An incident reminiscent of the television series M.A.S.H. took place at our bivouac near Inge in the fall of 1951. The company commander decided to modernize the relief facility which was sometimes referred to as the "outhouse" or "privy," but designated as the "latrine" in Army terminology. The carpenters dutifully constructed a nice plywood "8-holer" complete with hinged lids to control odors and prevent entry of insects. When completed the company considered that this was the most modern facility in Korea.

As an additional sanitary procedure, a Korean civilian employee of the camp was assigned the duty of pouring a few gallons of diesel fuel into the pit each morning. However, one fateful morning he was unable to find any diesel fuel, and being unaware of the properties of fuels, proceeded to pour five gallons of gasoline into the pit. Obviously, the mixture of gasoline fumes with the methane already in the pit set the stage for a very unpleasant surprise for the next visitor to the latrine.

Courtesy of Mack Vinson

Corporal Mack Vinson of Alabama's 1343rd Engineer Combat Battalion relaxes on a 340 foot long "Double-Single" Bailey, the unit erected over the Soyang River near Inge.

The unsuspecting victim was, unfortunately, a smoker. He raised the lid, sat down, lit a cigarette, and regrettably threw the lighted match into the pit. The resulting explosion not only demolished the facility, but rudely interrupted what was expected to be a moment of leisure for the victim. Fortunately, he was not seriously injured, but was quite embarrassed to have to seek medical attention for minor burns on his private parts and spent the next several days sleeping on his stomach.

While this event actually happened and may be added to the endless lists of latrine stories told by veterans, it well could have been part of the script of M.A.S.H. with the hapless Frank Burns as the victim of his tormentors.[16]

Home from Korea, Vinson worked for the Department of the Army and the National Aeronautics and Space Agency, at the Marshall Space Flight Center, in Huntsville, Alabama. Since 1980 he has been a private consultant with the United Nations.

In the spring of 1952, the National Guard engineers started to rotate home. They had completed every job assigned them, no matter how tough. They had more than lived up to the Corps of Engineers motto, "Essayons" [Let Us Try].

CAPTAIN DAVE MATTESON.
HEADQUARTERS, 378TH ENGINEER COMBAT BATTALION (NORTH CAROLINA).

February 28, 1952, the happiest day of my life. My wife's birthday and I'm standing on the deck of a ship leaving Inchon, Korea. After a day or so at Sasebo, Japan, we headed out across the Pacific and started home. After landing in San Francisco, I was sent to Camp Stoneman across the Bay for separation. Orders promoting me to captain caught up with me there. I was a captain for two days.

A few months later I was visiting my father up in Grass Valley, a small town a hundred and fifty miles or so northeast of San Francisco. It was the 4th of July and we went to a parade in Nevada City, a nearby town. As we were watching the parade, up the street came the local National Guard outfit, and it just happened to be an engineer unit.

The first thing I noticed was that all the jeeps and trucks were equipped with snorkel gear. The 378th had never had one piece of snorkel gear the entire time I was with them. Every time we had to ford a stream or river more than a few feet deep we had to unhook the fan belts lest the spinning fan would spray water back on the ignition wires and short out and kill the engine. We did this many times and it was a very time consuming and frustrating process.

Next a Caterpillar D-8 bulldozer on a huge trailer came up the street towed by a huge snorkel equipped prime mover. It appeared to be brand new. The cleats on the tractor were at least an inch and a half deep. This was much larger than the Caterpillar D-7s that we had in Korea and I had never seen one the entire time I was there. As it passed I mentally calculated how much work one of those monsters could do and thought how I sure could have used a few of them a few months earlier.[17]

CHAPTER 8

FOR WANT OF A NAIL

If little is known about the National Guard combat units that served in Korea, even less is known about the support troops. This of course is nothing new. The media has little interest in quartermaster clerks or ordnance mechanics. And while the best remembered outfit of the Korean War is the fictional 4077 M.A.S.H., no television series are being planned about a signal battalion. Yet as any student of military history knows, it is the caliber of these unsung units that often means victory or defeat for an army.

The United States Army has always had a high ratio of support troops to combat soldiers. In Korea, after the Chinese entered the war in late 1950, GHQ estimated that the Communists held a slim 6-5 manpower edge over the U.N. forces. But at the same time it reckoned that in frontline troops the enemy held a 5-1, if not more, superiority.[1]

The reasons for this disparity are many and complex, but can be distilled down to three main points. First: the American soldier has always been the best fed, best cared for, and best equipped soldier in the world. And if, as in Korea, there were shortages of clothing and other gear at the outbreak of hostilities, they were soon remedied. The picture of an infantryman, eating his holiday turkey dinner is one the American public has seen many times, be it in Korea, Vietnam, or some other distant battlefield. But few know of the logistics involved to get that bird with all the trimmings to the front. Meanwhile, a hundred yards away his enemy counterpart will be dining on a handful of rice and a fish head or some other local delicacy.

101

Second: in the twentieth century the Army's battles have been fought thousands of miles from the United States. Obviously the farther away from the source of supply, the more men are needed just to keep the supplies moving. While fighting a war in Korea, the Army also had the task of maintaining troops around the world. This global effort, that the Communists were not burdened with, diverted many potential riflemen to other duties.

Third: by the start of the Korean War the United States Army was, for the most part, mechanized. In Korea, soldiers traveled on wheels and tracks, be it in a jeep in some rear area delivering mail, or in a tank at the front taking on Russian built T-34s. Much of this rolling stock was of World War II vintage and nearing the end of its usefulness. That, along with the hostile Korean terrain and the extreme temperature variances on the peninsula, made for a horrendous maintenance problem. Thousands of men were kept busy repairing vehicles and components.

Because of their distinction as the first National Guard units to arrive in Korea the transportation truck units have been covered separately in chapter 3.

After the truckers landed in January, the next group of National Guard support troops to arrive in Korea consisted of three ordnance maintenance companies and an ordnance battalion Hq. and Hq. detachment. Arriving in the fifteen day period March 9–26, 1951, were the following:

106th Ordnance Heavy Maintenance Company (Missouri).
107th Ordnance Medium Maintenance Company (Michigan).
568th Ordnance Heavy Maintenance Company (Tennessee).
30th Ordnance Battalion Hq. & Hq. Detachment (New Jersey).

The designations "medium" and "heavy" refer not to the size of the equipment the units worked on, but rather to the type of work they performed. Eg.: while a medium maintenance company might replace assemblies such as axles and transmissions, a heavy maintenance company would completely rebuild them from the housing up.

Alerted for active duty July 29, 1950, Missouri's 106th Ordnance Company (HM) increased its drills to three nights a week before shipping out to Fort Hood, Texas. Alerted for overseas shipment in December, the 106th departed Fort Lawton January 16. Due to the combat situation in Korea, the unit's destination changed and they were sent to Japan where they stayed six weeks before taking a ferry to Pusan.

The Army assigned the 106th to the 1st Provisional Ordnance Battalion, and the company set up shop in an old fishnet factory near Pusan. The 106th missions were many and varied, including the removal of all combat vehicles and towed artillery from the Pusan docks, repairing and processing this equipment, and shipping it to forward artillery and vehicle parks. The unit also performed maintenance on combat vehicles, artillery, small arms, and fire control instruments for units in the immediate area. In May, the men dropped their tools and picked up their weapons as they helped quell a riot at POW compound 10.[2]

SERGEANT AMON BAUMGARTEN.
106TH ORDNANCE HEAVY MAINTENANCE COMPANY (MISSOURI).

I was a heavy artillery repairman; worked on the 155s and also on the 90mm tank gun. They'd come in all tore up and I'd rebuild them. My first hitch in the Army, I'd been in the infantry as a mortar crewmen, so I worked on the mortars a lot too. Later on I got sent back to Japan to an ordnance depot for eight weeks or so to learn how to repair the quad .50 cal. machine guns and 40mm guns that the light AAA units had.

When I returned to Korea another fellow and myself took a shop truck and went around to these units fixing them up. The quad .50's were in terrible shape. It wasn't all the gun crews' fault; this equipment was pretty old stuff. Some of the rings the guns traversed on were so dented the guns could only move a short distance. The firing solenoids also always needed repair. As we repaired the guns we showed the crews how to do it.

There were a couple of POW compounds near where we were based. When the big riots started out on Koje Island these guys also got involved. One morning they came out of their barracks in uniforms they'd made or smuggled in and started marching around the compound. They had made some billy clubs and were carrying them on their shoulders like rifles. Our unit got called to get them under control. We had some half-tracks we'd been working on, so we piled in and drove over. The half tracks mounted a .50 caliber machine gun, but we didn't have any ammo for them. We did have our rifles and a few .30 caliber machine guns.

There were fifteen or so of their officers on the roof of a barracks directing things. I pointed the .50 right at them and cranked it a couple of times. This got their attention and I think cooled things down a bit. While we were there I figured out how the North Koreans were getting information into the compound. Across the road there was a wash line and someone would put out different colored pillow cases, towels, and stuff like that in different sequences; a regular code, that's how they were doing it.

We had a real problem with thieves in the Pusan area. And the worst ones were the South Korean soldiers that were supposed to be guarding our area for us. They'd sneak into the tents and steal anything laying around. Finally we put a man up in a watch tower and he killed one of them. Another time I spotted five of them coming out of one of our work shops. I yelled "halt", but they kept running so I fired my .45 at them, and one went down. The others scooped him up and they got away. We told the South Korean MPs but never heard anything more about it.

Hailing from Pontiac, Michigan, the 107th Ordnance Company (MM) landed on March 9, and joined IX Corps.

WARRANT OFFICER (JG) JOHN BUSHART.
107TH ORDNANCE MEDIUM MAINTENANCE COMPANY (MICHIGAN).

We weren't supposed to go to Korea, at all. We landed in Japan and were going to Sendai, on the island of Honshu. The Eighth Army Ordnance Officer at this time was Colonel John Harbert, and Harbert had started his military career years before in the 107th Ordnance Maintenance Company, Michigan National Guard! When he heard we were in the area he naturally wanted us in Korea; so after thirty-two days in Japan, we packed up and headed over.

When we first got to Korea we set up near a Regular Army ordnance unit. We went over to ask a few questions; get the "lay of the land" so to speak. We weren't greeted with open arms to put it mildly. "You fellows are from the company. Harbert says will show us all how to perform ordnance service in the field?" is the reception we got. We had to play it by ear for a few days, but soon got into the swing of things. It was soon forgotten that we were a National Guard unit, and we became part of a unified army.

As the technical supply officer I had seventeen enlisted men to do the work, and in addition, we hired three Korean nationals as clerks. I had fifteen GMC 6x6's, eight $1^1/_2$ ton trailers and two jeeps. Twelve of the trucks were outfitted with parts bins; the other three were used to haul parts from the ordnance depot which was usually twenty to forty miles from our location.

The mission of the technical supply section was to receive, store and issue class II and IV ordnance to the units in the field. We stocked everything from sparkplugs to tank engines.

I usually had a two hundred square foot area of bulk storage—engines, transmissions, axles and tank track.

In addition, I maintained a "direct exchange" float of ten 6x6 trucks, five jeeps, five three-quarter ton trucks, one hundred watches, and ten binoculars. These were used to replace like items which could not be repaired by our shop sections.

When replacement or additional trucks or tanks would be shipped in from Japan for units we supported, it was my responsibility to pick them up from either the rail-head or the port at Inchon so that our repair sections could check them out before we issued them to the ultimate recipients. I loved to drive—the bigger the unit the better—so when I was notified I had some vehicles to pick up, I would arrange to take one less driver than I needed, so I would have to drive one back to our company. I availed myself of the opportunity to drive everything from a $7^1/_2$ ton prime mover to an M-46 tank.

The two other sections in the platoon were the service section and the recovery section. A lieutenant was the platoon leader. As a warrant officer I was second in command of the platoon in addition to my primary duty as technical supply officer.

The service section was the "blacksmith shop" for the company. They had welders and solderers, and canvas and leather workers. Anything we needed that we couldn't order, the service section would make it. When we first started operating in Korea there was a terrific shortage of front springs for the 6x6 trucks. The roads were in such poor shape broken springs were an everyday occurrence. Our service section perfected a method of taking two or more broken springs and making one good one.[3]

After World War II service in Europe, Bushart had become the first man to enlist in the reorganizing 107th in December of 1946.

The mission of Tennessee's 568th Ordnance Heavy Automotive Maintenance (HAM) Company was two-fold: first, to rebuild vehicles brought back from front line units; and second, to process and service vehicles rebuilt in Japan and to get them—and their own rebuilt vehicles—to distribution points for forward units as quickly as possible.

Prime movers and tow trucks of the 568th hauled the vehicles to a collecting point where company personnel made the decision to either scrap them, or send them to the shop for repair. If a truck or other vehicle was deemed unrepairable all salvageable parts were removed and put in the vast inventory of parts the 568th kept on hand. The Memphis outfit's ingenuity in reusing these parts paid off when in one 45-day period the 568th rebuilt 397 vehicles and processed another 1,960 that had been rebuilt in Japan.[4]

Little is known about New Jersey's 30th Ordnance Battalion Hq. and Hq. Detachment—possibly because when activated in August 1950, the Trenton unit only had twenty-two officers and men! After training at Fort Bliss, Texas, the 30th departed Fort Lawton, January 26, 1951, and after a short stop in Japan landed at Pusan March 21.

Moving north on the 25th, the 30th set up at Kumchon, joining the 8046th Ordnance Field Group. At this time three ordnance companies, including Tennessee's 568th were assigned to it. The unit's mission was to command, direct, and supervise administration of these three companies. The Army kept the unit moving; first to Taejon on April 4, then to Seoul, July 22.

On November 11, the detachment was assigned to the 59th Ordnance Group. The next thirteen months are a complete blank. Or, as the unit history dated November 12, 1954, states: "There is no information available at this time about the period from 11 November 1951 until January 1953." When the "Lost Detachment" was located in 1953 it was tending six companies whose primary mission was the repair of vehicles and artillery pieces. The 30th continued in this mission for the balance of the war.[5]

Landing at Inchon April 7, 1951, New York's 101st Signal Battalion became the only National Guard signal unit to serve in Korea. When mobilized in the first increment, the Yonkers unit was comprised almost entirely of employees of the New York Telephone Company. Moving to Camp Gordon, Georgia, the unit filled up to strength and shipped out in December 1950. Sent to Japan, the 101st waited there for their equipment before making the short trip to Inchon.

In Korea, the spring of 1951, a very thin line separated combat units from their supporting elements. As both sides attacked and counterattacked, support units that began the day five miles in back of the MLR might, by evening, find themselves manning front-line positions.

SERGEANT FIRST CLASS J. BRUCE COWPER, JR.
"C" COMPANY, 101ST SIGNAL BATTALION (NEW YORK.)

We had only been in Korea a couple of weeks and were running cable for the 1st Marine Division near Yongdungpo. One morning, just around daybreak, the area came under

Courtesy of J. Bruce Cowper, Jr.

Sergeant First Class J. Bruce Cowper, Jr. 101st Signal Battalion (photographed as first sergeant) played dead for two days and nights when his unit was overrun.

heavy fire and by mid-morning it was getting bad. The Marines pulled out and ran, leaving us with no machine guns, or other heavy weapons to hold off the enemy. All we had were our rifles, carbines, and side arms. You might say a signal company covered a Marine unit's withdrawal! I have not had much use for the Marines since that day.

We used everything we had to return fire. About noon when the word finally came to withdraw, the company executive officer gave me two men, Ray Russell from the 1st Platoon, and Ed Seaman from the 2nd Platoon, and ordered us to cover the withdrawal and protect the equipment left behind. The company pulled out using the $2^1/_2$ ton trucks only. They left behind the K-43 and K-44 telephone trucks that weren't very mobile and had a lot of trouble on the rugged Korean terrain.

I don't think our little fire power did much good; there were so many of them and they were getting closer and closer. Next to our position was a large shell crater, and after about half an hour the three of us got into it as we realized there was nothing we could do to stop the Chinese as they ran over us like ants. We played dead and the Gooks just walked around the top of the shell crater, and thank God, they must have assumed we were dead.

We had our canteens and I think I only took one drink the first night as I was afraid I would have to go to the bathroom more. I was scared that during the daylight hours they would look in the crater and notice we had wet our pants.

We laid there for $2^1/2$ days with no food and making no movement.

In the early morning hours of the third day it got very quiet, but we were afraid to get out of the hole. Then, after daybreak, we heard voices calling "Teapot Charlie" in clear English, so we crawled up and looked out. The Chinese had left the area and a squad from the R&M Company of our own outfit, the 101st Signal Battalion, was looking for a site to set up a relay station and saw the vehicles with our markings on them. The code name for the 101st was "Teapot" and "Charlie" for "C" Company. I recall Andy Santacross was the squad leader.

They took us back to the forward IX Corps CP and then back to our unit. We could hardly walk because of lying so still for so long. When our company got back to the original location, we discovered that not a piece of equipment or any of the trucks had been touched. Thank God the Gooks didn't know what they were doing![6]

The most daunting task facing the 101st was the installation of VHF stations and relays which provided combination radio and telephone communications. The placement of these units was a backbreaking job. The stations had to be situated in line of sight of each other at regular intervals; in mountainous Korea that meant at the top of 4,000 foot or higher mountains.

On May 23, 1951, I Corps ordered the radio relay team of the 101st to erect four VHF relays on Hill 1157. Lieutenant Jasper Lupo and six signalmen moved out the next day with three $2^1/2$ ton trucks carrying the equipment, and twenty-five Korean laborers. Leaving the MSR the detachment drove over a narrow rocky trail that led to the base of Hill 1157. After four miles the vehicles could go no farther and a base camp was established.

After dividing all of the equipment needed for two relays the men started climbing the hill, Lieutenant Lupo and an interpreter leading the way. After three miles scattered small arms fire from enemy stragglers was encountered but the small group continued on. At 1730 hours, after an eight hour climb, the bearers reached the mountain top. Lupo sent the Koreans back to the base and began erecting eight 25 foot antennas and reassembling the equipment. By 1900 the first two relays were ready for operation.

The Koreans returned at 0200 hours May 25, with the balance of the equipment, and the men spent the rest of the night setting up the remaining two relays. The VHF station and all four relays were operating by 0600. Eight tons of Signal Corps equipment and other supplies had been carried to the top of Hill 1157.

After the Chinese spring offensive stalled in May and U.N. forces once more began moving north, the 101st found a novel solution to the problem of getting signal equipment to the mountain tops.

The Chinese, who depended exclusively on pack animals to move their equipment in the forward areas, had abandoned a number of donkeys in the 101st area. When the animals were first found they were half starved and badly abused. A diet of candy, sugar, and cereal from 5 in 1 rations soon had the donkeys back in shape and six of them resumed their burdensome life, this time working for the radio relay platoon of the 101st Signal Battalion.[7]

During the Korean War the Army mobilized twenty National Guard medical units. For the most part these were separate clearing, collecting, and ambulance companies. Of the twenty units activated only one, the 217th Medical Collecting Company, from Booneville, Arkansas, served in Korea. And the 217th never served in the role it had trained for.[8]

PRIVATE FIRST CLASS WILLIAM CATLETT. 217TH MEDICAL COLLECTING COMPANY (ARKANSAS).

Our outfit's job was to get the wounded off the front line. I believe about three of us would be assigned to an infantry platoon, and as the people would got wounded we would move them back just off the front line, maybe only a hundred feet or so. From there other men in the company would pick them up and move them to an aid station.

We were at summer camp at Fort Robinson, at Little Rock, and one night at retreat the first sergeant steps out and says, "Boys, I've got some good news for you. We're going on a little trip." I was sixteen years old; I thought we were going on a fishing trip. Then he said, "We've been mobilized." I looked at my buddy standing there, and I said, "What the heck does that mean?" I had no idea.

They sent us to Fort Benning, Georgia, and filled us up to strength with National Guardsmen from, I believe, Mississippi or Alabama. The unit was all National Guard, no Regulars or draftees. For some reason they gave us airborne-infantry training instead of the regular basic training. We did everything but the jump training. I don't know why, and at the time I didn't have the guts to ask.

Part of the time they'd send us over to the post hospital and gave us medical training. It was good training, but a lot of it was reading prescriptions and things like that. I don't know why they did that because our job didn't call for it.

After our training they put us on buses and sent us back to Booneville for a fifteen day leave. Then back to Benning, and then to Fort Lawton, Washington, where we shipped out. It took twenty-seven days to get to Sasebo, Japan; two thousand men on a ship built to carry 700. The day after we landed the ship sank at the dock.

Next we were sent to a hospital where all the patients had hepatitis. No wounded at all, just men with hepatitis. I got assigned as a cook; I didn't even know how to boil water. We stayed there about ninety days and then went to Pusan, and as soon as we landed the company got broke up.

One platoon got sent to an Air Force Base where they unloaded hospital trains, processed the wounded, and sent them on to a hospital in Japan. Another platoon got sent to a hospital somewhere in Korea; I don't recall where, I never saw them again.

My platoon got sent to a POW compound eight or ten miles from Pusan, where the Army had set up a saw mill. I spent my entire tour there supervising POWs making wardrobes, cedar chests, shelving, and things like that. It was a regular eight to five job. They never told me but I'm sure it was all going to officers' quarters in Japan.

There were about 300 prisoners there, and they had a good deal and didn't give us any trouble. But we did keep the Chinese separated from the Koreans as they didn't get along. Once in a while there'd be a murder and we'd find a body in the compound. I recall we found one with a pick handle driven right through him. The guard duty was handled by infantry units that were back off the front in reserve.

I was mad as hell. Since they had sent me over there I wanted to get up to the front and fight; that's what I wanted. We were told we couldn't get out of there, and that we were doomed to stay there no matter what. And I thought, "If this isn't a hell of a way to fight a war I never heard of it." But being the low man on the totem pole there wasn't much I could do. We had taken what I thought was some real good hard training, and we never got to perform our mission at all, and that's what made me so damn angry.

Remaining in the Army, Catlett served three tours in Vietnam, before retiring as a first sergeant.

CHAPTER 9

THE THUNDERBIRDS

In the years following World War II, one topic was sure to arise whenever and wherever Army veterans gathered. Be it at American Legion or VFW halls, at unit reunions, or down at the corner saloon, sooner or later the topic would turn to the one big question: What was the best Army division of World War II?

Was it the 1st Infantry, the "Big Red One" that landed on beaches from Casablanca to Normandy? Or, perhaps it was the 3rd Infantry of Audie Murphy fame. And what about Matt Ridgway's 82nd Airborne or the 4th Armored that spearheaded Patton's drive across Europe?

Out in the Pacific, the Marines were getting most of the publicity, but the 32nd Infantry Division (Wisconsin-Michigan) was doing most of the fighting. After training for six months in Australia the Guardsmen began landing at Port Moresby, New Guinea, in September 1942. After New Guinea it was on to the Philippines, where the division took part in two campaigns. The 32nd spent forty-four months overseas before being inactivated in Japan in 1946.

In forty-seven states the argument could be heard. Only in the state of Oklahoma was there silence, for they knew. From Guymon in the panhandle, down to Altus and over to Lawton. Up to Oklahoma City, and east to Tulsa and Muskogee, they knew. They knew, without doubt, that the outstanding division of World

War II was the 45th Infantry Division, Oklahoma National Guard—
The Thunderbirds.*[1]

George Patton agreed with them. After the Sicily campaign he
told the men of the 45th: "Your division is one of the best, if not the
best division, in the history of American arms."

And at this point they were just getting started. Before the
Thunderbirds returned to Oklahoma, the division would be in combat 511 days, make four assault landings, and participate in eight
campaigns. The division suffered a total of 20,994 killed, wounded,
and missing in action, one of the five highest casualty rates suffered by any Army division in the war.[2]

Shipped home in the summer and fall of 1945, the division
began reorganization in the spring of 1946. Lieutenant General
Raymond S. McLain, who mobilized with the division in 1940, had
remained in the Army and now played a key role in reforming the
division as an all Oklahoma unit. With McLain's advice and considerable influence in the Pentagon everything quickly came together and on September 5, 1946, the reorganized 45th Infantry
Division received Federal recognition.[3]

The loss of the Arizona, Colorado, and New Mexico units necessitated a complete realignment of the 45th. The major change
being the formation of a new infantry regiment, the 279th, in the
northeastern part of the state. To give the new unit a nucleus, it
was necessary to transfer ten companies from other division outfits. This in turn led to a realignment of the entire division. New
companies were formed in towns that had not previously had National Guard units, while other, long established units had to switch
branches. By early 1947, the changes were completed.[4]

COLONEL FRED DAUGHERTY.
COMMANDING OFFICER, 179TH INFANTRY REGIMENT.

When I undertook the reorganization of the 179th Infantry
in 1946, a problem was immediately encountered. The 45th
had been located in four states prior to World War II: Oklahoma, Colorado, New Mexico, and Arizona. When the 45th
was reorganized in 1946 the whole division was located in
Oklahoma. This meant a complete realignment of units and
organizations in the state.

The southeastern quarter of the state historically belonged to
the 180th Infantry Regiment; this is where it had always been.

---

* Although composed predominantly of Oklahoma units when mobilized in 1940, the
45th also had Guardsmen from Arizona, Colorado, and New Mexico.

The 179th was to be located in the western part of the state. We now had a third regiment of infantry, the 279th Infantry Regiment; it started from scratch and was located in the northeast part of the state. The 180th remained in the southeast, and I got the west.

There were twenty companies in an infantry regiment at this time and I had to locate those twenty companies in that area of the state. That territory, before World War II, had been largely artillery, so I had to go into artillery communities. One of my problems was in finding infantry soldiers, particularly infantry officers who had some combat experience in World War II.

I had difficulties. As an example, in Perry, Oklahoma, which had been an artillery

Colonel Fred Daugherty, C.O. 179th Infantry Regiment, later commanded the 45th Infantry Division. (Photographed as a major general.)

town, my company commander, the only man I could find that I thought had the ability to put a unit together, had been a Navy LST Commander in World War II. Another problem was in Kingfisher, Oklahoma, another old artillery town. There I gave command to a former Navy flier. They were both good men, the right age, with good reputations in their communities. They had fine leadership qualities, and they could bring their units to authorized strength. This was important as we had to recruit our own men.

When we were called up for the Korean War one of the first things I did was send those two officers to the Infantry School at Fort Benning. When they returned to the regiment they were infantrymen.

Daugherty, who enlisted as a private in the 179th in 1934, led the regiment in combat in Korea. He went on to command the 45th Infantry Division from 1960–1964, before retiring as a major general. Appointed United States District Judge in 1961, Daugherty has been a Senior District Judge since 1982.

Command of the reorganized division went to newly promoted Brigadier General James C. Styron. After attending prep school in Washington, D.C., Styron missed his first appointment to West Point in 1915, because of his weight; at 125 pounds the rail thin Styron didn't have enough. A year of good eating solved the problem, and he joined the Corps of Cadets the next year. America's entry into World War I forced West Point to cut its curriculum to two years, and Styron graduated with the class of 1918, just ten days before the German surrender. Styron resigned his commission in 1920, later saying, "There were so many officers ahead of me it didn't look like much of a future."

Styron joined the 45th in 1922 as a first lieutenant. By 1940 he was a colonel and division chief of staff. Styron served with the Thunderbirds in Sicily and Italy in various staff positions. Awarded a Silver Star and the Legion of Merit, Styron returned to the States in 1944 due to illness. Promoted to major general just a month after receiving his first star, Styron would be fifty-three years old when he led the Thunderbirds to Korea in late 1951.[5]

MASTER SERGEANT FRANK BOYER.
G-2 SECTION, 45TH INFANTRY DIVISION.

I saw him all the time. He was a very outstanding person; I thought a very astute, scholarly man. Very calm. I never heard him raise his voice, although I heard him expound a little bit. I thought him a very level-headed type of guy. He had a lot of what you call "good old horse sense." For my money he was an excellent choice; I'm sure from his experiences in World War II, he had all the know-how in the world to lead the division in combat. He had a good staff, the "G" sections. I was head NCO in the G-2 section and I associated with them every day, and you can tell their capabilities real quick.

Boyer, who first joined the 45th in 1937, volunteered for the paratroops in World War II and fought in Europe with the 17th Airborne Division. He retired from the Air National Guard in 1959 as a first sergeant.

As noted in chapter 1, General Mark Clark had listed the 45th among the top six National Guard divisions in the country when Army Chief of Staff Collins asked for his recommendations in July of 1950. That, in addition to being the only originally recommended division located west of the Mississippi, made the 45th an obvious selection for mobilization.

Officially notified August 1, for a September 1 activation, the division commenced a statewide recruiting drive. Using the slogan,

"Go with the men you know," the drive netted some recruits, but most Oklahomans preferred not to go at all, and the division departed for Camp Polk, Louisiana, its new duty station, with only 8,260 men—over 10,000 troops short of its TO&E strength.[6]

If new recruits were hard to come by, the division did gain some combat veterans. Many of these were former Thunderbirds who had served with the division in World War II and didn't want to be left behind if there was a chance their old outfit was going into action. Other combat veterans who knew how the Army operated had a different reason for signing up.

SECOND LIEUTENANT CHARLES RICE.
45TH RECONNAISSANCE COMPANY.

I had served as an enlisted man during World War II with the recon troop of the 69th Infantry Division in Europe. After the war I attended Oklahoma University, studying petroleum engineering, and got a Reserve commission. When the war in Korea broke out they started sending second lieutenants with no combat experience as officers to Korea as replacements.

I decided that wasn't for me, so when I heard the 45th was being activated I called up Claremore, where the recon company was located, and talked to the C.O., and he said, "Come on up, we can sure use you." I did not want to go as a replacement, I wanted to go with a unit.

The recon company was in Claremore, because Oklahoma Military Academy was located there and had been forever. They taught cavalry, or armor, as their main branch, so there were a lot of OMA cadets who were members of that Guard unit. Within ten days after I joined I was with the advance party at Camp Polk.

Our company commander was Captain W. R. Landrum, who had been Commandant of Cadets at OMA. He was quite a bit older than I was. I was twenty-five at that time, and I'd say Captain Landrum was probably in his mid-forties which is old for a company commander. I think he had been a major at one time, but had to revert to captain to take this post at OMA.

Rice remained in the National Guard, then transferred to the Army Reserve; he retired as a lieutenant colonel in 1968.

Advance parties and service units went on active duty early, and began moving to Polk on August 15, to prepare the camp for the main body. On September 1, 1950, the 45th Infantry Division once again entered Federal service and headed south. For the third time in ten years the Thunderbirds would train in Louisiana.[7]

CORPORAL ROBERT FAKEN.
"C" BATTERY, 189TH FIELD ARTILLERY BATTALION.

As I recall, the first two or three weeks we made weekend drills, then the last week or two we made eight hour drills every day. We had to quit our jobs and be over at the armory every day. We spent this time checking our equipment and supplies, the things you'd normally do getting ready to go on active duty. We also did a lot of marching and started to learn Army discipline.

I was an assistant gunner. At that time we had three 155mm howitzers, which is half of what a battery has. I believe they were the M2A1, and I recall they were tractor towed.

September 1st, 1950, we were activated. We sent an advance party on down to Camp Polk, while the rest of the unit stayed at Blackwell for another week or ten days. Then we boarded a troop train in Blackwell; we took all of our equipment with us. When we got down to Dallas, our car, or several cars, came loose from the rest of the train. No one got hurt, but we got knocked out of our seats. The rest of the trip was pretty uneventful.

Transferring to the Army Reserve, Faken retired as a command sergeant major with thirty-six years service.

Camp Polk, Louisiana, one of the hundreds of Army camps constructed in the days just before World War II, is located on 198,000 acres of mostly cut-over pine forests in west-central Louisiana, five hundred miles from Oklahoma City. Closed except for short periods when Guard and Reserve components used it, the camp had fallen into disrepair in the five years of peace.*

Many of the officers brought their families with them only to find off-post housing almost non-existent in the small towns around Fort Polk.

CHIEF WARRANT OFFICER EMMETT STEEDS.
HEADQUARTERS, 179TH INFANTRY REGIMENT.

I'd first joined the Guard way back in 1936, or 1937, back in the days of campaign hats and wrapped leggings. When we

---

* Closed again after the Korean War, Polk reopened and became a permanent Army Fort in 1962. In the next fourteen years, over a million soldiers would receive their basic and advanced training at Fort Polk.[8]

went overseas I was a platoon sergeant and then got commissioned on Sicily when my company commander got killed and my platoon leader wounded.

When we got notified we were being mobilized for the Korean War, I was a captain and the regimental ammunition officer. I was told I could either take a line company or go into the S-2 or S-3 sections and remain a captain. Or, I could change my rank to warrant officer and remain the regimental ammunition officer. I liked the job and the pay was about the same, so I stayed with that all through Korea.

About three weeks before the unit moved to Camp Polk, Bill Willett and I and our wives went down to Louisiana to hunt for a place to live. We hunted all over the region and couldn't find anything. We'd given up, when coming back through Rosepine, we spotted what looked like some apartments over an old garage. Rosepine was about thirty minutes from Camp Polk. It turned out to be eight little two room apartments that belonged to a Baptist preacher. For one reason or another he didn't want to rent them to us, but we finally talked him into it.

There were eight small apartments and a big hallway with two bathrooms at the end of the hall. The first week or so, before we got stoves, we did all the cooking on a two-burner Coleman camp stove I'd brought along. All the refrigerators were out in the hall, and when everyone started cooking and opening them up at the same time, of course we'd blow the fuses. We put a rug, divans, and chairs out in this big hallway and whenever one of the kids had a birthday or we had a party we'd all get together out there.

I don't remember what we paid for those apartments, but it wasn't an awful lot. Then this guy that had the apartments tried to raise the rent on us. And me, being more or less in charge of things there, it was up to me to go talk to the man. I politely told him, "I'm down here fighting your war for you. We all have homes sitting vacant in Oklahoma that we're paying on while we're here in these little two room apartments, and now you're trying to raise the rent on us." So he didn't raise the rent any.

Following his Korean service Steeds resumed working for the post office in Oklahoma City. After retiring he took up photography as a hobby. His pictures have won awards throughout the southwest.

The Thunderbirds settled in at Polk and soon began receiving recruits to bring the division up to TO&E strength. The division assigned a thousand men to each of the regiments and to division artillery, while the separate units received troops as needed. Once assigned to a unit a soldier would remain with it, receive all of his training, and eventually be assigned a slot in the outfit.

But there was one big drawback. At this time National Guardsmen did not attend basic training. Two hours a week drill, and two weeks at summer camp, that was it. Other than the World War II veterans the NCOs were almost as green as the men they were preparing to train.

In the company grade officer ranks this same problem existed. Many junior officers were unqualified in their branches. If a man had led a tank platoon or artillery battery in combat and the National Guard outfit in his town happened to be infantry, it was not a big deal. Obviously the Guard wasn't about to let a combat veteran slip away if they had a chance to sign him up. When mobilized in 1950, many former Air Corps and Navy officers were leading company size units in the 45th Infantry Division.

This lack of branch training led to hundreds of officers and NCOs departing for Army service schools shortly after arriving at Camp Polk. Fort Benning, Fort Sill, Fort Riley, and other Army Schools soon became temporary homes for many of the Thunderbirds.

CORPORAL GEORGE BEWLEY.
"C" BATTERY, 189TH FIELD ARTILLERY BATTALION.

I was the battery instrument operator in the survey section. I worked the aiming circle which is used in laying the guns. I believe it was in November when I got sent to school at Fort Sill. They'd given me a choice of going to school at Fort Sill or taking a gun section, and I chose to go to school. I had been to Sill several times for summer camp and liked it down there. I was to go to school and then come back and teach the other guys in the unit. The course lasted three months, and I enjoyed it and learned a lot.

They taught me how to survey a position. At the battery level there was no training on survey work; they had the books, but that was all. I had never had that much math when I was in school, but I wound up in the middle of the class. The thing is, in Korea, everything was already surveyed in. It was already done; I imagine the 1st Cav did it. So they put me in the fire direction center. The only time I ever used what I learned at Fort Sill was in a test.

Back from Korea, Bewley went to work for the Federal Aviation Administration, as an air controller in the weather information department.

MASTER SERGEANT VERNON RIBERA.
"E" COMPANY, 180TH INFANTRY REGIMENT.

When we were mobilized we just had the nucleus; we were a long way from full strength. It was mostly the cadre NCOs and a few recruit type soldiers who had just joined. We had very few riflemen. This was September, and Camp Polk was rainy and hot, but we were in barracks, and all in all it wasn't a bad post. I was there for not quite a month and then went off to leadership school. They sent the senior NCOs to leadership school at Fort Riley, Kansas, and I was up there for six or seven weeks.

It was just like OCS; I mean it was daylight till dark, as fast as you could work. They taught us everything, but mainly leadership, how to lead and what to do in this case or situation, and to see how you would react. Then you'd be graded on how you reacted. You also had to teach classes and were graded on your presentation and knowledge of the subject.

There was one other senior NCO in the company who had been in World War II, Gerald Riddle. He was the first sergeant. So when I got back to Camp Polk, he went off to leadership school, and I took over as first sergeant while he was gone. I was doing double duty there for a while.

Courtesy of Vernon Ribera

Master Sergeant Vernon Ribera, pictured next to a knocked out Russian T-34 tank, led his platoon of the 180th Infantry through some of the heaviest fighting the 45th Infantry Division saw in Korea.

By the time I got back to Polk, the recruits had arrived. They came straight from the induction centers and we had to teach them everything, starting with close order drill. We had to teach them the bayonet, take them out to the firing range, etc. We did run through some squad problems, but we certainly weren't combat ready when we left for Japan.

I never had an officer for a platoon leader at any time. I was the platoon leader and the platoon sergeant the whole time, from beginning to end. We had the best company in the division, and of course within the company, mine was the best platoon. When I left Korea, my platoon had the most decorations of any platoon in the division so far as I know: Silver Stars, Bronze Stars, Purple Hearts, etc.

After receiving his master's degree at Rutgers University, Ribera taught mathematics and computer science at Central State University in Edmond, Oklahoma, before retiring in 1990.

While Bewley, Ribera, and other men left for branch schools across the country, the division established its own schools at Camp Polk. Units would continually be ordered to send soldiers to these classes. The absence of so many men created a hardship for the units and upset the training program that officially commenced November 7, 1950.

FIRST LIEUTENANT EDDIE COPE.
COMPANY COMMANDER, SERVICE COMPANY,
279TH INFANTRY REGIMENT.

I recall an incident at Polk. To me it was funny, but it got me in a lot of trouble. My first sergeant, Joe Knight, was a highly qualified individual; he could do most anything. He was very protective of his troops in Service Company as a first soldier should be.

Regiment was always calling on the companies to send so many troops to such and such a school. They had the special schools, and they'd say send two guys, five guys, ten guys, whatever. You still had all your work and all the training to do, even with the men in class, and a lot of extra duty had to be taken on by everyone. This went on day after day.

Finally my first sergeant got tired of it. One day I came in and he told me I was probably going to get into trouble. Regiment had called for two men to take a class in "Methods of Instruction." They would learn how to teach other men how to instruct and give classes. The first sergeant said he had sent "so and so." I said, "OK."

The next day I was down at regimental headquarters. The regimental executive officer saw me standing there and he hollered out of his office, "Cope, get in here!" I could tell by the sound of his voice I was going to get a dressing down. I stepped it off pretty smartly in there, saluted, and reported the way you are supposed to. He ate me up one side and down the other, never did give me at ease. He chewed me out royally. It ended up that he had never heard of such a dumb stunt in all his life; they had called for two guys to go to Methods of Instruction School, and we had sent two guys who could not read or write.

Cope retired in 1979 as a colonel with over thirty-nine years service. His last assignment was Chief of Staff of the Oklahoma Military Department.

Another Army concept that would eventually cost the 45th many excellent men now appeared. This was the plan to incorporate an Airborne Ranger Company into each infantry division. The Rangers, who traced their heritage back to before the Revolutionary War, had been organized in World War II into battalions and performed brilliantly on special missions around the world.

At Camp Polk, the call for volunteers went out in December, and over 500 Thunderbirds responded. A tough selection process weeded out over half the volunteers; the men that remained trained at Fort Benning and Camp Carson, before rejoining the division in Japan, July 1, 1951.

Two months later the Army decided attaching Ranger companies to divisions was not a good idea after all. Given their choice of assignments, two-thirds of the highly trained men transferred to the 187th Airborne Regiment, while only a third remained with the 45th.[9]

SECOND LIEUTENANT CARL STEVENS.
RANGER COMPANY, 45TH INFANTRY DIVISION.

I had just gotten my degree in May 1950 from Northwestern State College in Alva, Oklahoma, and had gone back to Stilwell. I was walking down the street, didn't have a job or anything to do, when the C.O. of the local Guard outfit, a guy named Rogers, walks up and says to me, "What are you doing now?" I said, "Nothing." And he said, "Why don't you get a commission in the Guard and make a little extra money?" I said, "That sounds good to me."

So I came down to Oklahoma City, took a test and walked out a second lieutenant in "I" Company, 279th Infantry. That was in August 1950, and in September we mobilized. We went to Camp Polk, and I knew I needed some training right quick as my World War II service had been in the Navy. They were forming an Airborne Infantry Ranger Company for each infantry division and asking for volunteers.

I had heard they were supposed to be pretty good, so I volunteered and was accepted. They took seven officers, and I think we ended up with 120 enlisted men. We started with about 190, but a lot of them got kicked out going through jump school and Ranger training down at Fort Benning. It was tough training. We rejoined the division in Japan in July 1951.

Stevens joined the Oklahoma Highway Patrol upon returning from Korea. He later became a member of the Federal Drug Enforcement Administration, and is now a Deputy U.S. Marshal at the Federal Courthouse in Oklahoma City.

As officers and men arrived and departed, the division continued to train. At times the lack of equipment caused the training to resemble the prewar days of 1940 and 1941.

SERGEANT FIRST CLASS TOMMY HAWKINS. "B" COMPANY, 245TH TANK BATTALION.

I'll tell you how bad it was at Polk. I remember at times we went out and used the company commander's car as a tank! Captain Stanley Coppage, he had probably a '49 or '50 Ford, and we'd use that for running formations, right out in the field. He'd let anyone drive it, whoever happened to be around. We didn't use it much, but we used it some because they just didn't have the tanks for us. And even with that some people had to walk, waving the flags to change from one formation into another. It was really something. That's about the only tactical stuff I remember doing at Polk.

Hawkins became a unit administrator with the Oklahoma National Guard. He retired with over forty-one years service as a command sergeant major.

In mid-December world events caught up with the 45th Infantry Division. In November, General MacArthur had sent the 3rd Infantry Division, the last major combat unit in Japan, to Korea. This move, made without authorization from the Joint Chiefs of Staff, left Japan without any ground combat troops. The Russians then increased their military strength, and commenced large scale maneuvers on Sakhalin Island, just twenty miles across the Soya Strait, from Hokkaido, the northern most Japanese island.

On December 18, MacArthur, now deeply concerned, cabled Washington requesting that the four National Guard divisions be sent to Japan to complete their training and reassure the Japanese populace. The JCS replied to MacArthur the next day. They informed him that the chances of any National Guard divisions being sent to his command were remote. Five star generals do not take no for an answer that easily. MacArthur tried again on December 30, insisting that the four Guard divisions be sent to Japan.

By January 9, the Joint Chiefs had at least partially come around to MacArthur's point of view. They notified Tokyo that, depending on events in Korea, two partially trained Guard divisions "could be deployed to Japan."

In mid-January, Army Chief of Staff Collins met with MacArthur for the fourth time in six months. The deployment of the four National Guard divisions was again a major topic. MacArthur stated that he could not "assume responsibility" for the security of Japan while at the same time keeping Eighth Army in Korea. He again urged that the Guard divisions be sent to Japan immediately.[10]

James Schnabel, in *Policy and Direction: The First Year*, relates the events of the next few weeks.

> *Under these conditions it seemed appropriate to carry out the half-promise, to send two partly trained National Guard Divisions to Japan. On January 23, Collins told General MacArthur that if things in Korea continued going as well as at present and the Chinese could be contained, two divisions might be sent him to increase the security of Japan. A week of continued successes in the field followed, and on January 30, Collins recommended to the other members of the Joint Chiefs of Staff that the 40th and 45th Infantry Divisions be ordered to Japan to bolster the defenses there. The Joint Chiefs of Staff agreed and forwarded the recommendation to the Secretary of Defense at once. MacArthur was informed of this development as soon as it took place. After a relatively lengthy consideration which involved weighing the interests of the European theater against those of the Far East, the Secretary of Defense consented to the transfer of the two major units. On February 25, the Joint Chiefs of Staff notified the U.N. Commander that the 40th and 45th Divisions would reach his command sometime in April.*

"He was specifically ordered to leave these divisions in Japan and not to employ them against the enemy in Korea."[11]

Many of the Thunderbirds first got the news of their impending departure over a radio broadcast at 1800 hours on the evening of February 24, 1951. The official word arrived on the 26th: the 45th along with California's 40th Infantry Division were deploying to Japan. Division units began sending men home on leave the next day, half a company or battery at a time. As soon as the first group returned, the other half departed. This plan enabled all the troops to get ten days leave before sailing for the Far East.

SERGEANT FIRST CLASS TOMMY HAWKINS.
"B" COMPANY, 245TH TANK BATTALION.

One night me and the first sergeant and one of the other platoon sergeants went over to Lake Charles. We went to a rodeo, and when we came back in, it was way late, after midnight. I told the old first sergeant, "Sign me back in, I'm just going on to bed." So I went to bed and about an hour or two later here come the cooks. They pounded on the door and came in there, saying, "Wake him up." My cadre room was right next to the cooks' room. I said, "What are ya'll up to anyhow?" They said, "We're celebrating, here have a drink." I said, "What are we drinking for?" And they said, "Well, we're going to Japan." And that's the way I got the word we were going to Japan.

MASTER SERGEANT FRANK BOYER.
G-2 SECTION, 45TH INFANTRY DIVISION.

I wasn't really surprised when the orders came. You could read in the papers what was happening to the Regulars in Korea. And I'll tell you something now, when you start seeing Regular Army people infiltrating a Guard division, then you know you're hot, because they are coming in to get those promotions, and we started getting them. All of a sudden new faces started showing up, and they started to show up pretty quick after we got down to Camp Polk. It was the West Point protective association operating. I guess I shouldn't say that, but it was so obvious. Which was fine, that's all part of the game. When the West Point protective association starts operating, you know then that you're getting hot.

We got a screwball; it didn't take long and we got one. He came to us right before we went to Japan. He was, of course, a Regular Army colonel, and he was bucking for the star, and he got his star when he came to us. This was Dulaney, the Assistant Division Commander (ADC), and he was a pain in the butt. We called him steel balls, steel balls Dulaney. He was a twenty-four carat . . . well, I better not say it. He exercised his authority in many, many ways. But that's all right, that's part of the game, too.

CHAPTER 10

LIFE WAS GOOD ON HOKKAIDO

Rather than send the 45th to the west coast for embarkation the Army decided to ship the division out of New Orleans. In late March the Thunderbirds boarded trains for the three hundred mile trip to the Crescent City, and the first of the six ships transporting the division sailed on the 29th. By April 1, the 45th Infantry Division, rated by the Army as forty-three percent combat effective, was once again on the high seas.[1]

SERGEANT FIRST CLASS WOODY HARRIS.
HEADQUARTERS & SERVICE COMPANY, 120TH ENGINEER COMBAT BATTALION.

We went down to New Orleans and got aboard the ship. Ours was the *General Weigel*, and this was the first time I had been on a ship that big; it held 5,000 men. We went through the Panama Canal and then up the coast to San Francisco. We were hoping to get off and see the town but it wasn't allowed. We picked up some more troops and headed out. The weather was fine until we got two or three days from Japan, and then we hit a pretty good storm. The head was full, and I was right there with everyone else.

Our quarters were the first compartment right behind the bow. The ship would come out of the water and hit down hard because it had a flat bottom there at the bow. There were only two covered decks, and a lot of people were on them. If I could have gotten outside, I think I would have

125

been all right. It was rough. If you went up three decks and looked outside all you could see were the waves, and you couldn't see the tops of them anywhere, and this was at the top of the ship!

We were in the bottom hold and there was a hatch down there, and the Navy guys hadn't battened it down very well. So our guys pulled back the canvas and climbed down into this compartment and found it was a dry stores compartment. They got a rope and sent up big cans of peaches and different kinds of fruits and soda crackers, stuff like that. The food on the ship wasn't very good, but we ate very well for a few days.

After the war Harris returned to college earning a B.S. & M.S. He later joined the staff at Oklahoma State University, becoming director of the Audio-Visual Center.

SERGEANT FIRST CLASS JOHN PETERS.
HEADQUARTERS COMPANY, 179TH INFANTRY REGIMENT.

I was the youngest of three brothers that served with the 179th in World War II. My older brothers were mobilized in 1940. I caught up with them in 1944, in Southern France. At this time the Army would not let brothers serve in the same unit and I was assigned to the 157th Infantry. My oldest brother talked to the C.O. of the 179th who he'd known for years and I was reassigned right before the regiment went back on line. After the war I stayed in the Guard and became supply sergeant of Headquarters Company.

We left New Orleans and went through the Panama Canal. At Balboa we were allowed off the ship for twelve hours; it was a madhouse, the beer was free and when they ran out of containers the men were putting it in their helmets. A helmet holds a lot of beer. Naturally a lot of men got drunk and there were some fights and a few injuries.

Our ship did not go up the coast to San Francisco, but sailed straight across the Pacific. We thought we were going to stop in Hawaii and get off for a while, but after what happened in Balboa, General Styron changed the orders and the ship didn't even slow down. All we saw of Hawaii were the lights as we sailed by.

Peters, who worked for Southwestern Bell for thirty-eight years before retiring, is now secretary-treasurer of the 179th Infantry Association.

Not all of the Thunderbirds sailed to Japan. Army regulations specified that certain requirements, such as weapons qualification and combat courses, be completed before a soldier shipped out. Four thousand new recruits had not advanced to this point in their training when the overseas alert arrived. To allow these men to finish their training at Camp Polk, the 45th formed a new unit, the 45th Division Training Regiment. Commanded by Lieutenant Colonel James H. Weaver, the unit consisted of 500 NCOs and officers.

As soon as the division moved out for New Orleans, the new unit set up in the eastern sector of the post. Each of the four training battalions formed four companies of 250 fillers, plus the cadre. Because the fillers had arrived in groups of a thousand men, ten days apart, they were in various stages of training. This worked out well as it freed weapons and facilities for each group in succession.[2]

A few Thunderbirds remained at Camp Polk to turn in buildings and equipment, both from the departed division and from the training regiment.

CORPORAL JIMMY TERRY.
700TH ORDNANCE MAINTENANCE COMPANY.

After about three months at Camp Polk, I got sent to a maintenance school at the Atlanta, Georgia, Depot. I was there about three months taking an automotive mechanics course; it was a great school and I learned a lot. I hadn't been back at Polk very long when the orders came to go to Japan. I wasn't too surprised. Even before they told us I figured we'd go sooner or later. I was sort of looking forward to it because I'd never gotten to go anyplace.

They left a small detachment behind to work with the training regiment—the men that were still training. Two of us from the ordnance company were selected to stay behind. I was disappointed. I really wanted to stay with the guys and the unit.

We were taking all the turn-ins: kitchen equipment, trucks, radios, everything that belonged to Camp Polk. We took it in and did the paper work; there was tons of paper work. Every day a truck load would come in or we'd be told to go and check out the kitchen equipment or something else at some unit. The stuff had already been cleaned and most of it had been inventoried. What we were doing was gathering up the stuff from the units and getting rid of it.

We were there about 60 days after the division left. We were about the last men to leave Camp Polk. Then we went by train to Camp Stoneman, near San Francisco. We stayed there a couple weeks and sailed to Japan. The first sergeant came over to the division replacement company where we were at and said, "I want this one, and that one; they belong to me." And just like that we were back in the unit.

Terry became a full time Oklahoma National Guard employee upon returning from Korea. He retired in 1986 as a chief warrant officer.

In late April the division landed at Otaru and Muroran, and set up headquarters at Camp Crawford, near the city of Sapporo. Other division units moved to camps near Eniwa, Shimamatsu, Chitose, and other towns on southern Hokkaido.

The decision to send the 45th to Hokkaido had caught the Army unprepared. Other than at Camp Crawford, with its brick barracks, the men lived in pup tents and later in squad tents at quickly laid out camps. Sixty-five hundred Japanese laborers were soon pouring concrete and assembling prefabricated living quarters for the Thunderbirds. Unfortunately, most of the troops would never see the interior of the new structures. The first units to occupy them had barely unpacked when the division received orders to Korea in November.[3]

As the division resumed training on southern Hokkaido, selected commanders and G-2 personnel headed to the far northern tip of the island. Their mission was to locate and draw up defensive positions and to keep an eye on the Russians, twenty miles across the Soya Strait on Sakhalin Island.

COLONEL FRED DAUGHERTY.
COMMANDING OFFICER, 179TH INFANTRY REGIMENT.

Our main mission on Hokkaido was training. But on top of that, one of the missions given to us was to be prepared to defend the island. The 179th Infantry Regiment was assigned a sector of the northern shore of the island. I reconnoitered the whole area. I recall you could see Sakhalin Island on a clear day.

I made plans to move and to occupy our sector. These were secret plans that I kept in my headquarters. I didn't have a safe, so every time I left my office, I'd cover the plans with a sheet and lock the door. The positions we would occupy if we had to go up there were plotted on a large map set on an easel.

We never moved the troops up there, but the commanders and some of their key people and the regimental staff went up. We had places for everybody to go. We knew where the regimental CP was going to be and the whole works. This information went down to the company commander level. The company commanders knew where their outfits were going to be located. We never stopped our training to do this reconnoitering. I didn't think there was a big threat. I never really thought they'd come across. But it was given to us as one of our missions, as well as our training, to prepare plans for defensive positions on the north shore.

MASTER SERGEANT FRANK BOYER.
G-2 SECTION, 45TH INFANTRY DIVISION.

We had an outpost up on the far tip of Hokkaido, near Wakkanai, about two hundred miles or so from Camp Crawford. It was a point of land, no town or anything. I think it was set up by the 45th Recon Company soon after we got to Japan. The outpost was manned by the 45th Recon Company and also by men from the various "2" sections of the battalions and regiments, maybe six or eight men at a time. They would stay up there a week or so, then rotate. This position was manned at all times and the men were fully armed. Their mission was to observe Sakhalin Island, across the Soya Strait, and to give the alert if anything happened. I recall from this outpost you could see the Russian MIGs taking off and landing.

As the men completed their advanced individual training, unit training commenced. First at the squad and platoon level, then progressing to company and battery exercises, followed by battalion and regimental maneuvers. The division combat units were continually in the field, moving from one training area to another. The job of keeping the troops fed and supplied belonged to the 45th Quartermaster Company.

FIRST LIEUTENANT REX WILSON.
45TH QUARTERMASTER COMPANY.

I was one of the officers that stayed behind with the training regiment. I had the job of clearing all the files and records with Camp Polk. It kept me pretty busy; I had no help, just me. I didn't get to Japan till August.

The special troops were at Camp Crawford, along with division headquarters. The quartermaster company was a good sized outfit, about 180 men and 11 officers at TO&E strength. Later, when we got to Korea, people kept getting attached to us. We called them homesteaders. By the time I left Korea we had 340 people in the company.

I was the Class I Officer working ration breakdown with about fifteen men. It was a pretty smooth operation. The strength reports and the ration requests would come in from the regiments and other units, and I would put my requests in to the Post Quartermaster. All of the food came in from the States. Later, in Korea, we did receive vegetables grown in Japan.

Also at Camp Crawford there was a large Class I cold storage facility; I don't recall how much it held, but it was huge. They also had a reconstituted milk plant run by some Department of Defense civil service people, and the stuff they turned out tasted just like fresh milk.

We'd break the rations down by separate battalions, separate companies, and regiments. The regiments then broke theirs down again to the twenty companies in an infantry regiment. It was kind of unusual in that we didn't haul the rations by truck but shipped them out by train every day to the units, wherever they were located. We shipped out four cars a day, the farthest unit being about fifty miles away.

The Japanese were very prompt with their trains; that's their main mode of transportation. If a car was supposed to roll at 1102 hours, you better have it loaded and sealed by 1100 because at 1102, whether you had it loaded or not, they were moving it. You can't imagine how timely they were.

I think we only went into the field once, stayed out there about ten days. We broke the rations down, loaded them on trucks, hauled them back to Crawford, and reloaded them on the train. The Army does a lot of stuff like that.

Wilson remained on active duty after his Korean service. Retiring as a brigadier general he is now National Secretary of the 45th Infantry Division Association.

The men who had remained at Camp Polk, along with those who had been attending service schools, now rejoined the division. One small group almost didn't make it to Hokkaido.

MASTER SERGEANT CHARLES BROWN.
MEDICAL COMPANY, 180TH INFANTRY REGIMENT.

There were twenty-five people from our company training at Fort Sam Houston, the Army Medical School, when the division shipped out. We had all been told we would rejoin the division in Japan. We got to Japan and were at Camp Drake, for two or three days and still under the impression we were going to be rejoining the division which by that time was on Hokkaido.

I was the ranking person from our company, and they came in one night and told me that we were not rejoining the division, that we would fall out the next morning at 0530 for rifle familiarization, and that we were being sent directly to Korea as replacements.

I got hold of a commercial telephone and placed a call to 45th Division Headquarters. It was easy; I got an English speaking operator and got right through. I got hold of someone in G-1 and told them what I'd been told. They said to "Hang on, everything would be taken care of." The next day we had to go ahead with the familiarization, but by the time we got back from the rifle range, orders had come down that we were not to be sent to Korea as fillers, and that we were to rejoin our unit. We left for Hokkaido the next day. I had made a good phone call.

Courtesy of Charles Brown

Master Sergeant Charles Brown (photographed in Japan) bought supplies for 1st Battalion, 180th Infantry, on the black market.

When we got to Hokkaido my assignment had been changed. I was no longer the dispensary NCO, but the platoon sergeant of the 1st Battalion aid station platoon. I was a little upset because here they'd sent me off to school and now they were taking my job away from me. Somehow that didn't match. But I found that I really liked the infantry battalion and the people I worked with. The lieutenant who was in charge of the platoon and I got along very well together and it turned out to be a very good move.

Japan was still an occupied country at that time and we couldn't eat in their restaurants. We could drink beer in their clubs, and I remember we could eat the french fries they served in the bars or cabarets as they called them, but that was all. I found the Japanese people very friendly and this was a surprise; I didn't expect to find them friendly. One of the men from my company, a man from San Francisco, was of Japanese ancestry. The Japanese people could not believe that he was wearing an American uniform, and they really could not believe that he didn't speak any Japanese.

Charles Brown, a common name for a most uncommon man. Ordained an Episcopal Priest in 1957, Brown remained in the Guard, and later the Army Reserve for over forty-two years before retiring as the senior colonel in the entire Army Reserve.

In late July or early August (the exact date was not revealed for security reasons) fifteen pilots from the division's light aviation section were transferred to Korea. The men, all from Oklahoma, would serve as artillery spotters and infantry liaison pilots.[4]

SECOND LIEUTENANT JACK RAY.
HEADQUARTERS, 45TH INFANTRY DIVISION.

When we mobilized, our pilot experience and capability were probably equal to or greater than the Regular Army. We had a lot of retreads and our equipment was the same as the Regulars. You have to remember that the majority of the personnel, at least in the key positions, were combat trained veterans of World War II. To a degree it was old hat and we were about as ready as anyone on active duty.

Life was good on Hokkaido. We worked hard and played hard. We picked up a rumor that a certain number of pilots were leaving the division to go to Korea for further assignment. It wasn't a rumor. They flew us down to Tokyo, and we grabbed whatever we could to get to Korea. I caught an old C-46 cargo plane loaded to the top and just crawled in, literally on top of the cargo.

I joined the 19th Infantry Regiment, 24th Infantry Division, and because they were short of pilots, I would say within a couple or three days of leaving Japan, I was being shot at— and then most every day thereafter. It was not unusual to fly multiple missions per day. Two good friends from the 45th joined me and flew for the 21st Regiment and the 5th RCT. My primary job with the 19th was to direct air strikes and adjust artillery and mortar fire. We flew behind the gun target line so we were over enemy territory at all times; the exposure was pretty high.[5]

Ray remained in the Army, retiring as a lieutenant colonel. He is now president of BS Aircraft Sales in Norman, Oklahoma.

Compared to the other three National Guard divisions mobilized in September 1950, the Army left the 45th pretty much alone in its never ending search for trained soldiers. The 40th, now stationed on Honshu, had been called upon, both in California and in Japan, to supply large numbers of replacements for Korea.

Highly upset, the 40th's commander, Major General Daniel Hudelson, complained to Congress. The lawmakers sided with Hudelson and told the Army that both Guard divisions in Japan should remain intact. While the Congressional order saved the National Guard divisions from being used as replacement companies, it also got Congress thinking about the future deployment of the Guardsmen.[6]

Meanwhile, in Korea, the peace talks had gotten under way July 10, at Kaesong. The talks progressed slowly, continually stalling and then resuming as the Communists changed positions, seeking to gain an advantage at the bargaining table. After a two month recess the talks resumed again on October 25, at Panmunjom. And on November 27, a truce line was agreed upon. With only minor changes, it would become the "final line" in a war that would continue for nineteen more months.[7]

Lieutenant General Matthew Ridgway, U.N. Commander, now kept Eighth Army Commander, Lieutenant General James Van Fleet, under tight control. Eighth Army would confine its operations to a defensive posture. Pressure would be kept on the enemy by patrols and artillery fire but no major advances were authorized. The war now became a battle of patrols and artillery fire broken by savage attacks and counterattacks to capture or hold key outposts.[8]

As winter approached, an advance party left to set up a winter training camp for the Thunderbirds in the mountains thirty miles north of Sapporo. Lieutenant Rex Wilson, 45th Quartermaster Company, was designated S-4 of the new camp and recalls having forty truck loads of winter gear, including skis and snow shoes ready to issue to the men of the 45th. The gear would soon be used, but not in Japan.[9]

The Guardsmen now had about nine months remaining on their active duty hitch and it was obvious their tour would end in Japan. Or would it? In Washington, Congress and the Army were once again debating the future of the two National Guard divisions in Japan.

When Congress saved the two divisions from being broken up for replacements they also expressed an interest in having the units committed to combat. Always anxious to please Capitol Hill, the Joint Chiefs of Staff, who on countless occasions had stated that the divisions would not be deployed to Korea, now changed their collective mind. In August they notified Ridgway that they wanted the divisions sent to Korea upon completion of their training.[10]

Walter Hermes in *Truce Tent and Fighting Front* best describes the turmoil surrounding the two National Guard units during the second half of 1951.

. . . But the development of the summer offensive caused Ridgway to again change his mind. He did not want to give up combat-wise divisions for untrained troops as long as there was any danger of an enemy counteroffensive. Besides, he told the JCS, a transfer would disrupt his ability to defend Japan for a period of three months while the transfer was taking place.

In Washington, the Army G-3, General Jenkins, disagreed. He thought the risk in leaving Japan partially exposed temporarily to be far less than the threat in Korea. Furthermore, he pointed out to Army Chief of Staff Collins, many of the National Guardsmen in the 40th and 45th would come to the end of their term of service in August 1952 and would have to be sent home. He recommended that one National Guard division be shipped to Korea and then, at an opportune moment, one of the combat divisions could be withdrawn and rotated to Japan. This process could be repeated later on with the second division. Both the JCS and the president approved of this procedure in mid-September.

But Ridgway was not convinced. He held that until at least 15 November the danger of a Soviet move against Japan would still be possible. The Russian reaction to the United States-Japanese peace treaty signed on 8 September was as yet unclear and the situation in Germany was also doubtful. He urged postponement of any movement until November when the matter could be reviewed. In the light of Ridgway's reclama, the JCS, with presidential approval, rescinded their directive to effect the National Guard transfer.

When early November arrived, Ridgway changed his reasons for objecting to the shift of the two divisions to Korea. Although the Eighth Army had completed the fall offensive by this time, Ridgway did not want to reduce its combat effectiveness in case other operations might be carried out to put pressure upon the enemy during the peace negotiations. Instead he once again urged that restrictions against using the National Guard divisions for replacements be lifted.[11]

To Matt Ridgway at his headquarters in Tokyo, this must have seemed like a reasonable request. In Washington it was a different story. General Collins definitely did not desire another fight with

Congress over the deployment of the two National Guard divisions in Japan.

Hermes continues:

General Collins would have no part of this. In his opinion an attempt to break up the divisions would invoke a storm of protests from Congress and imply that the National Guard divisions were not fit for combat duty after a year of training. He informed Ridgway that it appeared mandatory to use the divisions as units as soon as possible before their time expired.

The Chief of Staff's arguments settled the matter. On November 20, General Hickey, FECOM Chief of Staff, notified Van Fleet that the 45th Division would begin its movement in December to replace the 1st Cavalry Division.[12]

Militarily the decision to deploy the Guard divisions to Korea made little sense. Under Federal law the original Guardsmen, who comprised the bulk of the officers and key NCOs, had to be back in the States by July 1952. With the peace talks again under way, no large scale offensives had been planned nor could any be mounted in the dead of the Korean winter. Both sides had dug in; the front was static and casualties were light. Fresh units were not needed.

After eight months in Japan, the Guardsmen knew every foot of their assigned defensive area. They were far better prepared to defend Japan than any new units that might replace them. The argument that the 1st Cavalry and 24th Infantry Divisions should be replaced after months on the line also made no sense. Under the individual rotation plan then in effect, anyone that had survived those first bitter six months of combat in 1950 had long since been sent home. As the Guardsmen were to soon discover it was the battle-worn and neglected equipment of the two veteran divisions that needed replacing, not the men.

The alert order came on November 18. Almost six years to the day that they were deactivated in 1945, the Thunderbirds of the 45th Infantry Division were once more going "Up Front."[13]

SECOND LIEUTENANT BILL MARTIN.
HEAVY MORTAR COMPANY, 180TH INFANTRY REGIMENT.

Robert Kerr was our U.S. Senator at the time. I think he made the statement that the 45th would not have to go again because they were one of the first divisions activated in World War II. He kind of made the statement that the 45th would never have to be activated for the Korean conflict. Well, we were, and then he said we'd never leave the States, but we did.

I recall very vividly the night before the news broke that we were going to Korea. I don't know why we were chosen, but another Senator spoke to our company in the mess hall. I can't recall the name, but he was accompanied by Anna Rosenberg, the Assistant Secretary of Defense (and it may have been Kerr; in fact I'm pretty sure it was).

Anyway, he again made the statement that we would not serve any time in Korea. He did not know that the regimental commander, sitting right there with him, had already received his warning orders. We already had our warning orders. I didn't know it yet, but the colonel and the staff knew. That actually happened in the mortar company mess hall. The next day it was announced and we started preparations to leave.

Back home, Martin entered the education field, eventually becoming assistant superintendent of schools in Edmond, Oklahoma. Transferring to the Army Reserve in 1965, Martin retired as a colonel with thirty-six years service.

The first element, the 180th RCT, comprising the 180th Infantry and the 171st FAB, landed at Inchon, December 5. Also coming ashore that day were the 155mm gunners of the 189th FAB, the 145th AAA, and part of division headquarters which set up its CP at Taegwang-Ni.[14]

SERGEANT FIRST CLASS JERRY HARBERT. "A" BATTERY, 171ST FIELD ARTILLERY BATTALION.

It was late in the afternoon when we landed at Inchon. As I recall we marched to a train station and boarded a train. It was night when we arrived and the 1st Cav met us with trucks and transported us to our position. They had set up tents for us over the ice. It was bitter cold and I said, "Oh my, this has got to be hell." And it was hell, it was cold and miserable and there we were. To tell the truth, we really didn't know where we were, just in Korea.

That first night to me was a miserable night. Not only was I cold, I wound up with an abscessed tooth and felt I was about to die. I recall sitting there with a canteen cup heating water to put in my mouth to help soothe that tooth. I didn't know what it was, all I knew was that I was in pain.

I recall the next morning, after a miserable night, I tried to find a dental hospital or something like it. I was told that somewhere back fifteen or twenty miles or so there was a dentist. Understand we were quite busy at this time getting set up and they didn't have time to mess with me. I got out on the road and hitchhiked and caught a ride back to a little dental hut alongside the road. This was a one man operation. He said, "All I can do is pull, I can't help you in any other way, I can't even deaden it." I said, "Do it." He just pecked around and said, "Which one hurts?" And I said, "Owww." And he pulled it.

When that dentist pulled it he had to turn his head, there was that much stuff built up. No anesthetic, he just yanked it out and it gave me relief. I never bothered with it again. When I got home I got it filled in. The government paid for it. I had to hitchhike back; I had no idea where I was, or where I was going. I have no idea how I found my outfit.

Asked to rejoin the Guard in 1953, Harbert replied, "I wouldn't join the Boy Scouts!" Harbert later changed his mind and retired in 1987 as a colonel.

Years later, the poor condition of the weapons and equipment left behind by the 1st Cav still remains a sore spot with the Thunderbirds. While all the division units worked on the worn and neglected equipment, the major part of the repair effort fell to the division ordnance company.

CORPORAL JIMMY TERRY. 700TH ORDNANCE MAINTENANCE COMPANY.

I went over with the advance detachment. There was probably twenty-five of us and I recall we left pretty quick. We moved in and took over the 1st Cav's stuff, and it was in bad shape. Them old boys had been up and down the road a lot of times, so it was in pretty bad shape when we got there

Courtesy of Jimmy Terry

Jimmy Terry, and the men of the 700th Ordnance Maintenance Company, worked on the worn and neglected equipment the Thunderbirds had inherited from the 1st Cav.

and we had a lot of work to do. People worked some long hours getting stuff just to where it could move. Like I said, those old boys had had some rough times.

My portion of maintenance supply was mostly wheel bearings; the bearings and seals. I had the bearings for trucks, tanks, whatever. If it required a bearing, I had it. I had nearly the entire stock right there on my truck. The Cav had a lot better stock than they thought. It was just a mess. They'd made so many hasty moves and the stuff had just got thrown in the truck. It took me about a month to get it all set up and inventoried where I could handle it.

We set up three miles in back of the front. At night you could hear the artillery going over. Most of it going out, but once in a while one coming in. I don't want to belabor the point, but I was just a seventeen-year-old kid and that kind of stuff didn't register on me. I didn't worry about things like that.

The maintenance people had teams that would go out to the units and repair things in the field if they could. If not, they'd send it back to the shop. We had 310 men and we did everything from watch repair to cannon repair. We were good at our job. We had a lot of pride in our unit.

CHAPTER 11

UP FRONT AGAIN

After landing on December 5, the men of the 180th Infantry spent a week or so drawing equipment and shaking down before moving on line. Once there, Colonel James O. Smith's companies began sending out patrols.

MASTER SERGEANT VERNON RIBERA.
"E" COMPANY, 180TH INFANTRY REGIMENT.

We were in Korea a week or ten days before we went on line. I don't remember much of that time. So far as I know, "E" Company, my company, was the first one to relieve the 1st Cav. I believe this is documented, but I forget what unit of the 1st Cav we relieved. I remember I went up in the afternoon and spent the first night up there alone with the 1st Cav, finding out where I was going to put my men. The rest of the unit came up the next evening. We were in bunkers; they were a combination living and fighting bunker.

I know that in our sector I took out the first patrol that went out from the division. After a day or two, the company commander said, "Ribera, go to it, go out to Pokkae. Do a little reconnoitering and see what you can find out there." Pokkae was a small village out there in the middle of the Chorwon Valley. It was probably three or four miles across this big valley and we were told to go out a couple of miles. The Chinese were on top of a hill over there. They had to go about the same distance, about two miles, to get to us, like we had two miles to get to them.

139

I took a couple of squads; I don't remember for sure but it was more than a squad. I believe it was two squads. We moved out in the morning. I took a machine gun. I had a souped up platoon. We had two BARs in each squad; that was our heavy weapons. We didn't take any mortars.

Your heart is in your throat. You don't know what's going to happen. Dead Chinese or parts of dead Chinese all over, that's the first thing we saw. It was unbelievable, the bodies and body parts. Dozens and dozens and dozens of them all around. We didn't see any GIs, just dead Chinese. The carnage was unbelievable.

We hadn't seen any enemy other than dead and had gone out about as far as we were going when we came up this little hill. It had been an outpost for us or them, we really didn't know who. The 1st Cav may have been out posting there and a wave of Chinese may have tried to overrun it or it could have been a Chinese outpost that we shelled. We really didn't know what had happened, but there were a lot of dead Chinamen there.

That's when I saw the mailbox. This mailbox was an old ammo box turned upside down with slits cut in it, and it had little doves hanging all over it that someone had made. Next to it was a scraggly little Christmas tree and it also had these doves on it. It was propaganda. The wording on the box was kind of broken English. It said something like: "Put a letter in here to some of your friends that have been captured," something like that, and "End the war." Something like that, I don't remember all of it.

One of my men said, "Well, I'll get rid of that." And then I noticed down underneath it there were about three or four wires; that black telephone wire, coming down from it and a bunch of dirt piled up at the bottom. And I said, "Hold it." I said, "Look down there." And he said, "Oh my God!" So we left it and the next day Sergeant Merritt, one of my squad leaders, took the other two squads out and it was blown up.

We stayed out there till afternoon and had to eat lunch among all those dead Chinese. I didn't eat much; I don't know if I even opened my assault ration. I think a *Stars and Stripes* reporter came up and got the story about the mailbox from me the next day.

While the infantrymen started patrolling, other Thunderbirds went to work.

MASTER SERGEANT CHARLES BROWN.
MEDICAL COMPANY, 180TH INFANTRY REGIMENT.

I was scared to death not knowing what combat was going to be like. The first day we were on line a mortar round hit the C.O. of Mortar Company and it almost blew his foot off. I don't remember his name, but I do recall he was a West Point graduate. They brought him into the aid station and it was hanging there by just a tendon, and that made things very real. He lost his foot eventually.

Everyone was horrified at the poor supplies we inherited from the 1st Cav. They were short of plasma, gauze, tape, cotton, and other things we needed. This was a difficult situation because we immediately moved on line and we didn't have the supplies.

The biggest shortage was the mantles for the gasoline lanterns. I had to go back to Seoul and buy them on the black market. I would take a jeep and a driver and go into Seoul. It was just like a flea market; you could buy any type of military equipment you wanted. The mantles came in packages of several dozen. I don't recall what I had to pay for them, but it was exorbitant. Later on I wrote my parents to buy some and send them to me. At night the only way we could give any kind of treatment was with those lanterns. It took a couple of months before we got everything we needed.

We learned very quickly that it was hard for plasma to dissolve in cold water. We didn't know this, we had to learn it by experience. The plasma came in little plastic bags and you had to mix it with sterilized water which came in one pint cans. You injected the sterile water in it and then you had to work it with your fingers. It was really hard work getting it dissolved; it took five or ten minutes. At the battalion and regimental levels we only had plasma. Fresh blood was available only at the M.A.S.H. level. Later on we found out that the plasma was left over from World War II.

We set the aid station up at battalion headquarters. There was a doctor, a Medical Service Corps administrator, myself, and five other enlisted men. The other aid men were up with the line companies, one with each platoon. Casualties weren't that heavy with the line being static at that time. We did have a lot of people burned because of making stoves out of metal cans and using fuel oil in them, and they didn't always work properly.

We had trouble with the rats. You've never seen such large rats. I woke up one night and one was down by my feet; it looked like a cat. They came into the bunkers seeking food and warmth. We controlled them with poison. We had to get the word out about the disease that came from the rat urine as this was a major problem.

We had a doctor who was left behind by the 1st Cav and he was upset about that. He thought he had been in Korea long enough to rotate and he was unhappy that he was going to be with a rinky-dink National Guard unit. I kept contact with him and visited him a couple years later. He was still on active duty at Fort Leonard Wood, Missouri. When I saw him I said, "Wait a minute, what patch is that you're wearing showing who you were in combat with?" I said, "That's not a 1st Cav patch, that's a 45th Division patch." And he said, "I learned to respect the 45th."

I still have people here in Oklahoma City, who see me and say, "Hey Doc, how's it going?"

SECOND LIEUTENANT BILL MARTIN.
HEAVY MORTAR COMPANY, 180TH INFANTRY REGIMENT.

My platoon was attached to the 3rd Battalion. Normally our positions were located in the battalion headquarters area. The distance from the MLR varied somewhat, but it was probably not any more than two or three hundred yards, maybe five hundred yards at the most. In the beginning the 3rd Battalion relied very heavily on artillery support. I think they just didn't have much confidence in the mortars although Colonel Smith, our regimental C.O., was really high on the mortars because that was his artillery, so to speak.

I remember one day, I think it was in the latter part of December, I was up at this OP, and the battalion C.O. was there with some of his staff. They had a patrol pinned down out there and were trying to get them back. The artillery was trying to lay a smoke screen so they could come back under cover but they just couldn't get it done. The battalion C.O. kind of wandered up to me and said, "Martin, can your mortars lay down some smoke out there for us?" and I said, "Hell yes!" and he said, "All right, get it out there."

I'd already had the mission called in and they were just waiting back at the position for the order to fire. Of course I had tried to sound real confident and I was confident. The forward observer gave the command to fire and you could hear the thump, thump, thump of them leaving the tubes back there and it was beautiful. We knew exactly where the patrol was pinned down. The smoke came up in front of them and just completely covered them and they made it back in. From then on, every time they wanted a close support mission they called on the mortars.

As Christmas approached, more division units arrived to join the 180th RCT. Again it was the equipment left behind by the 1st Cav that made a lasting impression. And, in one instance, a trooper the Regulars had left for the 45th.

FIRST LIEUTENANT CHARLES RICE.
EXECUTIVE OFFICER, 45TH RECONNAISSANCE COMPANY.

After we landed we went by trucks to Uijongbu where the 1st Cavs recon company had their headquarters. If you watched the television series M.A.S.H., they were always located at Uijongbu. It was just a wide place in the road. We pulled in and it was a shock. The haphazard nature of all the equipment and how screwed up everything was. They had so much ammunition they could have fought the whole Korean War with it. I found out later that when the 1st Cav got to Korea they were short of all types of ammo and since then their units had been scavenging all the ammo they could get.

By this time I was company executive officer and responsible for supplies and maintenance. We were supposed to take over their tanks and all their equipment. Well, that equipment was in such bad shape. Oh, it was in terrible shape. It was all dead lined, just in a mess. We were working like mad to get the equipment in shape so we could go up on line and do something. It was terrible, there weren't even enough vehicles to move the entire unit and the equipment. You really can't blame the Cav, they'd been through hell.

The 1st Cav Recon Company left behind all their personnel that they considered screwups that had time remaining on their tours in Korea. One of these guys had been their former motor sergeant. His name was Sergeant Bowden. He was actually a private, he had been busted a bunch of times. I called him Sergeant Bowden because I thought he was great.

We had been there about a week, and it was obvious we needed more trucks. So I said, "Sergeant Bowden, there isn't any way we're going to be able to move this unit with the vehicles we have. Where do you suppose we could get a couple of 6 x 6 trucks that would run?" He said, "I don't know, Lieutenant, but I'll try, I'll see what I can do."

The next morning I went out to the motor pool, and he led me over behind a little rise, and there were two brand spanking new 6 x 6 trucks. They didn't have any markings on them so he took care of that; he marked them up. He'd gotten them from an ordnance unit, I understand. They were just sitting down there, so he got those two trucks and that helped us get ready and no one ever knew where they came from.

Shortly after this, Sergeant Bowden went AWOL. They picked him up and took him to the brig down at division headquarters. And he requested that Lieutenant Rice be his counsel. I got a jeep and went down there and said, "Sergeant Bowden, you don't want me, I'm not a lawyer." I didn't want anything to hurt his case, and he said, "Well, I know you'll do what's right." So I said, "OK." Now we had been in a staging area getting ready to go to the front when he went AWOL; consequently, he was in very serious trouble. I don't recall what type of court-martial he was facing, but it was serious. It could have been a general court-martial.

He told me one reason he hadn't been sent home was because his records had been lost; he'd been told this. I went to our division finance office and found out he hadn't been paid since he'd been in Korea, and he'd been there about a year and a half. I think he'd come over in July of 1950 with the division and with his "bad time" and lost records he was still there. All that time, he hadn't gotten his regular pay, just supplemental pay. I spent three days at division "rear" and I finally gathered enough evidence that everyone felt sorry for him and realized how screwed up his records were and he got off real light. I was as proud of that as anything I did over there.

We went on line Christmas Day. It was cold and miserable and we didn't get Christmas dinner. That's always bothered me, that I couldn't get a hot, somewhat traditional Christmas dinner for the men. They attached us to the 180th Infantry which was on the right flank of the division. There's a valley that's an offshoot of the Chorwon-Seoul corridor that came right past the right flank of the division. It's a natural invasion route and right there is where they set us up in a blocking position on the extreme right flank of the division.

On our right was the 9th ROK Division. For some reason the Chinks would shell the hell out of those ROKs and leave us alone a lot of the time. I felt sorry for those guys. I believe we were covering a mile or a mile and a quarter which wasn't too bad considering all the automatic weapons we had and that we were on slightly elevated ground. We kept all three platoons on line because we weren't really expected to do anything but block this approach. We did send patrols out into the valley every night just like the infantry.

We put the tanks in turret defilade and built bunkers for the riflemen. The scout jeeps stayed at company headquarters about three hundred yards to the rear in back of a big hill. That's the way we set up.

On December 17, the 179th RCT came ashore joining the 180th, and the Thunderbirds officially became a part of Eighth Army. The 179th moved up on the 180th's left flank and tied in with elements of the 3rd Infantry Division. The 180th and 45th Recon Company remained tied in with the 9th ROK Division next to the Chorwon River.[1]

SERGEANT FIRST CLASS JOHN PETERS.
HEADQUARTERS COMPANY, 179TH INFANTRY REGIMENT.

When we were ordered to Korea I sent my assistant supply sergeant over with the advance party. I stayed at Camp Crawford transferring the property to the 1st Cav people, then went over with the main body. When the regiment went on line the snow was so deep I couldn't get my supply trucks up to the front, so we set up near Service Company, about two miles in back of the MLR, and worked from there.

The biggest shortage was socks; getting clean dry socks for the men. At times rations would be a little short. This was because we had Koreans attached to us and had to draw rations for them and sometimes we weren't given enough. The books were a mess. I recall someone had signed for a jeep machine gun mount that we didn't have. The C.O., Captain Jack Blummer, let me have his monthly liquor ration; I went back to ordnance, did a little swapping, got the mount and got the books in balance. That first month I did a lot of trading; that's all part of a supply sergeant's job.

There were three men in my section: Archie Carpenter, Charlie Neid, and Jim Darling. We had two squad tents we worked out of. We kept them heated with diesel stoves; the diesel was outside in 55 gallon drums. One night the lines froze and Carpenter got a little frost bite on his toes. The cold was our biggest enemy, we never came under fire.

The 179th wasted no time in sending out patrols. "C" Company's First Lieutenant Joseph H. Gallant, from Ardmore,

Oklahoma, led one of the first. The patrol's mission was to force the enemy to disclose its position.

"The best way we could accomplish this was by forcing them to shoot at us," Gallant later said. Leading his men to the top of a hill, Gallant spotted a Chinese unscrewing the cap from a potato-masher hand grenade. "We saw each other at the same instant. I dropped to one knee and put three bullets from my carbine into his forehead. His grenade rolled down the hill and exploded a couple of yards away but didn't do any damage."[2]

With the landing of the 279th RCT and supporting units on December 28, all division elements were in Korea, defending the sector OMGOGAE-MOLTARI. This eight to nine mile sector of the MLR covered the vital Chorwon-Yonchon corridor, the main invasion route to Seoul, twenty-five miles to the south. The 245th Tank Battalion moved east, in back of the 9th ROK Division, blocking the most likely approach for enemy armor in the area.[3]

The prominent terrain feature facing the 45th in the eastern sector of the division front was a large hill mass, Hill 290, known as T-Bone. Two miles from east to west, the leg of the T was about a mile long and pointed directly at the Thunderbirds, ending somewhat over a half mile in front of the MLR. The Chinese occupied the top of T-Bone in force and had started to move down and construct positions on the "leg" about the time the 45th went on line.

The battles on T-Bone and for its outposts would be the most fierce fighting the Oklahoma Guardsmen would see during their time in Korea. All three regiments would suffer casualties on T-Bone and its environs. The 180th took the first crack at T-Bone. The 179th and 279th would soon have their turn.

MASTER SERGEANT VERNON RIBERA.
"E" COMPANY, 180TH INFANTRY REGIMENT.

Our first company size raid went out on January 12, 1952. We left the MLR about 0200 and very quietly went completely behind Hill 290; we called it T-Bone Hill. We came up the back side of it and jumped off in the attack about 0600. My platoon's objective was the farthest out and we obviously had the farthest to go. It was two hundred yards to the top of the hill and terribly steep.

The Chinese were dug in at the top and had us at point blank range. They began rolling grenades down on us and bringing in mortar fire from somewhere. Things happened so fast that the next thing I can recall it was about three o'clock in the afternoon. I don't know what happened to those six or eight hours. I only remember a few things.

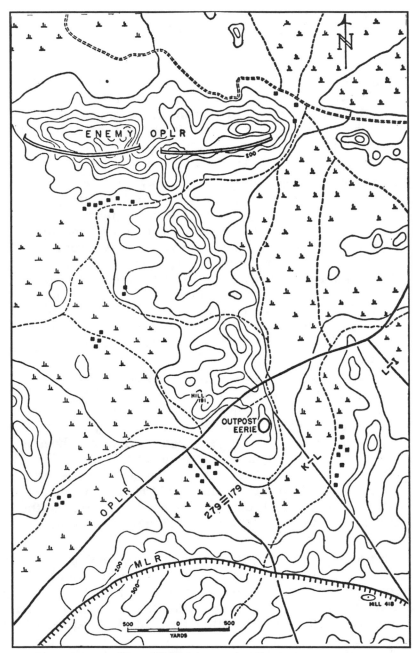

Courtesy of the Center of Military History, United States Army, Washington, D.C.

T-Bone and Outpost Eerie. The Chinese started to work their way down T-Bone soon after the 45th went on line.

I know we didn't make it to the top. One of my men got
within ten feet or so before he was killed. I remember seeing him kicking grenades away before a mortar round got
him. They gave him the Silver Star.

I know one time my 2nd squad leader and I were lying in a
trench, head to head, and he looked up and they shot him
right through the mouth. He had a partial plate, but that
bullet didn't hit his partial plate. It hit his good teeth and
knocked those out. When I went back to see him in the hospital he said, "Ribera, next time I'm going to let you look up."

Sometime in there I got hit too. It may have been at the
same time or even the same round that got my squad leader.
It was my knee. It barely broke the skin, but it was quite an
impact. That was during those eight hours I don't really
remember. We were out there about 300 yards beyond anyone else with about ten men wounded and four men dead.
All hell had broken loose. The forward 4.2 mortar observer
had a radio but it got shot up and then we had no communications at all. We were to fire a green flare if we needed
help evacuating wounded. I had two green flares and nei-
ther one of them would work. We felt we were lucky to get
out at all.

This isn't easy to talk about. You always want to bring your
men back if humanly possible. But I did not bring four of
my men back. I didn't want to jeopardize four more, or forty
more, to get those four men because I knew they were dead.
Whenever a man doesn't have a head on, his whole head is
gone, there's nothing more you can do for him. That's hard.
I couldn't bring them back. I tried. The next day they sent
out a platoon of tanks to get them and they couldn't make it
either. January 12, 1952. I well remember it because the
next day was my birthday and I didn't know if I was going to
live to see it or not.

Division Commander Styron initiated a plan of rotating the
three regiments from on line to reserve, then back on line in a
different sector of the division front. The first of these switches
occurred on January 15, with the 279th, the last regiment to arrive
in Korea, replacing the 180th three days after "E" Company's attack on T-Bone.[4]

The 279th established a listening post at the very tip of T-
Bone's "leg" at its closest point to the division MLR. This position
gave the 45th warning of any major Chinese movement from T-
Bone and also served as a rallying point for the patrols the division

sent out every night. The Thunderbirds manned the outpost continually, at times with nothing more than a reinforced squad, at other times with a full platoon. The establishment and occupation of this outpost neutralized the Chinese on T-Bone, their attempts to destroy or capture the outpost would make it the scene of heavy fighting in the months ahead. This was Outpost Eerie.

FIRST LIEUTENANT WELDON JACKSON. COMMANDING OFFICER, "A" COMPANY, 279TH INFANTRY REGIMENT.

We had twice the frontage we were supposed to have according to the Infantry School at Fort Benning. All I could do was establish strong points. I put all three rifle platoons on line. We had over a mile to defend, way too much to keep anyone in reserve. We had twenty-five to thirty yards between positions; two man rifle positions. I'm telling you it was spooky.

We were right in front of the T and every day you could see that during the previous night dirt had been moved and that the Chinese were moving down the leg of the T, digging trenches and constructing fortifications. The very first day we went on line, I was directed by Lieutenant Colonel Watkins, the battalion C.O., to establish a listening post at the base of the T. This was over a half mile in front of the rest of the company, and was too damn far out to provide good fire support.

Colonel Watkins came up to check my company, look at our positions, and see how we were enduring the weather conditions. Of course he was well aware how the enemy were extending their trenches towards "A" Company's position. The colonel wanted to go out to check the squad I had deployed at the base of the T. On the way out we met the squad that had been relieved and was returning to the MLR. Colonel Watkins said to one of the men, "Son, how was it out here last night?" and he said, "Sir, it was just eerie as hell." So that became Outpost Eerie.

Jackson, who had served with the 32nd Infantry Division (Wisconsin-Michigan) in World War II, now remained on active duty. The wounds he received in Korea required twenty-four operations and forced his retirement from the Army in 1968.

While Jackson's "A" Company occupied Eerie, other 279th units sent out patrols every night.

Courtesy of Carl Stevens

Lieutenant Carl Stevens led his Raider Platoon of the 279th Infantry on night patrols in -30 degree cold.

SECOND LIEUTENANT CARL STEVENS.
"F" COMPANY, 279TH INFANTRY REGIMENT.

After the Ranger Company disbanded, I had the choice of transferring to the 187th Airborne Regiment or staying with the division. I decided to stay with the division and joined Heavy Weapons Company of the 279th. When we got to Korea, I transferred to "F" Company of the 279th. This was, I think, in January. My first night with "F" Company, I took out a patrol. I didn't know the platoon sergeant or any of the squad leaders, but for some reason I took out a platoon size patrol my first night with "F" Company.

After the briefing, I went up to the MLR with my platoon sergeant to look over the terrain. When I got back to the hoochie, that's what we called the bunkers, the Battalion S-2, Major Baker, was there. He'd heard I was taking a platoon out on a patrol mission that night and he asked what I was going to do. I said, "Well, there's a machine gun out there that's been giving our rifle companies problems, and we're going to knock it out." This machine gun was about three quarters of a mile in front of the MLR, just past no man's land. Baker said, "I'm going with you."

He met me at the MLR, oh, about eight o'clock and he said, "Now this patrol is yours, you handle it exactly as you would if I wasn't along." You can imagine how I felt, a lieutenant, leading my first patrol and a major coming along. I told him we were going to knock out this machine gun nest and he said, "How are you going to do this? What are your plans?" And I said, "Me, you, and the sergeant are going to knock it out." He said, "That's very good. What do you want me to do?" I said, "Well, we're going to take it about ten yards at a time. One man will pass the other, then the other, and so on. We'll leapfrog until we're all up there, then we're going to throw grenades in there and knock it out." He said, "That's a good idea."

We left the MLR about nine o' clock. When we left, it was snowing. Damn, it was snowing; it was so cold. About three hundred yards out, I came to a single strand of barb wire. I looked down and it had a little sign on it that said "minefield." I called up the platoon sergeant and said, "Sergeant, there's a minefield here." And he said, "I've been through here before, it's OK." I said, "OK, but I want you to know I think this is a minefield."

We were in single file and the fourteenth man in the column stepped on a mine. It exploded and hit him in the back. The ground was frozen so damn hard it absorbed most of the blast. Some of the chunks of frozen earth hit him in the shoulder and paralyzed his arm a little bit. He was flopping around and I was trying to shut him up. He said, "My arm's gone, isn't it?" And I said, "No, it's not gone." He said, "Don't shit me, it's gone."

All this delayed us a couple of minutes. I detailed two men to take him back and we went on. I was hoping the snow had muffled the sound of the explosion and the Chinese hadn't heard it. I dropped a squad off about half way out to cover us and when we got fifty yards or so from the enemy position, I dropped off the rest of the platoon.

The three of us crept up there and you could hear them in there talking. I turned around and whispered to Baker, "You got a grenade?" and he says, "No." The only thing that guy had was a .45! I said, "Here, you take my fragmentation grenade. I'm going to take this white phosphorous grenade and when I throw it in there, you two guys throw yours in there and then we're going to get our butts out of here."

We threw the grenades in there and blew that thing up and started running. And boy, did we draw some fire; bullets were clipping all around us. Baker wasn't running fast enough, and I said, "Major, if you'll get your ass out of the way, I'll show you how to run."

Just as General Styron rotated his three regiments, Colonel Preston J. C. Murphy rotated his three battalions along their sector of the front.

FIRST LIEUTENANT WELDON JACKSON.
COMMANDING OFFICER, "A" COMPANY, 279TH INFANTRY REGIMENT.

We went off line for four or five days, then moved over to the extreme right sector of the division. This was about eight miles east of our previous position. The Chorwon River was the boundary between "A" company and the next unit on my right. This was the 9th ROK Division, and the Turkish Brigade. The Turks didn't believe in taking prisoners. They cut their heads off.

In this position we had about a mile of frontage. We didn't have an outpost in front of our battalion, so I was ordered to establish an outpost approximately five hundred yards in front of the MLR where we could still give them fire support if needed. Initially the position was occupied by a rifle squad reinforced with a .30 caliber machine gun and a 57mm recoilless rifle.

Our artillery forward observer had a battery commander's (BC) scope which is powerful; on moonlit nights with snow on the ground we could see a great distance with a BC scope. You could see out a half mile or more, particularly if we had fired some flares. We had been getting a lot of probes both at the outpost and at the MLR, and through the scope I could see a lot of activity out beyond the outpost. We'd requested artillery fire; I even got two air strikes. But when it stopped, the enemy would go right back to what they were doing, digging like moles. We knew they were getting ready for a big attack.

Thanks to new procedures, including the use of helicopters for evacuation, and the establishment of M.A.S.H. units near the front, the survival rate of men wounded in Korea was higher than in any previous war.

Lieutenant Jackson continues:

On the morning of 8 February 1952, about 0900, my first sergeant and I visited the outpost. I had approximately twenty men out there building positions with overhead cover. I was walking from one bunker position which was almost completed over to another one that they were working on, when this mortar barrage came in. I caught a mortar round about as close as you could and not get completely blown apart. I was the only man hit.

My damn ears rang. I couldn't figure out where in the hell I was. I couldn't move. I was numb. I just couldn't move. Thank goodness I had run a telephone line out there from my CP, so they called for a medic and a stretcher team, I guess. I don't know, I went out pretty quick. When they were carrying me back to the MLR it was through a rice paddy. Somebody stepped off the dike, and I heard this bang, and I told them to set me down. I thought we were getting an artillery barrage or a mortar barrage or something, but they said, No, they had just set off a trip flare.

I passed out, and when I woke up I was in the battalion first aid station and they were working on me. Colonel Watkins was there. He said, "Who do you recommend to take over the company?" I said, "Lieutenant Jim Wilson," who was my executive officer. The next time I woke up it was dark and I was in a bed and a sergeant was sitting there. I asked him where I was and he told me in the 45th Division Medical Clearing Company. About that time a major came in and he says, "Lieutenant Jackson?" and I said, "Ya," and he says, "I just came from having supper with General Styron and he sends his condolences."

Next time I woke up I was in a M.A.S.H. hospital and there was a NCO sitting beside me. I said, "Where am I?" He said, "You're in a M.A.S.H. hospital and you've been operated on." I asked for a cigarette. He lit it and I don't remember anything else. The next thing I remember I was awakened by a loud noise and I couldn't figure where in the world I was or what was going on. I was on a medical train. I didn't know it, but I was being evacuated to Pusan.

Next time I woke up there was this awful noise. I thought, "What is the enemy shooting at us?" What they were doing, they were lifting me up on a stretcher, over the side of a hospital ship with a winch. It was a Danish hospital ship staffed by Danish doctors and nurses, and they were good!

I was there a long time. They operated on me four or five times, then sent me to Tokyo Army Hospital and did four more operations. When I was finally able to walk they sent me back to the States and that was the end of the Korean War for me.

Supporting the infantry the division artillerymen were on call twenty-four hours a day. The redlegs fired on known and suspected troop concentrations and gave protective fires to the patrols as they returned to the MLR. At set times during the night the guns would fire harassing and interdiction (H & I) fire at preselected coordinates. This was usually only a few rounds, and rather than use a whole gun section one or two men would get up and fire the mission, allowing their buddies to get some much needed rest. This practice didn't always work out the way it was planned.

CORPORAL ROBERT FAKEN.
"C" BATTERY, 189TH FIELD ARTILLERY BATTALION.

We were about two miles in back of the MLR. We were closer to the MLR on our sides than to our front. Pork Chop and Old Baldy were right ahead of us. We were firing a lot. In fact, we fired our ten thousandth round in February, or it might have even been in January. We broke the gun crews in half and worked two twelve hour shifts. We fired the guns with half a crew.

One night we had a fire mission; it was just number three and four guns. I think it was an H & I mission. Anyway, this young man was doing it all by himself. He loaded a shell— and these shells weighed ninety-six pounds—into the breech, but he didn't get it sealed in there real good. Then he went to get a powder increment. The gun tube was slightly elevated, and while he was getting the powder charge, the projectile fell out and rolled away and he didn't see it. He put the powder charge in, closed the breech, and fired, and it lit up the whole valley. We got a little talking to about that.

SERGEANT JODY McLAIN.
"A" BATTERY, 160TH FIELD ARTILLERY BATTALION.

One time my howitzer section got pulled out and sent on a special mission. This was in March, maybe February; it was still cold. It was stabilized then while they were talking over at Panmunjom. They wanted to shoot about a hundred rounds of propaganda leaflets, so they pulled out our howitzer section and took us up right behind the 279th Infantry which was dug in up on a ridge. The leaflets were already in the shells, I don't know who packed them.

Courtesy of Bill Day (Shoza Koga); James Kercheval.

With the front static, both sides increased their use of psychological warfare.

OFFICERS AND MEN OF THE "UN FORCES"

Probably you are quite sure that the armistice negotiations at Kaesung will be brought to a success without fail, and you will be able to return to your dear parents and families at home.

Your folks will be of one mind with you, too. The "UN delegation," however, is hatching a plot to bring the Kaesung armistice negotiations to a rupture by every possible lawless act in their power and to expand the war in Korea.

Now you have no alternative but to follow either one of the two paths which lie before you:

Would you absently-mindedly look on like an idiot all the machinations of the "UN delegation" and in time meet a meaningless death here in Korea, so far away from your homelands? -- or otherwise would you be so smart as to come over to the side of the Korean People's Army or the Chinese People's Volunteers, and to be guaranteed your lives, thus winning back peace as soon as possible and being enabled to return to your loved ones at home?

Which path will you take?

The Korean People's Army and the Chinese People's Volunteers will obligate themselves to ensure all those who will surrender to their sides security of the person and welcome them as "Fighters for Peace."

GENERAL POLITICAL BUREAU OF THE KOREAN PEOPLE'S ARMY

914155

158

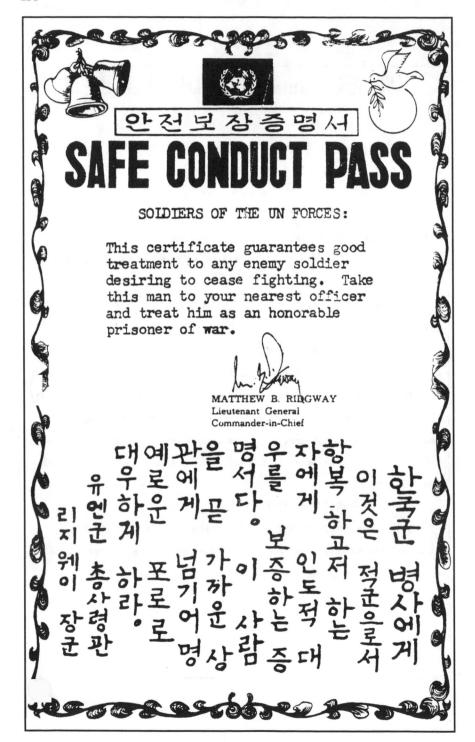

안전보장증명서

SAFE CONDUCT PASS

SOLDIERS OF THE UN FORCES:

This certificate guarantees good
treatment to any enemy soldier
desiring to cease fighting. Take
this man to your nearest officer
and treat him as an honorable
prisoner of war.

MATTHEW B. RIDGWAY
Lieutenant General
Commander-in-Chief

한국군 병사에게

이것은 적군으로서

항복 하고저 하는

자에게 인도적 대

우를 보증하는 증

명서다. 이 사람

을 가까운

관에 넘기어

예로운 포로로

대우 하게 하라.

유엔군 총사령관

리지웨이 장군

There was a place up there big enough to place a howitzer in. They gave us the deflection on the left section and one on the right section and they said, "Shoot 'em, couple up, and get out." So we fired those hundred rounds at maximum range, about 12,000 yards, coupled that gun up and took off. I don't recall how long it took but it wasn't very long. We went around a hill and as we looked back mortar rounds began to fall right in the area we'd been. It didn't take them too long to get a bead on where we were. The infantry didn't appreciate it at all.

McLain remained in the Guard, working as an administrator and personnel officer in the Oklahoma Military Department. He retired as a chief warrant officer in 1990, after 41 years service.

The dead of winter now set in. Temperatures dropped to -30 degrees, at times even colder. Contact with the enemy all but disappeared. The gathering of information about their intentions became a top priority. All commands drew up elaborate plans to lure the Chinese out in the open where they could be ambushed and prisoners taken. The Thunderbirds' plan, "OPERATION SNATCH," commenced February 10. Once again the U.N. high command underestimated the intelligence of their Asian adversaries. The results all along the front were about the same: a complete failure.[5]

CAPTAIN EDDIE COPE.
S-1, 3RD BATTALION, 279TH INFANTRY REGIMENT.

We had one period there when everything was real static. Division, and, I guess, Corps and Army too, everybody was wanting to get prisoners. We were to try anything we could to get prisoners. Somebody came up with the idea to shut everything down—absolutely no movement, no exposure, no smoke, no firing. Don't show any activity. Do all your moving at night. So that's what we did. We had to stand down. I remember we couldn't heat water and all the supplies came up under blackout conditions. I don't think it worked. I never heard of any prisoners being taken, at least in our area. I do remember that while this was going on, my old company, "I" Company, was on an outpost and they got into a little firefight one night.

The next morning they found one dead Chinese soldier. Normally the Chinese grabbed their casualties and evacuated them, but evidently they could not take this one with them. "I" Company sent the body back in a jeep trailer and it wound up right in front of my S-1 tent. I called graves registration to come get him, but no one showed up. Of course it was colder than "Old Billy" so he didn't get too unpleasant, but I wanted him out of there. The next night when the division message center people came up to our position, I just had them load the Chinaman's body in their jeep and sent it back to the message center. I got two or three harsh words for that, but at least I got rid of the dead Chink.

Division Commander Styron continued to rotate the three regiments in a triangular pattern. On February 6, the 180th went back on line relieving the 179th. Then, after three weeks in reserve, the 179th replaced the 279th in front of T-Bone. The next move came on March 17, with the 279th relieving the 180th. When the regiments rotated off line, the first order of business was a hot shower and a clean set of clothes.[6]

MASTER SERGEANT VERNON RIBERA.
"E" COMPANY, 180TH INFANTRY REGIMENT.

We were rotated off the line every forty-five days and would go into division reserve for a few weeks. One of the first things we did was head to a shower point; forty-five days is a long time to go without a shower. What you'd do is take off your uniform at one end of this tent, go in, take a shower, and get a clean set of underwear and fatigues at the other end of the tent.

Well, this one time, I think it was in March, the clothes we got were infested with crabs and the whole company got them. I remember our administrative assistant, Otis Starns, and I comparing crabs to see who had the biggest. I found a giant and Starns said, "Ribera, did you glue two of them together to get one that big?" We finally got some DDT and got them cleared up. Those are the kind of things you like to remember.

While Styron rotated his regiments, other Thunderbirds stayed on line continually.

FIRST LIEUTENANT CHARLES RICE.
EXECUTIVE OFFICER, 45TH RECONNAISSANCE COMPANY.

The infantry regiments rotated back into reserve. A regiment would go back and another one come up, but we stayed right out there on the division's right flank. About every ten days we got to send men back to a shower point the engineers had set up at one of the infantry battalion headquarters. This was probably two miles back to the west via a hilly, winding road. I shared a five man tent with Leo

Marshall, the unit administrator; he was one of the older fellows. We called him Frosty, since his hair was totally gray. Because the line was static we usually got three hot meals a day. Things really weren't too bad.

We sent out ambush patrols into the valley nearly every night, usually a squad, sometimes a platoon. While I was there, we made two raids across the valley with our tanks and, or, dismounted troops. On the first raid, we were supposed to guard the flank of Easy Company of the 180th while they made a raid on Hill 290. The Chinese were dug in from one to two miles across the valley from our MLR and we were going out about half way where we could cover the infantry attack. The tanks and armored personnel carriers went out into the valley and two of them hit mines and we had some guys wounded.

We got the men back and I called Colonel Smith, the 180th C.O., and asked him if he would mind sending a platoon out to guard those tanks until we could get a tank retriever out there. I didn't know much about higher echelon thinking or planning in those days. Anyway, he said, "Hell no, Lieutenant, you can take care of your own tanks." He was kind of a crusty old devil. That really made me mad, but, in retrospect, I can understand why he didn't want to do it.

The tank retriever in the 180th's Tank Company was broken down; it usually was. So, Warrant Officer Harry Willett from the 279th came up to help us out. He took a tank retriever out there and we put down covering artillery fire and smoke and he pulled one of those tanks back in. By the time he made it back it was dark. That night a Chinese plane came over, dropped some flares, then dropped bombs or some sort of explosives on the remaining vehicle still in the valley. It was totally destroyed.

CHAPTER 12

OUTPOST EERIE

The division conducted no large raids during March, but maintained contact with the enemy through patrols and listening posts, set up in front of the MLR. Then, on the night of March 21–22, the Chinese hit Outpost Eerie.

Manning the outpost that night were twenty-six men from the 3rd Platoon, "K" Company, of the 179th, under the command of Lieutenant Omer L. Manley. The soldiers, who had all previously been on Eerie, went out the afternoon of the 21st for their five day stint at the outpost. It was a cold rainy day and almost dark before the platoon arrived.

In the previous six weeks the units assigned to Eerie had worked on improving the outpost. Three separate barbed wire obstacles now ringed the upper part of the hill. Thirty-five yards inside the last wire an egg shaped trench, studded with fighting bunkers, encircled the hilltop. Sound powered telephones connected the nine bunkers Manley and his men occupied, while four different telephone lines plus a SCR 300 radio maintained communications with "K" Company and 2nd Battalion headquarters.

Shortly after dark two patrols, "King" and "Raider," going out to scout and to set up ambushes passed through Eerie. Both patrols were to maintain contact with Manley by means of sound powered telephones tied into the outpost system. After eating their rations, the men settled in for what looked to be a long night.

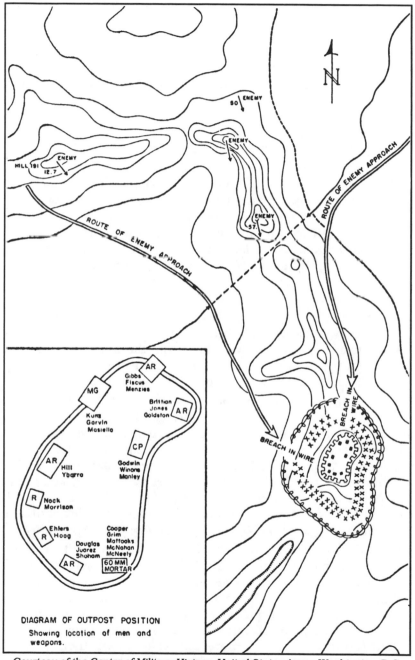

DIAGRAM OF OUTPOST POSITION
Showing location of men and
weapons.

Courtesy of the Center of Military History, United States Army, Washington, D.C.

The battle for Outpost Eerie, March 21–22, 1952.

About 2300 hours both patrols requested flares and reported heavy enemy activity in the area. Raider patrol then called and said they were "returning to the MLR, for there were too many Chinks for them to handle." They failed to tell Manley if they were going to return through his position or take a more direct route back in.

Soon after, Platoon Sergeant Calvin Jones, guarding the "back gate" of the outpost, reported movement in front of his position. Manley told him to hold his fire as it was probably Raider patrol coming in. "If it is they're speaking Chinese," Jones reported. "Kill a few of them," Manley replied. The battle for Outpost Eerie was on. Manley later wrote:

> . . . I tried to move from position to position to make sure everything was going as well as possible. The men were fighting so well, the spirit was unbelievable! When a man was hit, Godwin (the aid-man) was right on the spot. After perhaps an hour the positions to the north and east began to run out of ammunition. As I moved from the machine-gun position on our left, a round from the enemy weapons hit the machine gun.

> The concussion knocked me out of the trench upon the ground behind. I was dazed and stunned, but as soon as I regained my consciousness, I crawled back into the trench. As alertness returned to me I called out to the men, "Take care of your ammo! Make sure of every shot! We're running low!"

By this time the enemy had managed to cut the wire and were in the trench. All of the platoon's grenades had been expended, and .30 caliber ammunition was almost gone. Knowing two of his men were dead, and at least two wounded, Manley yelled for them to scatter and bug out. Manley now decided to surrender and tell the Chinese that he had called for artillery and air strikes to shell the hill. With the Chinese taking cover, there was a chance his men could make it back to the MLR. Lieutenant Manley continues:

> . . . I waited awhile longer and prayed. I thanked God for the lives that were spared and for the fact I was still in one piece. After my prayer, I stepped out. There were several Chinese immediately above me. I fired four rounds, . . . Chinks fell. I ducked back into the bunker, my helmet had been shot off and a bullet had grazed my left hand. After I had said thanks to God that it was no worse, I shot my last four rounds. I saw four more Chinks go down; then, stowing my rifle, wallet, papers, and dog tags in the bunker, I stepped out and yelled, "Surrender!" in Japanese.

The Chinese grabbed me; I began making motions that I had called in for an air attack and that all my men were gone. The Chinese must have understood me, a horn was blown three times and the Chinese began moving off the hill, taking me along with them. . . .[1]

It was 179th Infantry Commanding Officer, Colonel Fred Daugherty, who made the courageous decision to bring artillery fire down on the beleaguered outpost.

COLONEL FRED DAUGHERTY.
COMMANDING OFFICER, 179TH INFANTRY REGIMENT.

When I started manning Outpost Eerie, I had a serious discussion with the division commander in which I complained about the vulnerability of this position to enemy night attack with a superior force. I learned that the manning of the outpost was ordered by I Corps over a similar protest from the division commander. In these circumstances I continued to man Outpost Eerie.

This was my only experience in combat to deliberately bring artillery fire on one of my own occupied positions. But I authorized this when we had lost both radio and wire communication with the outpost, and from our various observation posts it appeared the outpost had been overrun. In our telephone discussions about this the battalion and company commander and I concluded that our men would probably be in the bunkers, which turned out to be the case. It appears that we caught the enemy in the open, not only on the outpost, but on the surrounding area and likely enemy approach and return routes.

One lesson we learned was the need for better understanding, with signals and other communications, between the outpost and friendly patrols we had out at night in the area. This, no doubt, reduced the outpost fire power in the very early stages of the enemy assault when our outpost wire was being breached.[2]

At daylight when the 179th reoccupied Eerie, they found thirty Chinese bodies in and around the outpost. Manley, now a prisoner and masquerading as an enlisted man, saw and counted twenty-eight more bodies that the Chinese had recovered and carried back to their lines. The 179th lost eight men killed, four wounded, and two captured, Manley and Corporal Joel Ybarra. Belatedly, I Corps realized that Styron and Daugherty were correct in their assessment of the vulnerability of Outpost Eerie. The position would now be abandoned and not occupied again until June.[3]

The night after the Chinese hit Eerie, the Raider Platoon of the 279th, operating to the west of the 179th, ambushed an estimated Chinese company.

FIRST LIEUTENANT CARL STEVENS.
RAIDER PLATOON, 279TH INFANTRY REGIMENT.

They sent out a call for a raider platoon for night fighting. There was one in each regiment and I volunteered to lead the 279th's. I picked two of the men that had been in the Ranger Company. I made one the platoon sergeant and the other one of the squad leaders. The problem was there wasn't any TO&E for the platoon and you can't have four or five master sergeants as riflemen. The platoon had thirty or thirty-two men; all but six of us got hit at one time or the other. I ended up with fourteen men.

I trained them for three weeks before we went on our first raid. All the training was at night; we trained every night. Discipline was tough, but they liked it because there was nothing chicken about it. I let the sergeants, the squad leaders, discipline their own people. I didn't bother them. If there was anything chicken I wouldn't put up with it. But those people were good. They were very good. Some were holdovers from the 1st Cav, some National Guard, but all out of the 279th. We were close, very close.

We were under regimental control and got our missions from the Regimental S-2, Major Dugger. The first mission was an ambush. We went out, probably a quarter of a mile past our lines, and set up an ambush and got in a pretty good firefight. No problem. We did a job, we killed a bunch of them and came back. I think we had one man wounded.

We had a Sergeant Anderson, he was from Boston, I think, and had been with me in the Ranger Company. He could smell those people. He could smell the garlic, he could damn sure smell it. He'd call back and say, "I smell garlic." And there they'd be. Now people laughed at that, but he saved our butts two different times.

The last big fight we had, we were going out and set up an ambush because the Chinese were moving ammunition or mortars or something, I'm not sure what, down to positions in front of their lines. Major Dugger had got this information from the line-crossers or somebody.

This was March 22, 1952, and there were probably about twenty-five or twenty-six of us guys. We got out there and

Sergeant Anderson was on point ahead of the lead squad. He radioed that he thought he had seen some movement against the snow, but that he wanted to make damn sure of what he saw. And about that time he said, "Lieutenant, I smell some garlic up here." And about that time I saw them. They were in the next rice paddy, about ten or fifteen yards away.

I counted about thirty-five or forty of them, then I quit counting and I got on the radio and told my people to spread out. I said, "We're going to have some problems." They were right in the next rice paddy and we were on one side of it. We had them boxed in pretty good. Somebody tripped a flare and we got a bunch of them.

Ray Seals, from Drumright, Oklahoma, was my platoon sergeant. A Chinaman charged us from about fifteen or twenty yards and Ray shot him with his carbine. A carbine doesn't have a lot of stopping power and the Chinaman didn't go down, so I put a round in him. Seals calmly set his carbine down and said, "Lieutenant, there's enough of these son of a bitches to go around, shoot one of your own."

I lost some men that night. In fact, I was talking to a BAR man named Don Rust when he got it. I turned around and I told Rust to fire a little lower—to sweep it—and he got it right then. Right through the head and it killed him.

About that time I got hit by a piece of shrapnel. I got hit in the head and blood was all around on the snow and I thought, "Oh, my head's been knocked off." There was so much blood and I couldn't see. Then, I realized I wasn't hit very bad and thought, "No it's just my eye." But it wasn't.

Then they told us to get out of there. Major Dugger radioed, and said, "Snowball, get out of there." I lost one man killed, and I think seven or eight wounded. The next day Dugger heard from a line-crosser that we had hit a reinforced company. We got credit for eighty-five of them that night.[4]

In March the first Thunderbirds rotated home. To the first men to depart Korea, Division Commander Styron said:

I couldn't let you people leave without expressing my sincere and heartfelt appreciation of the fine things you've done for the division these past nineteen months. We've developed the finest division ever to be sent to Eighth Army. That's because of what you and the other men of the division have done . . . I hope to see most of you back in Oklahoma myself soon. We'll all meet at the division reunion in September.[5]

During April contact with the enemy remained light. On the 11th, the 20th Philippine Battalion Combat Team joined the 45th. Styron attached the Filipinos to Daugherty's 179th Infantry.[6]

On May 21, 1952, Major General James C. Styron relinquished command of the 45th Infantry Division to Major General David L. Ruffner, Regular Army. General Styron retired from the National Guard that September with over thirty-one years service. He died January 2, 1989, at the age of ninety.[7]

COLONEL FRED DAUGHERTY.
COMMANDING OFFICER, 179TH INFANTRY REGIMENT.

I first met him [Ruffner] briefly, when he came to the division CP and I was called back to meet him. The next time I had contact with him was when I had an attack operation in which I used the 20th Philippine Battalion Combat Team. He wanted to observe it.

So I met him to take him up to the front to observe this attack by the Philippine BCT. He got out of his jeep and I put him in the front of mine. I had a couple of sand bags on the front floor of my jeep. They were there for two reasons: one, if you hit a mine it would give you a little protection; and two, it made it a little bit warmer down there on your feet. When he saw them he raised hell. He said, "This is no way to clutter up your jeep." I explained what they were there for, and he said, "You can leave them there today, but take them out tomorrow." Which I didn't do. That was my first real encounter with him. He didn't make any major changes, but he was a very critical man. I understood that he had never had any combat experience. He basically left us alone, but he was still critical.

Another story on him. I was getting ready to rotate home, just a few days left. We had a fire fight that lasted all night and we came out of it very good. There were about twenty dead Chinese to our front who had not been carried away by the enemy. Ruffner insisted on coming up and seeing it.

This was an outpost under Chinese observation and I tried to talk him out it. I told him, "It's hard to get to. They've fought all night and the Chinese have the place zeroed in with artillery and mortars. They've got observation on it and if they see a lot of commotion up there and it looks like brass, they are going to start shelling the place and you're going to bring shells down on your own men. But I'll take you to it if you want to go." He wouldn't have it except to go out. So I met him, this time without sandbags, and drove him as far as we could. Then we got out, crossed a valley and started up the hill. It was at least a half mile from where we left the jeep to the position.

We got up there. They'd been fighting all night and the position didn't look very pretty. I can't recall what company this was. It was not a full company, but a platoon. They had a Smith fence around the position. A Smith fence is straight up and down, about six feet high, made of interwoven wire. We had found that a Smith fence was a better barrier than an apron fence.

If I'm not mistaken, I counted nineteen dead Chinese on or in front of that fence. The Chinese had gone off and left them, which was unusual. They'd begun to draw flies, but they weren't smelly yet. If our men went out to do something about these bodies in the daylight, the Chinese would start shelling the position. They weren't going to start smelling for a while, so we just left them alone and would do something about them at night when our men couldn't be seen.

Ruffner saw these dead Chinese and he wondered why we didn't evacuate them. We explained why to him. Then he went up to a soldier in a foxhole. This soldier's knife was stuck in the dirt on the edge of his foxhole. Ruffner chewed his ass out, saying: "That is no way to take care of a knife." The soldier told him, "It has to be where I can get it. If they get through that fence, it's hand to hand."

Then, sure enough, in just a little while mortar and artillery fire started coming in because Ruffner was stirring around. You can tell when you've got some brass around. In came the shells and I finally told him: "Sir, you're bringing mortars in on your troops and you've seen enough. I think we ought to get out of here." He finally agreed, so we started down the trail off the hill. The mortar shells were right behind us, following us all the way down that hill.

I thought, "I'm going to rotate in two or three days and this silly so and so is going places and doing things he shouldn't be doing." Getting out of there we followed the trail till we were in defilade. But they were still firing mortars around us and some of them got a little bit close. We got across the valley and back to my jeep. That's the last I saw of Ruffner.

All these months, as the infantry went out on patrols, and the artillery fired their howitzers, other Thunderbirds continued their job of supporting them. Some of these tasks—that no one ever hears about—were anything but pleasant.

FIRST LIEUTENANT REX WILSON.
45TH QUARTERMASTER COMPANY.

We set up initially near Chorwon at the end of a railroad line about four miles behind the MLR. All the supplies and ammo came into this railhead. That's where the 1st Cav Quartermaster Company had been set up. Somewhere along about this time I became the purchasing and contracting officer. The purchasing and contracting officer also had responsibility for the field service platoon which included the shower unit and the laundry unit. I was also the division graves registration officer.

I had a five man graves registration section. Each regiment had a graves registration officer and they would get the bodies back to us. What we did then was identify the bodies, do the paper work, dust them down with DDT powder, and put them in the body bags. I had one mortician in my section. He had been a mortician in civilian life, but it got so bad that he was wanting to get out, wanting a transfer out of the section. I wouldn't let him do that. I told him if he did he'd never be able to go back and perform as a mortician when he got home.

It was about June of 1952, when we took Old Baldy back from the Chinese. They'd had it for about a week and they'd left all the American bodies lying out. We got about thirty-five of them in one day and they were pretty ripe. The mortician had to wear a gas mask to work on them, but he toughed it out and did all right.

My name was the only name that went on the records. When a family got the body and paper work back home, my signature was on the documents. If the family had a problem, they had one name and that was mine. Thank goodness the Army had a regulation that the graves registration officer was precluded from contacting the family. So, if I got a letter from the family, I forwarded it to an officer the Army called the memorial services officer, and he handled all the correspondence.

I got lots of letters. "What happened to Johnny's gold watch? We got his personal effects and his watch wasn't there. What happened to the bath robe that I sent him?" We did a lot of things; we had a guy named Jerry Spencer with us from Mississippi who was the graves registration sergeant. I had him screen all the personal effects, take out all the Japanese girlfriend pictures and syphilis and gonorrhea records and all those kind of things. Then I'd check it over and we'd burn anything I didn't think should go to the family. We also processed the wounded guys' stuff and did the same thing. I'm sure we saved a lot of families a lot of misery.

On the morning of May 18, a recon patrol noticed activity near the site of Outpost Eerie. The position had been abandoned since the battle in March, but the 45th was not about to let the Chinese occupy it. Over the next three days raids by the Philippine BCT resulted in the destruction of six enemy bunkers, and seventy-six Chinese dead.[8]

Ruffner continued Styron's practice of shifting the regiments along the front. On June 2, after a fifteen day rest, it was back on line for the 180th.

SECOND LIEUTENANT BILL MARTIN.
HEAVY MORTAR COMPANY, 180TH INFANTRY REGIMENT.

There were times right before I left there, and this would have been in May and June, they were really having a struggle in holding the outposts. We'd kick them off, then they'd kick us off, back and forth. We had some really major attacks by the Chinese during that time.

I remember one time we were firing so rapidly that we had to take burlap bags and wrap them around the tubes and keep them soaked. We were firing as fast as we could and after about ten minutes of sustained firing the tubes got so hot the powder increments would pre-ignite. This caused the shells to go a little ways up the hill, maybe twenty or thirty feet, and start rolling back down. Well, you knew they weren't supposed to be armed because they hadn't hit the bottom of the tube, but it got everybody moving. At this time all three platoons were firing as fast as they could all along the regimental line. In the 2nd Platoon, a round exploded in the tube and I know one man was killed and two or three wounded pretty bad.

June would bring the heaviest fighting the 45th had seen so far in Korea and the return home of most of the Guardsmen who had been activated in 1950. As the peace talks dragged on, the enemy became more aggressive. It became obvious that a stronger outpost line was needed. This led to OPERATION COUNTER in which the division seized and held key terrain features in front of the MLR.

The first phase of the operation, June 4–12, went smoothly, catching the Chinese by surprise. But Outposts 10, Pork Chop, and 11, Old Baldy, received counter probes minutes after being occupied. On the 12th the second phase of COUNTER began with elements of the 180th and 245th Tank Battalion attacking objectives on Pokkae Ridge. And then on the 14th, after bitter fighting, the 45th Infantry Division once more held Outpost Eerie, and the new outpost line was complete.[9]

As June ended, the last National Guardsmen were on their way home. A few had transferred to the Regulars, and a few with bad time still remained. But for all intents, the men who had arrived at Camp Polk, Louisiana, in September of 1950 had left Korea. One of the last Thunderbirds to leave tells of his thoughts as he started home.

SECOND LIEUTENANT BILL MARTIN.
HEAVY MORTAR COMPANY, 180TH INFANTRY REGIMENT.

I suppose the thing that really made me feel fortunate and lucky was when I was getting ready to come home. I was relieved and went back that night to battalion headquarters. There were bunkers there and I was going to spend the night and the next morning go on back to the rear area. I remember it was just about dark when I got there.

Anyway, I'll never forget, as I got back there I looked over by the battalion aid station and there was a long line of bodies on stretchers. They were in body bags. I'd never seen anything like that before. We might have seen someone wounded and being moved back, but never in our position really seen any bodies. It looked like probably fifteen or twenty of them.

That was pretty sobering; to know that people were getting killed up there on the line and there they were. That night I don't think I got any sleep at all. There was some shelling in the area and the thought crossed my mind, "Here I am, this close to being home and just my luck, a round is going to come down through the middle of this thing and I'm going to be out there laying with those guys." But nothing happened and the next day I went down to the staging area at Inchon and started the trip home.

On July 18, the Thunderbirds went into Eighth Army reserve. In October, reassigned to X Corps, the division moved onto Line MINNESOTA where for a period of time their left flank would be held by the 40th Infantry Division with whom their destinies had so long been entwined.[10]

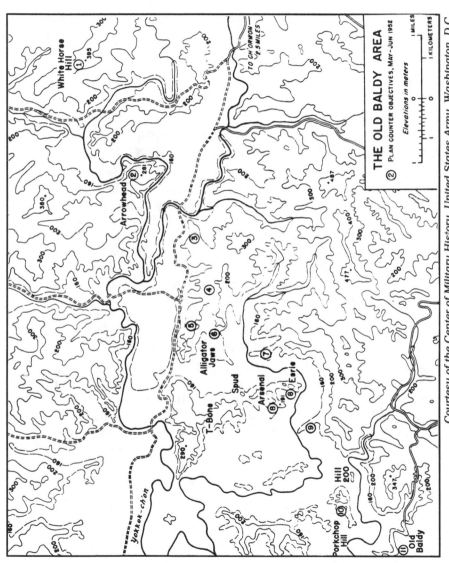

Courtesy of the Center of Military History, United States Army, Washington, D.C.

OPERATION COUNTER, which strengthened the outpost line, was the last action for many of the Thunderbirds who went to Korea.

The third Korean winter came and went and with it new names entered the history of the Thunderbirds. Heartbreak Ridge, No-Name Ridge, and the Punchbowl joined Outpost Eerie, T-Bone, and Old Baldy. The "cease fire" on July 27, 1953, found the 45th on the left flank of X Corps in the area TONGSONGOL-PAEAM.[11]

April 1954 saw the 45th Infantry Division return to the United States. The official ceremony, "OPERATION COLORBACK," was held at the Oklahoma State Fair, September 25, 1954. The Thunderbirds were officially home.[12]

Before we leave the 45th Infantry Division, one last story, a tale that began on the beach at Anzio and ended eight years later in the mountains of Korea.

CHIEF WARRANT OFFICER EMMETT STEEDS. HEADQUARTERS, 179TH INFANTRY REGIMENT.

On the Anzio beachhead a fellow I knew named Cruickshank got captured. I can't recall his first name, but I believe he was C.O. of "I" Company. When we finally pushed off the beachhead he managed to escape. At that time if you were captured and then escaped you weren't sent back to the fighting in the same area, so he was being sent back home. I met him at a hotel in Rome. I'd been detailed by G-4 to kind of help him out and get his things organized. At this time all of his uniforms and stuff were back in Naples in storage, and there was no way for him to get it before he left. So he said to me, "Steeds, I'll write you a letter and let you know where to send my Valv-Pak and stuff."

I said, "Fine, when I get back down that way I'll pick it up and send it to you." Well, I never did get a letter; never heard from him again. Keep in mind that I had been commissioned on Sicily. I had no dress uniforms or any other officer's gear. Shortly after that we pulled off line and went back to the Naples area for training prior to the invasion of Southern France.

They had a big officers' party in Naples at the Orange Club. This was a club the Army had taken over. By this time I'd picked up Cruickshank's Valv-Pak. I thought, "I'll just look and see what's in here." I pulled out his "pinks and greens" [officers' dress uniform], and it fit me. Even his shoes fit me. I put all that stuff on and went to that party. I walked in and these guys saw me, who knew me, and one said, "I've heard of people being optimistic, but here you are with a battle-field commission and walk in with a full dress uniform on."

But here's the unbelievable part. I never heard from Cruickshank, so I kept all that stuff. There was never an occasion for me to wear a full dress uniform so I just left it in the bag. When we got mobilized and sent to Japan, I took it with me. When the orders came to go to Korea, all dress uniforms were to be sent home. I was still the regimental ammo officer and, with all the things to do, I just never found time to ship mine home. As our trucks headed for the port area, I threw the box with the uniform in it on one of them. I was probably the only division officer in Korea with a dress uniform.

One day my phone rang; it was Cruickshank. He had joined the 45th as a replacement officer. He said, "Steeds, where in the hell is my uniform?" I said, "Well, I've been listening and waiting all these years for you to tell me where to send it." I said, "Do you still want it?" He said, "Sure." I said, "I'll bring it right up." Of course, he didn't believe me. Ten minutes later I walked into regimental headquarters with his Valv-Pak, uniform and shoes. I sat it down in front of him and said, "Here's your damn uniform and I don't want to hear anymore about it."

In the years following their Korean service the 45th Infantry Division was reorganized many times as the Army and Congress continually contracted then expanded the National Guard. Today the 45th Infantry Division is no more. But its legend will never die. Out on the wind swept plains of Oklahoma a new generation of Thunderbirds, now organized into three brigades, stands ready. Like their fathers, their grandfathers, and their great-grandfathers before them they train and they wait. They wait for the call they hope will never come. The call for the Thunderbirds to once more head "Up Front."

CHAPTER 13

KOREA REVISITED

When sleepy-eyed Southern Californians opened their *Los Angeles Examiners* on Sunday morning, February 3, 1952, they were greeted by three inch headlines: "40TH IN KOREA." The *Examiner* could hardly be credited with a scoop; Chinese Communist radio had broadcast the news three weeks previously.

But now the worst kept secret of the Korean War was official. The second and last National Guard Infantry Division to serve in Korea, the 40th Infantry Division (California) had arrived. From Barstow to Santa Monica, from San Diego to Ventura, from all over Southern California, the "Sunshine Division" had returned to the "Hermit Kingdom."

This trip promised to be even less enjoyable than the first one, a little over six years earlier. To the Guardsmen who were making their second trip to Korea, the place looked and smelled about the same, but at least back in 1945 no one was shooting at them.

Actually, after what had been planned for the 40th the summer of 1945, going to Korea wasn't all that bad. After the capture of Negros, the fourth largest island in the Philippines in June, the division went into training for the OLYMPIC Operation, the forthcoming invasion of Japan. The 40th's role in this gigantic endeavor would be to land on and secure several small islands off the southern coast of Kyushu, five days prior to the main landing.[1]

With Japan's surrender the Army reassigned the 40th to XXIV Corps for OPERATION BLACKLIST, the occupation of Japan and South Korea. By mid October, the majority of the division had landed and set up headquarters at Pusan.

The mission of the 40th was twofold: first, the disarmament and evacuation of all Japanese personnel, and second, to establish military government offices in the three most Southern Korean Provinces. The first part was easy, the Japanese had already put their weapons down and just wanted to go home.

The second part proved more difficult. Setting up headquarters in Taegu, military government teams of the 40th set about to restore some semblance of a civil government. After forty years of Japanese rule the Koreans were eager to participate in the democratic process, in fact, very eager. Representatives from no fewer than ninety-six political parties badgered the teams in the first weeks of the occupation.[2]

Meanwhile, the division received notice that it would be sent home for inactivation. Men with long time service had already started to be discharged and now the pace accelerated. The final group of thirty-four officers and twelve men departed Pusan in early March 1946. Released from active duty April 7, the 40th was the last National Guard division to return to the United States from World War II service.[3]

Prior to World War II the division, although primarily composed of units from California, included elements from Arizona and Utah. The National Guard Bureau now felt that Southern California could support a division by itself. The Arizona and Utah units were converted to separate battalions and a new division, the 49th Infantry, was formed in Northern California.

Brigadier General Daniel Hudelson assumed command of the division December 1, 1947. Promoted to major general in April of 1948, he would lead the 40th to Korea four years later. Hudelson first joined the 40th in 1925 as a private in the division's 160th Infantry Regiment. Commissioned soon after, he served with the regiment and division in various assignments for the next sixteen years, and was Division Assistant G-3 when the 40th went on active duty in 1941.

In 1942, Hudelson left the division and received command of the U.S. Commando Training Detachment at Achnacarry, Scotland. From there he joined the 14th Armored Division, leading a battalion and later a combat command in heavy fighting in France and Germany. An outspoken man with a touch of George Patton in him, he would at times, like Patton, voice opinions that may have been better left unsaid. In the summer of 1950, he would be 48 years old.[4]

How did the 40th come to be one of the four divisions selected for September 1 induction? The answer is politics and geography.*

As noted in chapter 1, on July 27, General Mark Clark gave Army Chief of Staff, General Joe Collins, his recommendation of the six best qualified National Guard divisions. Of the initial units Clark listed five were located on the east coast or in the South. Only the 45th Infantry Division (Oklahoma) was located west of the Mississippi. Four days passed. It was now July 31, 1950, a fateful day in the history of the 40th Infantry Division. In *Policy and Direction: The First Year* James Schnabel describes the curious chain of events of that day, events that started the "Sunshine Division" on the long road to Korea.

> On 31 July, General Ridgway notified General Clark that the Secretary of the Army and General Collins were fearful of the political repercussions unless there was a better geographical spread among the divisions selected.**

> Clark said that he and his advisers had considered this point very carefully, but had given more weight to other factors. . . .

> Ridgway then asked Clark to consider the readiness status of divisions on the west coast since it might be desirable to choose one division from that area.

> Later that same day, General Clark learned that four divisions would be chosen. He was asked if he had adjusted his recommendations to conform with the necessity for a geographical spread.[5]

And so he had. There on the revised list, squeezed in between the 37th and the 43rd (another addition), it read: 40th Infantry Division.

Receiving word that the division would be mobilized September 1, Hudelson, and his unit commanders got busy. A number of Guardsmen went on active duty to start the paper work flowing, and a recruiting drive got under way. By the time the division mobilized, its ranks had grown to 9,866 men; this still left it almost 9,000 troops short of TO&E strength.[6]

Concurrent with the recruiting drive, division units busily prepared to move to their new duty station, Camp Cooke, California, 130

---

* Many of the men who contributed to this and the following three chapters stated that soon after war broke out in Korea, Hudelson flew to Washington and begged that the 40th be mobilized. While nothing could be found to substantiate this claim, many former members of the division swear it happened.
** With whom this thought actually originated with is unknown.

miles up the California coast, from Los Angeles. Upon arriving at Cooke, the Army planned for the 40th to quickly fill up with draftees and other personnel. A twenty-eight week training cycle consisting of basic, advanced, and unit training would then commence to bring the division up to Regular Army standards.

As in all the mobilized Guard units considerable work had to be done before the division units could depart their home stations. Processing of personnel, including the separation of a large number of soldiers who suddenly realized they were underage for military service took a tremendous amount of time. Preparation of equipment, transportation arrangements and a myriad of other details also had to be completed before the division departed for Camp Cooke. Completed or not, on September 1, 1950, the 40th Infantry Division was back on active duty.[7]

PRIVATE HARRY NELSON.
"I" COMPANY, 160TH INFANTRY REGIMENT.

I joined up back in late 1948 or early '49; I was sixteen years old. We had a very close knit unit, we had all went to or were in high school together. Nesto Castillo was the one who instigated everything. He got Danny Castile and Frank Villarruel to sign up and then they talked me in. So when I went in, I talked Ernie Rodriguez, and Mike Garcia into joining. Our outfit was located in Maywood. We didn't have a regular armory, but had a building at an old Army supply depot.

I was a mortar man on the 60mm mortars, but I didn't get to handle one for eighteen months. We didn't have one in the company. I think I saw one at summer camp, but didn't get to fire it. When the war broke out in Korea we didn't think we would go; then we started hearing rumors that we might be called up. Then I received a telegram saying to get my things in order because we were being mobilized. We started to have more drills and take things more seriously.

I was out of the house when another telegram arrived. I got home and my mother gave it to me. She was very upset. It said to report to the armory immediately. I had no transportation to get to the armory which was fifteen miles from my home, so I called the L.A. Sheriff's Department and they sent a squad car to pick me up. My friends and the officers couldn't believe it when I pulled up in a squad car. As it turned out I would not have had to be in such a rush as we stayed at the armory for several days. We were then trucked to Exposition Park, in downtown L.A., where we boarded a train for the trip to Camp Cooke.

Returning home, Nelson became a metal plater. He is currently an inspector at General Inspection Lab in Cudahy, California.

FIRST LIEUTENANT CALVIN SAMPLES.
EXECUTIVE OFFICER, "L" COMPANY, 224TH INFANTRY
REGIMENT.

We started to attend drills full time at the armory. The armory was nothing more than a barracks with a room about three or four times as big as a living room: a little office, a little place where we put our weapons, and a toilet. I guess we had a three or four burner stove in the kitchen; that was it.

By then we had grown to something over a hundred men, so we had to get somebody to come in and cook for us. We had a couple of cooks but not enough equipment for them to work with. The ladies' auxiliary from the American Legion came in and cooked for us. They cooked down at the Legion hall and brought the food in.

The first Saturday night after we were activated they had a big party for us down at the American Legion hall in Santa Anna. About ten o'clock, the company commander came up to me and said, "You had better go home and get your clothes, I want you to take a convoy up to Camp Cooke and you're leaving at twelve o'clock." What really astonished me was there had been no real planning; I didn't even know where Camp Cooke was. I just knew it was up the coast.

I went home, got my clothes and came back. The battalion headquarters was in another old building about a block away. They had me take the company jeep and go up there. By the time I got there trucks were filling in from the other companies in the battalion. We were taking the equipment up in trucks; the troops would go later by train. I went to a Texaco station and got maps for everybody. The battalion exec was there and I asked him how many vehicles were we going to have. He said, "Well, we'll have to wait till they all get here and see."

I just couldn't believe that the thing was being handled that way, that they really didn't know how many trucks the unit had. So finally, shortly after twelve that night, he said, "Well, evidently that's all of them." I went up with the convoy and met the rest of the regiment at the Rose Bowl and then we went on from there, me leading the whole regiment.

They didn't tell me speed or anything. We just took off up the coast and kept going. We didn't have any gas with us and they hadn't told us how to gas up. We stopped in Santa Barbara and filled up the vehicles at a regular service station.

I told them we were activated and we needed some gas, so we just pulled in and I signed for it. I never did hear if the guy got paid.

We went on into the camp and found the supply rooms. One in particular I remember, it was so covered with sand and bushes we couldn't find the door. We unloaded, slept that night, then drove back to Orange County, reloaded and made another trip back to Cooke before the troops arrived.

In Korea, Samples commanded "K" Company of the 224th. He remained in the Guard, retiring with 36 years service and wearing the star of a brigadier general.

Activated in October 1941, Camp Cooke covered ninety thousand acres along the central California coast. An unidentified division signalman wrote: "Seen from the air Camp Cooke was a sometimes rolling, sometimes flat, mostly unpromising stretch of sand and dark green, set in scrawny struggling hills, bounded on three sides by easy-going towns and almost towns, and on the fourth by a rough ocean, with a savage undertow, a danger to swimmers."

When the base was deactivated in June of 1946, the blowing sand and corrosive salt air had taken their toll on its facilities. Camp Cooke now had the eerie appearance of a ghost town, complete with rattlesnakes, spiders, and other assorted creatures. The experience of Sergeant George Buttner was not unique. When ordered to string telephone lines in the 981st FAB area, he requested a snake bite kit from the medics. They refused. He then brought back four live snakes and a dead rattler to prove the need.

Taken over by the Air Force in 1956 and renamed Vandenberg Air Force Base, it is now America's western missile test center.[8]

FIRST SERGEANT HESTER PARKER.
"B" BATTERY, 140TH AAA (AW) BATTALION.

It was a camp that had not been used. The plumbing, that type of thing, was beyond repair; we had to go through everything. Fortunately enough, the National Guard has a group of people that's a mix of all trades and we did most of our own maintenance. I recall the lights in our barracks we rewired ourselves.

Parker later became State Command Sergeant Major, the top ranking NCO in the California National Guard.

SERGEANT MAJOR ED STROM.
980TH FIELD ARTILLERY BATTALION.

The barracks, generally speaking, were deplorable. There were construction crews working all through the camp trying to get things in shape. This was an adequate camp, but not designed for a large organization like an infantry division. There wasn't sufficient open area at Camp Cooke for the type of training you need for a division.

Strom, who in World War II landed on Omaha Beach with an AAA outfit on D+7, remained in the Army and retired in 1967 as a command sergeant major.

The lack of adequate training space meant that the division would continually be fragmented. In the next six months all of the artillery battalions and support units would move up the coast eighty miles to Hunter Liggett Military Reservation where they could fire their heavy weapons. After the division arrived in Japan in April of 1951, the various units were scattered to a number of camps across the island of Honshu. At no time did the division train as a unit.

By the time the 40th arrived in Korea, the war had turned into a battle of patrols, and outposts; consequently the lack of large unit exercises had minimal effect on the division's performance.

Soon after the division arrived at Camp Cooke the first group of fillers reported for duty. They came from all across the country, and with varied military backgrounds: Guardsmen, draftees, Reservists and a handful of Regular Army personnel. A few seemed to suffer from culture shock.

PRIVATE FIRST CLASS FRANK SARIÑANA.
B" BATTERY, 980TH FIELD ARTILLERY BATTALION.

The guys were afraid; the new guys that came in. I made friends with a few of them from Massachusetts. I asked one of them, "Look, what's bothering you?" He said, "I heard about the Mexicans. Have you heard about them? I heard that they all carry a knife." I said, "I know, don't worry about it." I said, "You guys have to relax and take it easy. We'll protect you." He didn't realize I was Mexican because I didn't speak Spanish around Angelos. He eased up a bit and we became good friends.

Home from Korea, Sariñana worked in the research department at the City of Hope Medical Center before becoming a high school teacher.

Photos courtesy of Frank Sariñana

Best friends Mike Gallegos (left) and Frank Sariñana (right) had planned to join the border patrol, but instead wound up in Korea with the 980th FAB, 40th Infantry Division.

PRIVATE GEORGE NITIS.
"C" COMPANY, 140TH TANK BATTALION.

We took our physicals, and processing at Fort Lewis up in Washington took about ten days. At the end of the physicals a doctor would look you up and down and then hand you a card. My friend in front of me showed me his; it said 160th Inf. Regt. When I told him what it meant, he said, "Oh God." Mine said 140th Tk. Bn. I thought this meant truck battalion because I'd been driving a truck in my Guard outfit in Tacoma. We got on a train and into Camp Cooke about ten o'clock at night. Hardly any lights, everything being done by flashlights.

They got us up at daybreak the next morning. I looked out the window and it looked like a thousand tanks were parked there. It didn't take long to figure out what 140th Tk. Bn. meant. The barracks were dirty; on one of the walls someone had wrote: "Hitler, here we come!" We had to clean up the whole camp. And that's how it started.

In Korea, Nitis would be wounded twice and receive a Bronze Star.

The new tanker and the other replacements that now started to trickle in made a welcome addition to the units of the 40th. Unfortunately, there were not nearly enough of them. On September 5, the Army informed Hudelson that the division would be brought up to war strength plus 10 percent prior to October 15, 1950. That the Army could find 10,000 men, process them and ship them to Cooke in that period of time was a Pentagon dream. By now the majority of the Army clerks that did the paper work, and the medics that gave the physicals were carrying M-1s and aid kits in Korea.[9]

The Army had more pressing problems the week of September 5, 1950, than finding men for the 40th Infantry Division. In Korea the fighting had reached a crucial point. The thinly held Pusan Perimeter finally broke, and NKPA troops penetrated the line in the 2nd Infantry Division's sector. The 5th Marine Regiment, already being pulled off the front to spearhead the Inchon landing, rushed back and managed to close the gap.

By now the situation had reached the point that General Walton Walker, Eighth Army Commander, notified GHQ Tokyo: "If I lose the 5th Marine Regiment I will not be responsible for the safety of the front."[10]

Teams of Regular Army personnel now arrived at Cooke to give instruction on a variety of subjects from heavy weapons to administration. At the same time officers and men departed for Army Service Schools to learn the latest doctrine. Meanwhile, work continued on improving the camp.

FIRST LIEUTENANT DONALD McCLANAHAN. COMMANDING OFFICER, HEADQUARTERS COMPANY, 1ST BATTALION, 223RD INFANTRY REGIMENT.

> It was all just blowing sand. The buildings had been closed up pretty well, and we had to get some utilities working and get the place fired up. I remember the first thing I did as Company C.O. was to plant a little lawn in front of the company headquarters building.
>
> This attracted a gopher who started to make short work of it. We tried everything to kill that gopher, even broke off all the points on our mine probes, nothing worked. So one day I shot him with an M-1. Unfortunately, the MPs were across the yard from us in formation, and when I fired the M-1 I attracted a lot of attention, but I got the gopher.

McClanahan, who had received a Purple Heart while serving with the 37th Infantry Division (Ohio) during World War II, would go on to serve with the National Guard Bureau, and on the staff and faculty of the U.S. Army War College at Carlisle Barracks. He retired after thirty-two years service as a brigadier general.

Hudelson and the division staff took the Army at its word and planned to commence the eleven week basic training cycle on October 30. This date passed with only a handful of men having joined the division. Another week went by and still no sign of the promised 10,000 fillers. By now all concerned realized they had best get started with the troops on hand if they were to have any chance of meeting the April 14, 1951, target date for operational employment. On November 6, 1950, the division commenced training with a strength of 12,065 officers and men.[11]

FIRST SERGEANT DAVID HARRIS.
"E" COMPANY, 223RD INFANTRY REGIMENT.

The hard part about this was finding the right man for the right spot. We came up short of officers. Some people didn't go on active duty, and some of those that did were found physically or mentally unacceptable. At the same time they needed cadre to be teaching the recruits and everything else.

At this time we had a lot of high ranking NCOs with no real military experience. That's the way the Guard was in those days. Some of these men in key positions couldn't handle their assignments. Then there were those of lower rank who could handle these positions so they were promoted. Some of the officers left for school. It was very unsettled.

Then they started to switch around commanding officers. We lost Captain Stagg who I'd known since when. They pulled him and put a Captain Jackson in command of the company. He had his own ideas on how to run the outfit. By this time I was a little bit upset with the Guard. How do you put it? They were wishy-washy about the whole thing. Nothing was firm, you didn't know where you were going.

Then I saw on the board they were going to form an Airborne Ranger Company within the division; this was to become the 40th Division Ranger Company. And I thought, "Boy, I'd like to take this. I'd like to go airborne." So I went down there for testing and I was the first master sergeant to pass. This was a little before Christmas. There were about a hundred and fifty of us and we went back to Fort Benning. After Benning we were sent to Fort Carson, where we went through mountain and cold weather training. We rejoined the division in Japan.

Harris, a Marine during World War II, remained in the Guard, retiring as a major with twenty-seven years service.

Enlisted men were also transferred in and out of the division those first hectic days at Camp Cooke. One of these was Sergeant Herbert R. Temple, Jr., of the 160th Infantry Regiment. Assigned to

Courtesy of Buddy Hall

Buddy Hall, 981st FAB, 40th Infantry Division, standing next to a load of 155mm projectiles. As the front stabilized in 1952, thousands of rounds were fired every month.

Post Headquarters at Cooke, Temple was still there when the division sailed for Japan in March of 1951. But Temple beat the 40th to Korea, going over as a replacement and joining "B" Company, 5th RCT, 24th Infantry Division. On August 19, 1986, President Ronald Reagan appointed Lieutenant General Herbert R. Temple, Jr., Chief, National Guard Bureau.

RECRUIT BUDDY HALL. SERVICE BATTERY, 981ST FIELD ARTILLERY BATTALION.

I joined on August 8th, 1950. I knew I was going to get drafted. My buddy said, "Come on, go with us, join the Guard," so I did. I went with all my friends. I was a recruit, lower than a private. We went up to Camp Cooke and started our basic training. We took infantry basic and at the same time took some artillery training. The 981st was a 155mm artillery battalion.

The wind came up every day at 1:30, and it was cold. I was a raw recruit, didn't know what the hell the score was, but I felt we were going to have a good outfit. We had a lot of World War II officers, retreads was what they called them; they were good officers. I'd say half our outfit were veterans. The fillers were mostly from the east coast, a lot from New York. They probably came in around November.

I was assigned to the ammo section. We'd take the ammo up to the firing batteries. We trained hard. We did a five mile hike in the morning and another five miles in the afternoon. We got really hard; I was in good shape. We had a good outfit, and we had a lot of pride.

In 1952, Buddy Hall returned to Santa Barbara as a sergeant first class with two Army Commendation Ribbons.

CAPTAIN T. K. TURNAGE.
S-3, 1ST BATTALION, 223RD INFANTRY REGIMENT.

There was a lot of lost time initially simply because you had such an influx of guys that were draftees who had been brought into the division. You virtually had to start from scratch instead of starting with unit training which is the initial objective of a mobilized Guard unit. But even so, all these things considered, the training was intensive. I know that people really put their shoulders to the wheel and did what they were supposed to do because they felt that ultimately they would be going to Korea.

By the time we got to Camp Cooke we could see what was happening with the Pusan Perimeter and the rest of it. We had sufficient knowledge to understand that there wasn't much that the active Army had to draw on. Knowing some of the people that were called up from the Reserves and shipped straight over we felt the situation must be rather desperate and ultimately we would be going. And, we did. Not only were we doing the normal routine that you would expect from battalion operations, but we were also required to attend classes in the evening on leadership. There was also a big thrust on physical fitness. You had to get up early in the morning and take those physical fitness walks that General Hudelson initiated.

The days were long and the days were intense. I don't recall having heard any great dissent or bitching other than that which is normally associated with the Army. I recall those days as being long and busy, but essentially achieving the objectives we were assigned.

Twenty-four years later Major General Thomas Turnage assumed command of the 40th Infantry Division (Mechanized). He would command the division on two separate occasions, a total of almost three years. In October of 1981, President Ronald Reagan appointed Turnage, Director of the Selective Service System, a post he held for four and a half years. In March of 1986, he was named Administrator of Veterans Affairs by the president. Turnage headed the VA until his retirement in January of 1989.

SECOND LIEUTENANT DONN STAFFORD.
HEADQUARTERS & SERVICE COMPANY, 578TH ENGINEER COMBAT BATTALION.

I was a brand new 2nd lieutenant; the papers came in the night before we left for Camp Cooke. When we got up there they put me in charge of the bridge platoon. They filled us up with draftees and we started basic training. Our basic included some engineer training; it was sort of a mixture. I was staying one night ahead of the fellows in my platoon. I'd study the problem, then give the lecture the next day. I'd been in the Army before, but this time I really learned basic training.

Stafford, who had served in the Pacific during World War II, returned to California after his service in Korea. A civil engineer, he helped design the California Aqueduct.

SERGEANT ROBERT HOLTBY.
"E" COMPANY, 223RD INFANTRY REGIMENT.

We only had about thirty men in the company when we were activated; it was very small. Then they brought all these fillers in to fill us up. At that time in the infantry all you had were rifles, machine guns, mortars, and a few radios, nothing real technical like now. I had the 60mm mortar section in the weapons platoon, then shortly after we got to Cooke I became the platoon sergeant.

The weapons platoon had the mortars and the machine guns. Most of the time we didn't have an officer and I ran the platoon. We didn't train that much on the mortars, most of it was simulated. They had a range there but we only used it once or twice. Fact is they tried. They got dummy rounds for us to fire, but the ground up there is so soft that you'd fire out three or four hundred yards and spend the rest of the afternoon looking for the damn things. They'd go down, almost out of sight, in the sand.

The infantry training was very realistic in our company. Periodically, we would have a twenty mile hike with full field equipment. To get to the rifle range we had to hike about two or three miles; the abutments were right next to the ocean. We had to cross the railroad tracks, the one that runs all the way up the coast, to get out there. Early in the morning we'd be at the rifle range and everybody would look and say, "I wish I was on that train."

A veteran of World War II service in Italy, Holtby remained in the National Guard. He retired after thirty-one years service as a command sergeant major.

For a number of reasons the training program never really lived up to Hudelson's expectations. The departure of officers and

NCOs for branch schools left many units with only a company commander and a few sergeants. A large percentage of the junior officers brought in to fill up the division were recent ROTC graduates with little training and no experience.

To remedy this the division organized a school just for junior officers. Named "The Killer School" for Hudelson's penchant for always talking about wanting a division of killers, it taught infantry fundamentals and the use of heavy weapons, such as the bazooka, which many of the young officers had never seen, let alone fired.

The arrival of fillers over an extended period meant that in any unit there would be men with varying degrees of training. This problem was temporarily solved by setting up provisional training organizations to give basic training to the fillers who arrived after the division had progressed to AIT.

These units conducted a six week streamlined basic training course in order to allow the late arrivals to catch up with the men in advanced training. All this, coupled with the limited facilities at Cooke and the continual movement of units to and from Hunter Liggett, complicated the effort to form the companies and batteries into cohesive fighting units.[12]

On December 2, the division assembled in mass formation for the first time. General Hudelson spoke:

This division is going to fight on the field of battle . . . it is my responsibility to see that you men learn to endure hardships and reach top physical condition . . . and I will keep that responsibility. I congratulate you draftees and recruits on being a part of the 40th . . . I am proud of this division . . . it has an outstanding history and a remarkable record . . . with fillers from throughout the entire Country training with the 40th, the division can be a mighty force to fight and protect this great Country of ours.[13]

Hudelson's training program had a single purpose: to make the men of the 40th Infantry Division the toughest soldiers in the United States Army. He visited the units and spoke to the men often, and his message never varied. "Look at the man on the right, look at the man on the left, you're going to fight the Communists and they may not be coming back, so train and train hard."

The training program had a single foundation: "Guts, more guts, and still more guts." To emphasize this point and improve physical conditioning Hudelson instituted a program of speed marches. They started with four mile, one hour hikes with full field gear and worked up to twenty-five mile, eight hour marches.[14]

FIRST LIEUTENANT DONALD McCLANAHAN.
ASSISTANT S-3, 1ST BATTALION, 223RD INFANTRY
REGIMENT.

As officers came and went I was moved to the battalion staff. We had the speed marches. They started short and slow and became longer and faster; Hudelson was great on that. Our battalion S-3, Captain Tom Turnage, was also a bug on that. He organized the marches for the battalion. My job was to get the battalion lined up and ready for the march.

The thing that sticks out in my mind was that Tom didn't care much to make the marches himself. All of us officers had our packs in the battalion headquarters and they were packs made up special for the speed marches. Tom always used to wait till the last minute to put his on and usually he would say, "Bring out my pack." Then he'd turn around, stick his arms out and we'd put his pack on him, and then he would lead the battalion on the march.

So I remember one day, the wags, we thought we'd do something special for Tom and his speed marches. So we loaded his pack with about thirty-five pounds of nails. When the day came for the next speed march, he said, "Don, get my pack and we'll go." So we dumped his pack on him and started out. Tom was in real trouble on that speed march.

PRIVATE FLOYD MOODY.
HEAVY MORTAR COMPANY, 224TH INFANTRY REGIMENT.

We had the 4.2 inch mortar, 12 guns in the company. Most of our training was in the company area learning how to use the guns, the basic stuff. We also did the regular infantry basic, a lot of physical training and marches; it was tough basic training. I was seventeen years old, the youngest man in the company and in good shape, but I found out I couldn't walk as far, or as fast as I thought I could.

Our C.O. was Captain Al Barron. He had been a mortar man in World War II with the 45th Infantry Division. He was tough, strictly Army, very serious, very professional. We didn't realize at first how lucky we were to have a man like him. We fired the guns some at Cooke, but really didn't do a lot of firing till we got to Japan. The NCOs were observing us to decide who would be assigned to what job. I wound up in a firing squad as an ammo bearer; by the time we came home I was a squad leader. Hudelson didn't confide in me but there was no doubt in my mind we would be going overseas.

Moody later joined the Air Force. After participating in the hydrogen bomb test at Eniwetok, and service in Thailand, he retired after twenty-two years as a master sergeant.

As the foot sloggers of the three infantry regiments tramped across the sand dunes and through the sage brush of Camp Cooke, the division artillery battalions and support units were traveling up and down Highway 101 to Hunter Liggett Military Reservation, eighty miles to the north.

SERGEANT MIKE GALLEGOS.
"B" BATTERY, 980TH FIELD ARTILLERY BATTALION.

We couldn't fire at Cooke, we just did gun drill and practiced with dummy rounds. Then we went up to Hunter Liggett; it took about four hours in convoy. I slept in the back of a truck the whole way. The Army really picked a miserable place for a firing range; it rained the whole time we were there. Real rough terrain, trucks and howitzers kept sliding off the roads; the retrievers really kept busy pulling them out of ditches. It was nothing but mud.

I was a forward observer. One day some cows wandered into our impact area. I called back and it happened that the battalion commander was there. He said to let him know when the cows left the area. When the cows went up a ravine, I called back and gave the all clear. Then, just when we opened up, they came back down again. We got at least three of them. Pretty soon the owner showed up; he knew he was in the wrong for not watching them better. He said if we would gather up the remains we could have them. The next night the battery had steak.

Badly burned in a bunker explosion in Korea, Gallegos would spend three years in Army hospitals.

FIRST SERGEANT HESTER PARKER.
"B" BATTERY, 140TH AAA (AW) BATTALION.

We had the quad .50 machine guns on half-tracks and the towed 40mm guns. We went up to Hunter Liggett and qualified the gun crews a battery at a time on the .50 calibers;stayed about a week. It took us about twenty-four hours to get up there. We had to take the back roads; they wouldn't let the half-tracks out on the highway. About twenty percent of the tracks would break down on the way.

At that time they didn't have an AAA range at Liggett, but the Army leased part of a large ranch near King City, and that's where we fired. We fired at ground targets at ranges from five thousand to ten thousand yards.

Later on, in early February of 1951, we went down to Camp Irwin in the Mohave Desert, to fire at towed targets. We got some really good work in. I do remember one day somebody miscalculated a bit and shot the target off about twenty-five feet in back of the L-19 tow plane. The pilot just wagged his wings and kept going; he didn't come back that day.

Things were not all work and no play for the men of the 40th. Training only a few hours' drive from their homes, family and friends could come up to Cooke for visits, and the troops could make a quick run home if they could wrangle a pass. Being from Southern California meant a continual parade of Hollywood stars came up to entertain the troops. Dorothy Lamour, Debbie Reynolds, Vic Damone, and other show-biz personalities performed for the troops. While the proximity of home and loved ones kept morale high it did nothing to enhance the training program.[15]

REGIMENTAL SERGEANT MAJOR RALPH STOCKWELL. 223RD INFANTRY REGIMENT.

We were too close to Los Angeles; that was another problem. Everybody and his brother wanted to go home every weekend. You couldn't get a thing done on weekends. I don't know how many people were injured or killed going back and forth to LA. In one sense we were glad to get away from Cooke; we weren't happy to go to Japan, but we knew it was going to happen anyway. It was just a matter of when.

Stockwell, a full time Guard employee, had served in Italy during World War II.

A hint of what the future might hold for the 40th occurred in January when the Army pulled 600 to 700 men out of the division and shipped them to Korea as replacements. Hudelson appears to have accepted their departure with unaccustomed good grace as he commented:

It should be clearly understood that this levy in no way upsets the tactical integrity of this division. We brought thousands of National Guardsmen into active service with us last September. Our ranks were soon increased to war strength with additions of draftees to our rolls. Recently we started receiving 4,000 more men.

A few months later when the Army again pulled troops from the division, his comments would be somewhat different.[16]

SERGEANT ROBERT HOLTBY.
"E" COMPANY, 223RD INFANTRY REGIMENT.

We sent the first batch of replacements to Korea. They had finished basic and were qualified infantrymen. They took about fifty or sixty from our company, out of a total of a hundred and ninety-eight.

We went to Japan and were there almost a year before we went to Korea and on line. When we went on line I went up to see the first sergeant of the company we were replacing (by this time I was first sergeant). It was at night; infantry usually relieves at night. Anyway, he was one of the replacements that we had sent out of my platoon a year before. We both said, "What the hell are you doing here?" Here he was, first sergeant of a line infantry company; he'd gone from buck private to first sergeant in a year's time.

CHAPTER 14

NO, WE'RE FROM CALIFORNIA

The first news that the 40th would be deploying to Japan arrived at Camp Cooke in rather strange fashion. At 1100 hours, February 24, the division public information officer (PIO) received a phone call from the Public Information Section, Sixth Army Headquarters in San Francisco. He was told of the impending movement and ordered to release the news to the media at 1300 that afternoon.

The PIO notified the Division ADC, Brigadier General Homer Eaton, and the Division G-2 of the message. An astounded Eaton confirmed the message with the Sixth Army Chief of Staff, and, as ordered, the news was released to the media at 1300 hours. The movement readiness date designated as March 23, was later changed to March 28.[1]

While some of the troops were surprised and disappointed in their destination, the majority had assumed they would be shipping out eventually, if not this soon. Many men felt as Corporal Albert DiJerlando, "D" Company, 160th Infantry, "We can't all stay home while others are dying for us."

ADC Eaton expressed his views: "It was somewhat disappointing that we didn't go the other way [Europe], but the news has been a lift, and for overall morale a shot in the arm." Eaton then estimated that the division had reached 60 percent combat readiness. In this estimate Eaton erred somewhat. Regular Army inspectors graded the division at 45 percent combat effective when it deployed to Japan.[2]

The next day Division Commander Hudelson spoke to the division:

We are going to Japan and Japan is not very far from Korea. The last time I addressed the full division I told you we would fight and this time I repeat that we are training to fight on the field of battle. We will complete our training in Japan but all phases of battle indoctrination, village fighting, close combat, infiltration and overhead artillery fire courses will be completed before we leave Camp Cooke.

Every attempt will be made to see that all men get home, a policy of seven to ten day leaves, depending on the distance of your home from Camp Cooke has been established. I am depending on you—men of the 40th—to do and do well whatever duty we are called on to perform. You will be ready to leave for Japan in the latter part of March.[3]

And now the failure of the Army to bring the 40th up to strength the previous fall, and the resulting delay in commencing the training program came back to haunt the division. For, along with the receipt of the overseas movement order, Sixth Army notified the division that soldiers who had not completed fourteen weeks of training could not ship out. If held to this requirement the 40th would embark with less than 15,000 troops. A request was made to allow men with six weeks training to go with the division. The request was denied. So, like the Thunderbirds at Camp Polk, the division formed a training unit.

The newly formed unit, designated the 40th Division Rear Detachment, comprised approximately 560 officers and men. Their mission was to organize and staff training battalions to instruct the fillers the division had received during the first three months of 1951. It was anticipated that the 40th Division Rear Detachment would operate until June 1951. Then having completed their training, the approximate 3,000 fillers, together with the cadre, would ship to Japan to rejoin the division.[4]

With a month to prepare for an overseas movement thousands of things had to be done. The requirement that all men complete the various combat courses, and qualify with their individual weapons before shipping out caused problems. With all vehicles being prepared for shipment, many men on pre-embarkation leave, and the necessity of fatigue details for the packing and crating of the division's equipment, just getting everybody out to the firing ranges constituted a major logistical headache.[5]

Lieutenant Colonel Dallas Downs, division engineer, estimated it would take 6,500 boxes of four standard sizes plus an undetermined number of special boxes to pack up the division. Before it was over close to 10,000 boxes were used including two standard piano boxes to hold the division band's two pianos. Somehow it all got done, and then it was time. On March 29, 1951, the division climbed aboard trains and headed north to San Francisco where they boarded Navy transports.[6]

As the troops climbed up the gangplanks, a reporter discussed with General Hudelson the training cycle completed at Camp Cooke, and the additional eleven weeks training to be received while on "occupation duty" in Japan. Asked whether the "Sunshine Division" would be "theoretically ready" for combat in Korea after that, Hudelson cheerfully replied, "Theoretically, hell, we'll be ready period!"[7]

And on that note the 40th Infantry Division sailed out under the Golden Gate Bridge and to whatever lay ahead.

*   *   *   *   *   *

Life aboard a troopship consists of lines—long lines. Not the 20 and 30 minute lines of training camp, but three and four hour lines. Lines that wind up and down ladders, through dark passageways and dank compartments, past overflowing heads and thirty gallon garbage cans, their contents making small waves as the ship rolls back and forth. And, at the end of these torturous trails, a gray glob or two of an unidentifiable substance slopped on a stainless steel tray, then quickly wolfed down in a standing position. If a man has a real passion for cleanliness, he may avail himself of a cold saltwater shower. Most troops opted to wait until arriving at their destination before bathing, giving the sardine-can-like troop compartments an aroma that Chanel never bottled.

And this is how the trip to Japan went for the soldiers of the 40th Infantry Division—at least for most of them. In every outfit there are individuals who know how to make the best of any situation. These men can readily be identified by the six stripes on their sleeve. With these six stripes comes a lot of responsibility and on occasion, a few privileges.

REGIMENTAL SERGEANT MAJOR RALPH STOCKWELL. 223RD INFANTRY REGIMENT.

We were on the *General Meigs*. As I got on board, over the loudspeaker I heard, "Troop sergeant major report to the troop commander's office." I didn't pay any attention; I didn't know who the troop sergeant major was. Then they called me by name. We were the administrative office for all the troops on the ship. We set up the K.P. and guard rosters, solved problems, that sort of thing. I really enjoyed the trip. I ate in the Navy mess, had my own chair and even my own waiter.

I met a couple of Navy chief petty officers who said, "If you need anything at all, let us know." We had no supplies to run the office, so I told them I needed some stencils, scotch tape, that sort of thing, stuff we could never get from the Army. They got me everything I wanted. I thought one of those big mirrors that hang in the ship's latrine might come in handy. I asked them, and they got one for me.

When I asked them how I was going to get all this stuff off the ship, they took me to the ship's carpenter and he built two nice boxes to hold everything. Someone said I came aboard with a match box and left with two coffins, which is true. I did. I got enough office supplies to last six months, maybe longer.

On April 10, the first troopship landed at Yokohama. On the dock an Army band played "California Here I Come," but the ship didn't turn around. More ships docked on the 12th, and in a matter of days the entire division had landed in Japan. From Yokohama, the division moved by train to training sites scattered across the northern half of the main Japanese island of Honshu.

Division headquarters went to Camp Schimmelpfennig near Sendai, 170 miles north of Tokyo. They were joined there by the 223rd Infantry, and division artillery which also had units at Camp Younghans. The 224th Infantry traveled to Camp McNair on Mount Fujiyama, while the 160th Infantry settled in at Camp Haugen. Other division units took post at Camps Palmer, Fowler, Matsushima, Zama, Fuchinobe, Whittington, and McGill.

During the nine months the division stayed in Japan, most of the units would move at least twice. This gave the troops the opportunity to train in different types of weather and on different terrain. Many of the troops thought the camps, former World War II Japanese military installations, a distinct improvement over Camp Cooke.[8]

PRIVATE FIRST CLASS KENNETH ERCKENBRACK. "B" BATTERY, 140TH AAA (AW) BATTALION.

We went over on the General *Nelson M. Walker*. About a hundred miles out of Oakland we hit a big storm. The ship would come half way out of the water then slap back down. It was miserable. I guess it didn't slow us down any—when we got to Yokohama the Navy said we had set a speed record for that type of ship. We were greeted by the cherry blossoms in full bloom; it was a fine sight to see.

We got on a train and went to Camp Whittington, a former Japanese air base. We stayed there a short time and then went to Katakai to fire our 40mms and .50s. In two days we destroyed all the targets they had for us. We stayed at Camp Palmer awhile and then in June moved on to Camp Schimmelpfennig, our permanent base. The camp had been a kamikaze training base and there was still a lot of bomb damage visible. The barracks were all right, but they had been painted with a fish oil base paint and didn't smell so good.

After about a month my brother who was in the Navy came up. I got a pass and he took me to see Tokyo. We had a great time, but now I realize I was too young to appreciate it. The politeness of the Japanese people was something to see.[9]

Active in veterans' affairs Erckenbrack has been instrumental in raising money for the Korean War Memorial.

PRIVATE FIRST CLASS HARRY NELSON. "I" COMPANY, 160TH INFANTRY REGIMENT.

We had anticipated going over and I think everybody wanted to go. I know I for one wanted to go. When you're young you don't think of death or being wounded. You just think, "Well hey, this is an experience, something new. I want to go see it."

We landed at Yokohama and boarded a slow moving troop train to take us to Camp Haugen, our new home in northern Honshu. I remember it was terribly cold. We saw women with babies and little kids out in the frozen rice paddies. They kept yelling "Ohayo." We thought they were saying "Ohio" and we yelled back, "No, we're from California." We later learned this meant "good morning" in Japanese.

We thought we'd had some good training at Cooke, but it was nothing compared to what we got in Japan. The training there was really advanced. Japan helped us a lot; we really grew up in Japan.

After arriving in Japan, the three regiments reorganized into regimental combat teams. The attachment of artillery, engineer, and other units to infantry regiments had been used in Korea since the start of the war. The new formations in effect gave the regimental commanders a mini-division.

PRIVATE FIRST CLASS FLOYD MOODY.
HEAVY MORTAR COMPANY, 224TH INFANTRY REGIMENT.

We went to a place called Zama; I believe it had been a Japanese officer's training area. We only stayed there a week or so, but our C.O. took us right out on some forced marches to keep us in shape. I can remember we went to town, had our first taste of Japanese beer, and generally acted like crazy people.

After a week or so, we moved to Camp McNair up on Mount Fuji. By this time we had all of our equipment and really went to work. The whole time we were in Japan we were continuously training. We would go out four or five days at a time with the battalions and the regiment. The training was far better and tougher than in California.

At Camp Cooke the emphasis had been on physical conditioning, personal weapons, real basic stuff; we weren't well trained on the guns. Now it was more on squad training, working as a team on the mortar, we learned to use them real well. We fired them all the time, in all kinds of weather. We lived in squad tents, but spent most of the time in the field. We went up and down those hills and all around the island of Honshu. We did a lot of marching; like I said, we were out in the open a lot.

The completion of the division's training was the first priority; at the same time Hudelson and his senior commanders spent many hours planning the defense of Honshu. This was what the now departed MacArthur had wanted the Guardsmen for in the first place. While no one expected two understrength, partially trained divisions to stop the Russian army, President Truman and the Joint Chiefs felt that the presence of the Guard units would demonstrate to the Communists America's determination to defend Japan.

So while the newly formed RCTs began the prescribed Army training routine, other division units commenced on the job training. The 40th Reconnaissance Company, and the pioneer and ammunition platoons of the infantry battalions traveled all over the island photographing key bridges and tunnels to facilitate their demolition in case the Soviets invaded. They would be gone for weeks at a time, living in pup tents and eating "C" rations. The division artillery battalions also sent men out to reconnoiter the bridges and roads.[10]

CAPTAIN JAMES GRIFFITH.
COMMANDING OFFICER, "A" BATTERY, 625TH FIELD
ARTILLERY BATTALION.

> Lieutenant Bob Gregory and I took two jeeps, two trailers, and two drivers and we went from Camp Younghans down the middle of Japan to Fukushima, about two hundred miles. Our mission was reconnaissance: can we get out of there with our guns? We were out almost two weeks. We plotted every bridge and every road all the way down, and saw what the engineers would have to do to get our equipment out of there. At night we camped out alongside the road. We were out in the boonies, there was nobody out there.

> That road down the middle of Japan was about eight feet wide. And the bridges, well, we would stop our jeep and tenderly walk across because we didn't think they would hold the jeeps up. We would watch and see a truckload of wood, which is about ceiling high on a truck about seven feet wide, come down the road rocking and tilting. They would go across these bridges just a bouncing away and nobody ever went down. These bridges were over little ravines. They weren't wide like going across a river, they were fifty to a hundred feet across, but they were deep. One thing I will say, it was the most beautiful country I ever traveled through.

Griffith, who had served in the Aleutians and the Philippines during World War II, remained in the Guard upon returning from Korea. He retired as a colonel in 1974.

At the center of all this activity was Lieutenant Colonel Dallas Downs' 578th Engineer Combat Battalion. Day and night, the line companies of the 578th constructed new bridges and roads and shored up old ones all over Honshu. One company at a time went out on these week-long build and repair excursions.

MAJOR WILLIAM GEISSERT.
EXECUTIVE OFFICER, 578TH ENGINEER COMBAT
BATTALION.

> It was mainly bridge work. The so-called Japanese bridges weren't designed for tanks. A lot of the work was done just so the tanks and other heavy equipment could get to the training areas. I was never officially told to expect a Russian invasion, but it was in the back of everyone's mind. When the RCTs were formed we had to attach a company to each of the regiments, so the battalion was spread out all over Honshu. It made training very difficult.[11]

Geissert would take command of the 578th upon its return from Korea.

If the officers and men of the division had any questions as to why they were in Japan, they were quickly answered. Less than a month after the 40th arrived in Japan, they were visited by the new U.N. Commander, Lieutenant General Matthew Ridgway. Wearing his familiar rumpled fatigue cap, Ridgway spoke to a formation of 2,300 troops at Sendai.

There is eminent threat of war [in Japan]. Referring to Korea, he continued, You are here in a war. I hope you will never forget it. However good you think you are, and I know you are good, you have a long way to go.

I expect am and confident that under Major General Daniel H. Hudelson you will use every minute of the time you have. You don't know, and I don't know, when the chips will be down.[12]

CAPTAIN T. K. TURNAGE. S-3, 1ST BATTALION, 223RD INFANTRY REGIMENT.

It was an overcast day. We were in regular duty uniform, fatigues. Everybody felt it was a significant visit. Here was the Commander in Chief back from Korea to see us. We felt that our ultimate dispossession would be Korea, that we would be deployed there, and he was coming for a look see.

I recall one thing very vividly, and I thought a lot of other people had the same impression, that he was overly melodramatic, showing up there with hand grenades hanging from his suspenders. We didn't think that was necessarily appropriate for

Courtesy of T. K. Turnage

Captain T. K. Turnage, 223rd Infantry Regiment, 40th Infantry Division. Twenty-four years later Turnage would command the division.

Sendai, Japan. We weren't in a war zone and when a guy shows up in that kind of a format to talk with troops in Japan at their division headquarters, we thought it was a bit much.

I guess the big thing I recall was that first of all everybody knew Ridgway. His name was the magic word; he was the foremost personality in the Far East. The fact that he came there to talk to the troops provided significance to the prospects of the division being redeployed to Korea.

Ridgway's confidence or not, Hudelson had problems. The Army's policy of pulling troops out of the division for replacements that had started at Camp Cooke continued in Japan. Hudelson soon exploded, he had not brought his division to Japan to become Eighth Army's replacement company. Using his favorite phrase, "They can go piss on a flat rock," Hudelson defied the Army and vowed to send no more replacements to Korea.

Politics, which had played such a large part in getting the division mobilized in the first place, now came riding to the rescue. A Regular Army general who told his superiors to piss on a rock, flat or otherwise, would soon be counting parkas at the North Pole with gold oak leafs replacing his stars. But Hudelson wasn't Regular Army, and in this instance he played his cards perfectly.

Congress, already concerned that National Guardsmen were being used as replacements for Regular Army units, acted swiftly. While a Congressman from Texas or Nebraska might not care what the Army did with the 40th Infantry Division, he knew that what the Army did to the 40th it could do to the unit from said Congressman's district—and that could cost votes come next election. An order went out to the Army to terminate this practice at once.

Ridgway reassured Congress that the two divisions in Japan would no longer be tapped for replacements. Hudelson had saved his division, but in doing so had ruffled the feathers of his Army superiors. More problems between Major General Daniel H. Hudelson's 40th Infantry Division and the Regular Army soon surfaced.[13]

Boots and clothing became the next area of contention. The troops had arrived in Japan with a full TO&E issue of clothing, but the rough terrain and constant training quickly tore up boots and fatigues. The volcanic rock and ash on Mount Fuji proved extremely rough on the clothes and boots of the units training at Camp McNair.

The division experienced extreme difficulty in obtaining replacements. A time lapse of four to six weeks from requisition to issue became common. Soon men were going into the field wearing their dress shoes. That the Army could not supply sufficient clothing almost a year after the outbreak of hostilities defies explanation. Certainly the men on line in Korea came first, but after their needs were met the troops in Japan should have been next.[14]

WARRANT OFFICER (JG) JESS CARRANZA, JR. HEADQUARTERS, 160TH INFANTRY REGIMENT.

The logistical tail was not there. They sent the troops over, but no logistical support. Ridgway came into our training area and Colonel Benoit, our regimental commander, made the statement that there was a problem so far as uniforms were concerned. The logistics were not there to support the hard wear and tear on the uniforms that we took from California.

After all the training at Camp Cooke, plus all the training in Japan, the uniforms were not holding up too well. Benoit told Ridgway, "We need uniforms and we need boots." It got blown all out of proportion, of course, by the media. First thing you know here it is, equipment shortage. They can't go to war because they don't have boots; they don't have helmets.

Then Governor Warren got involved, "They're not going to send California boys into combat." He gave a regulation growl to the media; I think for publicity. He made a name for himself. He came over and visited us and had lunch with us when we were in the field. We had stew and it was raining so hard you had to eat real fast in order to keep your tray from filling up with water.

My boss, Colonel Benoit, he was a tough guy. He said, "He can come and join us, but we're not going to have anything special for him." We treated all the VIPs that way, we made no special preparations. The Governor was invited to come and eat lunch out of a mess kit. If the regimental C.O. was eating out of one, why not the Governor? It was raining cats and dogs, whether he caught cold, I really don't know.

Commissioned in Korea, Carranza remained in the Guard, eventually commanding the 3rd Battalion, 160th Infantry. Transferring to the Army Reserve, he became a brigade commander before retiring as a colonel. Active in the Retired Officers Association, Carranza spends much of his time assisting veterans and their dependents.

Warren, a veteran of World War I, tried to visit all of the division units. As with the 160th, he went into the field and ate with the men. At one of these field meals he asked a jeep driver what part of California he hailed from. "Ahm from Texas, suh," the soldier replied.[15]

As Hudelson fought his battles with the Army establishment, training continued. Once again, as at Camp Cooke, the big problem was lack of room. The division artillery and armored units were especially cramped for space in the small Japanese training areas.

CAPTAIN JAMES GRIFFITH.
COMMANDING OFFICER, "A" BATTERY, 625TH FIELD ARTILLERY BATTALION.

We didn't take the guns to Japan; we took over the equipment of the division that had been there. One of my people had been in ordnance as an artillery repairman. When we got over there he took the weapons we got and overhauled them completely. We were forbidden to do this, but we did it anyway. Every one of my weapons was perfect, perfect and beautiful. Six guns and every one was spit polished.

Japan was not really that satisfactory as far as artillery was concerned. At our firing area at Camp Younghans, we had a postage-stamp to shoot on; the impact area was only about 3,000 yards out, which is pretty close. There just wasn't room to do more, but we did pretty good.

As a battery commander my main concern was training the gun crews and gearing up for the Army battery test. At the time I took over and became the battery commander I had a lot to learn. I had learned artillery from a battery commander's viewpoint. Now I had to relearn it as a forward observer, which is a little different. I had some pretty good gun sighters in the battery. Another thing, we created section six which was the dumbbells, I gave that to one of my best gun sergeants and by the time he got through with them they were the best crew in the bunch.

CORPORAL ROLFE GLASHAN.
TANK COMPANY, 160TH INFANTRY REGIMENT.

Our regiment went up to Camp Haugen in Northern Honshu, near the town of Hachinohe. Our quarters were in large barracks much nicer than at Camp Cooke. We stayed at Haugen about three months; it was a terrible place for tanks, no room at all. We couldn't fire the 76mm gun at all, just the machine guns. We still had some of the tanks with us from the armory back in Lancaster. In fact, we took them all the way to Korea.

Then we went down to Camp McNair. At McNair we finally got to fire the main gun, but not very much. They needed the ammo in Korea and the shells were expensive. The Japanese would follow behind us and pick up the brass shell casings. They'd make ash trays and other things out of them and sell them back to the GIs.

Being the tank company, we were the oddballs of the regiment. We would go out and play aggressor for the infantry, that was our main job. I was underage when I first joined the Guard, many of us were. When we got to Haugen, I was still seventeen years old, a gunner on a tank. It was all a big adventure to me.

Commissioned in 1956, Glashan served a four year tour with the National Guard Bureau in Washington, before retiring in 1986 as a brigadier general.

SERGEANT GEORGE NITIS.
"C" COMPANY, 140TH TANK BATTALION.

The tanks were special troops. We had the M4A3E8, the "easy eight" with the 76mm gun. Because they didn't have a camp set up for us when we first got to Japan, we went to Camp McGill and took over a Navy installation. From there we went to Camp McNair up on Mount Fuji. We didn't train too hard. One of those 76mm shells cost $475, and that was a lot of money in those days. You're not going to keep putting those shells in the breach of a "76" and keep firing all day; you're talking taxpayer's money going down the drain.

The tank training area was not real good. There were only a few trees left in the area and if we harmed them in any way with our tanks the U.S. Government had to pay Japan for that tree, $100 or $150 or whatever it cost at that time. We were told we were there as occupation troops and to defend Japan.

CORPORAL BUDDY HALL.
SERVICE BATTERY, 981ST FIELD ARTILLERY BATTALION.

We went by train up to a place called Camp Younghans, right out of Jimnachi; it was a big town, 5,000 people or so, about thirty-five or forty miles from Sendai. It's where the artillery ranges were. They rotated the other three artillery battalions through, but we stayed there because we were the 155mm battalion, the big gun outfit.

We fired a lot, an awful lot. We also did night firing which is something to see for the first time. It was much better training than Camp Cooke. We figured we'd be going to Korea and we learned our jobs well. If you don't learn your job well, you're in trouble.

The engineers built their bridges, the artillerymen fired their guns and the tankers rode their tanks. For the infantrymen of the three RCTs none of it mattered, they just kept marching.

FIRST LIEUTENANT DONALD McCLANAHAN. COMMANDING OFFICER, HEADQUARTERS COMPANY, 1ST BATTALION, 223RD INFANTRY REGIMENT.

In Japan, the speed marches continued. When we first got there, the biggest shock was the concrete cisterns used to hold the human waste that the Japanese used for fertilizer on their fields. The stench from these cisterns was just fantastic, particularly to our untrained noses.

Captain Williamson, the weapons company C.O., especially couldn't stand the smell. So as we marched, the battalion C.O., Major Hervey, set up a system where someone would signal him when Williamson was next to a cistern. Hervey would then call a break. I remember Captain Williamson telling Hervey after a march, "You just won't believe it, but every time we took a break I was in front of one of those cisterns." He was looking pretty green.

Our main field training area was about twenty miles from Schimmelpfennig, a place called Ojo-Ji-Hara. This field training area was adequate for battalion training. We had RCT exercises out there, but my feeling is that it was probably a pretty limited area for an RCT. It rained a lot of the time, a lot of mud. It was very realistic and excellent training for what finally happened in Korea.

We trained very hard. Hudelson pushed the division very, very hard. In fact, I remember we even trained on the 4th of July. One day we did get off was California Admission Day. Imagine being on Federal duty and celebrating California Admission Day! By the time the division was committed to Korea, I thought we were in relatively good shape. We had trained for a long time.

In August the division participated in amphibious exercises. After instruction by Marine Corps NCOs on the technique of scrambling up and down landing nets the troops once again boarded Navy transports. Rough water and several accidents marred the operation, but the landing of nearly 15,000 men at Chigaski Beach was deemed a success.

PRIVATE FIRST CLASS FLOYD MOODY.
HEAVY MORTAR COMPANY, 224TH INFANTRY REGIMENT.

It was tough. We had to go out in the field somewhere and learn how to climb up and down these big wooden towers that had these cargo nets strung over them. You first practiced without any equipment on your back, and with the instructor (I think he was either Regular Army or Marine Corps) hollering at you the whole time. "Use your legs, not your arms, use your legs, not your arms." You'd go up and down this damn thing a few times and then put on your pack and helmet, grab your M-1, and climb up and down the damn thing some more. It was hard work.

I can't remember too much about how we got out and on to the boat. I can remember going over the side. They called your number or your squad number or whatever it was and over you went. The ship seemed to be steady, but the landing craft was bouncing all over. You kept stepping on the next guy and everybody was screaming at everybody else. As I came down the net the landing craft was just at the right spot and I didn't have any problems.

We played infantry that day. We didn't take our mortars with us. Getting onto the beach you're running through the water, the sand is coming into your boots, and you're thinking this is one hell of a job, running through this Goddamn sand with this damn pack on your back, and this M-1 in your hand and getting yelled at, at the same time. It was a tough job and you can imagine how difficult it would be if someone was shooting at you.

I know we had one guy fall in, one of our commo guys. The way I heard the story he was getting off his landing craft and something was wrong with the ramp or something and he had to go over the side. He dropped his M-1 in the water and had to go diving for it; he came up with it too. At one of our reunions we gave him a rusty rifle award.

CORPORAL FRANK SARIÑANA.
"B" BATTERY, 980TH FIELD ARTILLERY BATTALION.

It was very interesting. We went out on this amphibious vessel, and then we transferred to a large landing craft and went back in. We took the guns and everything with us. We did a lot of work on the guns and trucks getting them ready. We had the guns hooked up to the trucks so when we landed we were ready to take off.

It was a very rough landing, real bad. After we landed, one of the landing craft turned over on the way back to the big ship. Some of the sailors from the other craft jumped in and tried to save the men, but two of them drowned. We saw it all from shore. We couldn't go back to the ship, so we had to drive around to a Navy base. We hadn't had dinner, so they fed us. It was the best food we ever got.

After the amphibious exercise the Air Force visited the division. The men now received training in air assault techniques and learned the intricacies of loading and unloading the C-119 Flying Boxcar. By September 1, 1951, one year after their mobilization, the 40th Infantry Division had completed its twenty-eight week training and a lot more. The Army classified the division combat ready.[16]

The next blow to hit the division came not from the Regular Army, but from Mother Nature, and it was one to remember.

SERGEANT FIRST CLASS CLAUDE ALLISON. MEDICAL COMPANY, 160TH INFANTRY REGIMENT.

After we made the amphibious landing the regiment moved to Camp McNair, about two thousand feet up Mount Fuji on the inland side. We lived in eight man squad tents. The training was tougher at McNair because of the weather. It rained like crazy up there.

On October 15th we were just getting up; it must have been 5:30 or 6:00, when a typhoon hit. Typhoon Ruth. No one had warned us and we were totally unprepared. It was blowing like crazy and I thought I'd better get out of here because this tent is going to blow away. There were eight men in the tent and we all got out and none of us got hurt. We lost some stuff; things were blowing all over for miles.

I ran over to the medical Quonset hut. There was this huge beam running down the center and the darn thing lifted up and I thought, "The roof is going to come off this building." But it didn't. The typhoon lasted a couple of hours. Some of the men from the line companies were injured and came in for treatment. It was a couple of weeks before things got back to normal.

For the past fourteen years Allison has been chairman of the Medical Company, 160th Infantry reunion committee.

CHAPTER 15

WE GO NEXT

While Congress, the Joint Chiefs of Staff, and Ridgway spent the summer of 1951 debating the future of the Guardsmen, command and staff officers of both divisions had been going to Korea to observe the fighting first hand. These visits lasted four or five days and enabled the training programs to be adjusted to reflect conditions in Korea. Then in September the duration and purpose of these visits changed.

CHIEF WARRANT OFFICER JESS CARRANZA, JR.
HEADQUARTERS, 160TH INFANTRY REGIMENT.

I went over in September of 1951, as a filler to the 19th Infantry Regiment, 24th Division. I was sent by the 40th Division. We needed somebody to infiltrate, to find out and see what was going on. So I went over as a replacement through the pipeline. When I got over there, two days after I was with the 19th, a house boy back at regimental headquarters said, "You 40th Division." By this time I had my 24th Division patches on my uniforms. But he said, "Naw, you 40th Division, you come soon." Their intelligence net was unbelievable.

Within a week of Eighth Army commander, Lieutenant General James Van Fleet, getting the word on November 20, that the Guard divisions would be joining his command, more Californians arrived in Korea. This was still a month before the 40th received their marching orders, and three weeks before the first elements of

Oklahoma's 45th Division arrived in Korea. Obviously, the impending move had been planned for some time.

Warrant Officer Carranza, continues:

> Another big element flew over before Thanksgiving. General Eaton, the ADC, led this group. It was the people who were going to sign for property and some of the training folks. We met them at tent city out of Inchon. Let them know what was going on, what was happening, what we had to do. What the plans were so far as replacement on line.

On Honshu the men of the 40th sensed what was coming. An unidentified soldier later wrote: "For a month the rumors had been coming, softly at first, but growing stronger, more persistent." An article in *Newsweek* said the 45th was in Korea. Throughout the division the word went around. "The 45th is there, we go next."[1]

CORPORAL HARRY NELSON.
"I" COMPANY, 160TH INFANTRY REGIMENT.

> We didn't know what was going to happen until we started to get new equipment. All of a sudden, around the first of October, we got new uniforms and were issued new weapons, everything was brand new. Then we knew something was up.
>
> About a week before we left for Korea we had a bad fire. I was asleep and a gong woke me up. I looked out the window and could see little sparks flying by. I remember thinking, "The Japanese must be having a celebration or something because they have these fire works going off." The fire had started in the boiler room of Headquarters Company. The firemen thought they had it out, but they didn't check the walls of the barracks for sparks, and with the wind blowing, the fire started again.
>
> I ran out wearing just my trench coat and with my boots untied. That's all I took with me. I went across the street and watched the fire. It jumped to the barracks next to Headquarters Company and took that one. Then it got the barracks in back of us, then it took two more. Before it was over, the only barracks standing was ours. All of the new equipment was destroyed and they had to issue us new equipment and weapons all over again.

Then, on Sunday morning, December 23, 1951, the orders everyone had been expecting arrived. The 40th was alerted for quick movement to Korea where they would replace the 24th Infantry Division on the central front. To facilitate the move only personal gear and weapons would be taken, everything else would be exchanged with the 24th. An advance detail of about a thousand men left for Korea right after the Christmas holiday.[2]

Sixteen months of training had ended. The armories of Southern California; Camp Cooke; Hunter Liggett; Zama; Schimmelpfennig; McNair, and all the others were behind them now. The 40th Infantry Division was going to war.

* * * * * *

The first increment—the 160th Infantry, 143rd and 625th FABs, and a battery of the 140th AAA—left Sendai on January 6, 1952. By the 28th, the bulk of the division was on line. Assigned to IX Corps and flanked on both sides by ROK divisions, the 40th assumed responsibility for a twenty-seven mile sector in the KUMSONG-CHWAPRE-RI area of the central front.[3]

FIRST SERGEANT DAVID HARRIS.
"H" COMPANY, 160TH INFANTRY REGIMENT.

When they broke up the 40th Division Ranger Company in Japan, my C.O., Captain Rudolph Jones, went to something called air transportability. I went with him as operations sergeant. We taught air transportability technique to the units in Japan.

The 40th was still training in Japan at that time. Then they got their orders to go to Korea. I knew they were going, rumors were flying all over the place and that's the time I volunteered to go back to the 40th Division.

I couldn't have been with the outfit more than two weeks before we shipped out. They moved us down to Yokohama and we loaded up. I do remember this, it was about the 1st or 2nd of January and the snow was coming down all over the docks. I mean it was really cold. We loaded aboard the vessel and got off at Inchon, and from there they loaded us on trains to go up towards the front. It was cold, mucky, dirty, but what really impressed me was the mountains. I'd never seen such mountains.

SECOND LIEUTENANT DONN STAFFORD.
"B" COMPANY, 578TH ENGINEER COMBAT BATTALION.

When we were alerted to go to Korea it was decided we weren't going to need the bridge platoon so I was transferred to Baker Company as a line platoon leader. I was in the advance party for my company and left without really knowing my platoon sergeant and men. I don't remember the date; it was right after New Years and we still had hangovers. They flew us over and then trucked us to the front.

I went out with the engineers from the 24th, seeing the whole area we were responsible for and what they were working at which was mainly rebuilding roads through the rice paddies. In about three weeks my company showed up and we started in. We blew up tons of demolition breaking up rocks. We had Korean laborers who then put the rocks into the roadbed. We were trying to build these roads up so that we had some kind of footing for the trucks in case the infantry had to get out.

In Japan we had been given a lot of brand new equipment; the equipment we got from the 24th was in terrible shape, falling apart and shot up. Our headquarters were immediately behind the infantry positions, maybe half a mile back. We could be shelled and we were shelled by enemy mortar fire. It was winter time and everybody was bunkered down. There were nighttime patrols, but the line wasn't moving. It had settled down by the time we got there.

FIRST SERGEANT ED STROM.
HEADQUARTERS COMPANY, 40TH INFANTRY DIVISION.

It was very late in the day when we landed and very cold. We had the old shoe pacs that weren't very good in really cold weather. After we got organized we got in a convoy. Most of us crawled into our sleeping bags in the back of the $2^1/_2$ ton trucks and sat on the side seats in our sleeping bags trying to keep warm.

Division headquarters was at the foot of what they called "Million Dollar Hill" at that time. We were a bunch of little nervous nellies. We were on a salient on the front. The MLR on both flanks was actually to the rear of division headquarters. There was a bulge on the MLR and the 40th was on the bulge. Everybody was a little nervous because at that time the ROK troops didn't have the best reputation for staying and hanging in, so we pretty much prepared to depart hurriedly should the situation arise.

I was responsible for four morning reports and had to keep track of over 650 men. Some of these people were at the front, some at division rear, some at Pusan, and some at other places. It was a job keeping track of everyone. I didn't see much of General Hudelson in the headquarters area. He spent a lot of time at the front.

Soon after we got to Korea, the division postal section, about eight or ten miles behind the front, lost seven men killed in a strafing run by Marine Corsairs [A Navy and Marine Corps fighter plane used in a ground support role in Korea]. The Marines didn't know where they were apparently. A couple of Air Force colonels and Marine Corps officers came to see General Hudelson and to apologize and they weren't really very welcome.

Radio Peking broadcast that the newly arrived 40th was composed of "convicted felons and murderers" and that the 40th "has been trained in torture and murder and that a killer division had been formed." That last line must have brought a smile to the face of General Hudelson.[4]

After a few days in the rear area the infantrymen of the 160th Infantry went on line replacing the 19th Infantry Regiment. Nothing in their long months of training had prepared the Guardsmen for what they found.

CORPORAL DAVID PRESSEY.
"F" COMPANY, 160TH INFANTRY REGIMENT.

We were trucked up a valley through pine forests and snow covered hills until all visible human activity disappeared. The trucks stopped at the cul-de-sac of the valley and we began the approach march to the front. Off in the distance I could hear the occasional chatter of an automatic weapon and the crump of artillery explosions. Then the word came back down the line: we had arrived.

Each NCO was assigned to a trench or bunker and introduced to the combat veteran he was replacing. I was assigned to the machine gun section of a platoon. I crawled into a dirty, dark, cold hole in the ground and found myself in the company of four or five men.

The filth was beyond description, and the bunker was crawling with lice. The cleanliness and order of normal military life had long vanished. One soldier spat and rolled over in his own spittle as he lay in a vile looking sleeping bag. His companions were grizzled and dirty. These men had degenerated to a primitive cave man existence.

And to top it off I was told that the machine guns were inoperable. The front had been blown off one gun while the other was so frozen nothing moved. As I looked out down the ridge leading to the Communist positions, I asked what they would do if attacked. The contemptuous answer was "Run."

To them I was a greenhorn, a dummy that needed to learn the facts of combat. As a trained soldier I began to clean the waste and debris out of the dugout. I was derided with comments that in a few weeks I would be like everyone else. I would accept the animal-like existence and just learn to survive.[5]

Pressey later earned a MS degree from the University of Southern California, and entered the educational profession.

CORPORAL HARRY NELSON.
"I" COMPANY, 160TH INFANTRY REGIMENT.

We were in the rear a short time, maybe a few days. We didn't do anything, just sat around and waited. The thing I recall about this time is that an old friend, Frank Villarruel, stopped by. Frank and Danny Castile were the guys that had got me to join the Guard a couple of years before. In fact, his brother and I were best friends.

After we were mobilized Frank was one of the men pulled out of the unit and sent to Korea as replacements. Now Frank was a sergeant in the 19th Infantry, and going home. I later heard he had won the Bronze Star for saving his company during an ambush. That hurt, Frank was going home and we were moving on the line. I remember telling him to stop by my house.

We took over from the 19th Regiment on Hill 714. We got up there and they gave us some spikes to put underneath our boots because it was nothing but ice. There was a large rope coming down from the top of the hill we were going to occupy, and we had to pull ourselves up it for a hundred yards or more. It was quite a climb, pure ice all the way.

We got up to the top of the hill. It was cold and miserable, I don't think I was ever so miserable in my life. We were from California and not used to that cold stuff. That night the Chinese welcomed us; they hit us with a mortar barrage. A bunker about five or ten yards above mine took a hit and two guys in there were wounded. They evacuated them the next morning. One came back, the other never did return.

Credit for the first shot fired in anger by a 40th Division soldier in Korea went to SFC Gary Ducet of "B" Battery, 143rd FAB. After Ducet pulled the lanyard that sent a 105mm shell heading north, he commented to reporters, "It seemed like half the brass in Korea was watching me."[6]

And then the infantry. This somewhat dramatized account of the first kill scored by a division rifleman appeared in *Stars & Stripes*:

At 3 P.M. on a mid January day the crack of an M-1 rifle echoed through little valleys that crisscross the Korean landscape, from atop a high finger of a hill a Chinese soldier tumbled, rolling over and over, clumsily to the bottom. This first shot fired by a soldier of the Sunburst Division sounded when its first combat patrol met a small enemy group. The shot fired by Cpl. Pete Romas killed a red.

First mission of the division was delegated to the 160th Regiment "Los Angeles' Own." Company A of that unit sent out a reinforced squad to contact and harass the enemy. Led by SFC Loren Knepp, the small group wound their way about 800 meters into enemy territory when Romas developed a cramp in his leg.

They couldn't stop for one man so they left him and continued on their mission. The group had advanced a short distance and were climbing a finger of a high hill when Romas sighted an enemy patrol of about fifteen men climbing the other side of the finger.

He called to his comrades but they were out of earshot. Picking up his rifle he took careful aim at the lead man of the enemy element and fired. The man fell and rolled down the steep sides of the hill.

That shot warned other Angelenos and they took up the fight. It only lasted about 30 minutes but the enemy force was broken and forced to retreat, leaving several of their number behind.[7]

By early February all units were on line and sending patrols out both day and night. The purpose of these excursions was to maintain contact with the enemy, reconnaissance, and, if possible, to take prisoners. Ranging in size from a squad to a full company, some were successful, some not.

CORPORAL CLARK FINKS.
"L" COMPANY, 223RD INFANTRY REGIMENT.

After a couple of weeks our C.O. took most of the company out on patrol, a "reconnaissance in force." By this time I was carrying the captain's radio and was set to go out at 0500. But, I was not the only one "Gung Ho" for action. A buddy talked to our platoon leader and switched places with me, much to my chagrin. So I sat atop our hill manning my radio and watching through some very strong binoculars as our captain mis-read his map and ended up attacking an outpost of the Chinese MLR.

Only two of our men made it to the top of the hill: A Texas German known to all simply as "Otten," and a wild ass of a kid who somehow found a home in the Army at age 14. That was "MacNutt," too young to be afraid and too wild to care. He actually made it to the top twice, went down for more grenades and went back up. Like the man grabbing a buzz saw we pulled back the bloody stump and got out of there with our dead and wounded leaving behind a trail of abandoned arms and equipment. I was told that the C.O. took a round through the scrotum, and my "substitute" got badly shot up. I learned not to be so "Gung Ho" from then on.[8]

The regiments set up company-sized outposts on key hills as far as two thousands yards in front of the MLR. These outposts denied the enemy the opportunity of permanently occupying ground south of Line BILL, a line parallel to, and 1,000 to 3,000 yards in front of the MLR. Well dug in and covered by artillery and air support, these strong points also served as rallying points for patrols.

FIRST LIEUTENANT CALVIN SAMPLES.
COMMANDING OFFICER, "K" COMPANY, 224TH INFANTRY REGIMENT.

I took command of the company a few weeks before we left for Korea. I started taking them out on forced marches right away, two or three times a week. They really hadn't done as much physical training as I would have liked, but they improved immensely during the short time before we departed for Korea.

As soon as we got to Korea and up on line we went out to a company size outpost about a mile in front of the MLR. There was a granite mountain right in front of us we called Chalkface and a smaller mountain to the northwest that we could observe. While we were on this combat outpost an operation called OPERATION CLAMUP went into effect.

They brought all the trucks up to the MLR under blackout conditions, then turned them around, turned their lights on and headed south. They wanted the Chinese to think we had pulled back. We were supposed to be real quiet and get the Chinese to come right on past our outpost toward the mainline and then cut them off. But they were just as smart as we were and it didn't work. It was a complete flop.

We had an interesting few days and nights while CLAMUP was going on. We had to stay out there, right where we were, and we couldn't use the normal artillery support that was assigned to us. At times we were in hand-to-hand battle, tossing hand grenades back and forth, keeping the enemy out of our foxholes, in some instances with rifle butts, that sort of stuff.

The failure of OPERATION CLAMUP led to the decision to throw the Chinese off the small mountain northwest of Chalkface. Planned for February 18, it would be the largest division operation to date and a day the men of the 224th Infantry would never forget. "L" Company, reinforced with tanks and supported by mortar and artillery fire, made the assault.

Lieutenant Samples continues:

While I was out there on this outpost I could also look out behind this little mountain next to Chalkface where all the Chinese were coming from. Battalion, or someone, decided we had to go out and take that little mountain beside Chalkface. They got all the information from my company on where the enemy activities were generally located and what approaches looked to be the best for our attack.

When I came off the line this attack plan had been completed and my company was supposed to be the one that made the attack. But because they couldn't coordinate all the details of it in time with my unit, and since "L" Company was sitting on the MLR and easy to reach to coordinate all the details, "L" Company was assigned the attack mission and my company went into battalion reserve.

The attack went off almost as soon as we got to our rear area reserve position which was some 1,500 yards in back of the MLR. In no time at all it came over the radio that Lieutenant Inglesby had been hit. Lieutenant Inglesby was a good friend of mine, he had stood up for me at my wedding. There was some confusion because they had assigned the platoon leader's last name as the radio call sign for the platoon. We didn't know if Inglesby was hit, dead, or his whole platoon wiped out. I received orders to load up my company and that we would have to go and reinforce them. By the time we got on the way to the line of departure the attack was called off and "L" Company was coming back.

Colonel Richardson, the regimental commander, was out there with "L" Company, and his radio operator got killed right off. Richardson walked all the way up to the enemy position; he never hit the ground once, he stayed up on his feet. He got Inglesby's body and some more of them loaded on a tank and got them evacuated. He then picked up his radio operator and the radio, slung them both over his shoulder and carried them off the hill. I'd never seen a man do that, pick up another man and a radio. He had blood all over him and then he went back up the hill and helped some more men.

To this day there's still one man missing in action from that operation. I think "L" Company took more casualties than any company in the division, at least while I was there. It was a real personal thing for me because "L" Company was my old outfit. I knew everyone by their first name.

"L" Company's first sergeant, William Cathcart, of Garden Grove, California, also went up the hill that morning. For his actions he would be awarded the Distinguished Service Cross. Cathcart had also seen that Inglesby had been hit and that the platoon was pinned down.

The citation said:

Without hesitation, he rushed to the men, rallied them and personally led them toward the crest of the hill, only to be met with such a tremendous volume of fire that withdrawal was necessary to save them from annihilation.

Upon reaching the base of the slope, Sergeant Cathcart realized that several wounded men were still on the fireswept hill. Without regard for his personal safety, he traveled back up the slope directly in the face of heavy enemy fire to evacuate the men.

Six times Cathcart made his way almost to the edge of the enemy bunkers and six times returned with a wounded man.

The extraordinary heroism displayed by Sergeant Cathcart on this occasion reflects the greatest credit on himself and is in keeping with the most esteemed traditions of the military service.[9]

The company size raids by the 223rd and 224th demonstrated to the commanders of the 40th the futility of attacking the well-dug-in Chinese with infantry. For their remaining six weeks in the Kumsong area the division infantry units restricted their activities to patrolling and manning the outposts in front of the MLR.

CORPORAL HARRY NELSON.
"I" COMPANY, 160TH INFANTRY REGIMENT.

We went out our first full day on line and manned a listening post two thousand yards in front of the MLR. That's where we stayed the whole time we were in this sector. I have no idea why we were never relieved or rotated; at the time I never gave it a thought.

We took the entire 3rd Platoon, all three mortars, the heavy .30 caliber machine guns, some 57mm recoilless rifles and bazookas. By the time we got out there it was dark. They should have hit us that first night but it was kind of quiet. The outpost was on a knoll at the end of an arm coming down from the MLR. There were three fingers leading off the knoll towards the Chinese.

We set up the mortars in a little gully below a ridge. We were told to set up at the bottom of this gully, but we dug out a firing position maybe five or six feet from the top of this ridge, and it was a good thing we did because it gave us a much better angle of fire. Once we were dug in we set up our concentrations.

We were out there for quite a while, then one night they hit us really hard with mortars. They hit us all night long. There was nothing we could do with our little 60mm mortars because they were way out of range. By this time we were dug in real well and didn't have any casualties.

Then a couple of nights later, about midnight, they attacked. They hit us on our left flank and we were holding them off pretty good, then they hit us on our right flank. Mortars one and three were firing to the left and number two was firing to the right, then they came right down the center. We were shooting right in front of our positions. My tube was straight up and down.

I remember John Esposito, one of the infantrymen, kept yelling, "Give us some light, give us some light, we can't see anything." We had been given orders not to fire a flare because flares leave a trail and can be zeroed in on. But John kept calling and kept calling, "We can't see them, they're at the wire, they're at the wire!"

So I grabbed a damn flare, I didn't give a damn. I grabbed it and dropped it down the tube. When it burst, it caught them on the wire. They were just coming through and the riflemen opened up and stopped them, at least for a while.

Later that night they broke through; I have no idea what time this was. The riflemen had to leave their bunkers and fall back to a secondary position but managed to hold them there. The next day we went back to the bunkers. The Chinese had left before it got daylight. They must have been hungry, they took all the food that was in the bunkers with them. Esposito came up to me and said, "You know if you wouldn't have fired that flare they would have tore the shit out of us."

While the three infantry regiments continued to man outposts and send out patrols, division artillery and tank elements fired on suspected enemy assembly areas and targets of opportunity. With the peace talks again under way any firing other than of a defensive nature had to be cleared by higher headquarters. To the men on line it was a frustrating way to fight a war.

CORPORAL ROLFE GLASHAN.
TANK COMPANY, 160TH INFANTRY REGIMENT.

We were mainly in defensive positions. Because of the terrain there was little place for tanks on the line. We had one platoon on line, another one in a secondary position, and the balance of the unit maybe two miles back from the line. The platoons rotated every week.

The peace talks had started and we had to call back to get permission to fire unless we were fired on first. With the peace talks going on they didn't want to rock the boat. We could see the Chinese tunneling through the hills. If they could see us they would fire, otherwise it was pretty quiet.

One day, with the telescope on the tank, I could see the hole from where they were coming out of a hill. It was out there about 1,600 yards. We called back to see if we could shoot at them. We called regiment, they called division and so on. They said we could fire two rounds; it took about a half hour to get permission to fire two rounds! The first one was a little wide, but the second one I put right through the hole.

Many Guardsmen have told of the harsh discipline imposed in the South Korean Army for minor infractions. Soon after going on line one unit of the 40th observed an extreme example of this discipline.

FIRST SERGEANT ROBERT HOLTBY. "E" COMPANY, 223RD INFANTRY REGIMENT.

We set up a company size outpost about a thousand yards in front of the MLR; I think it was hill 607 or 608. During the day it was pretty quiet, but at night the Chinese were very active and we would button up and wait for them to probe our position.

Courtesy of Robert Holtby

First Sergeant Bob Holtby, "E" Company, 223rd Infantry Regiment, 40th Infantry Division (photographed as a sergeant first class), instructing on a 60mm mortar while training in Japan.

All of our supplies were brought up to us by Korean civilians called "chogie bearers." They were commanded by a South Korean captain and would bring everything up in the morning and then go back in the afternoon. At this time all of the men were given two cans of beer a day. They couldn't hoard it, but had to drink both cans the same day.

As first sergeant the beer was delivered to me, then the platoon sergeants would come over and I would distribute it. I soon noticed that one or two of the cases always seemed to be broken open and a few cans missing. It was no big deal but it meant that one or two men would be short their beer and I mentioned it to the Korean captain.

The next morning as the Koreans were bringing up our supplies we heard a shot. The ROK captain had spotted one of his men "accidentally" trip and break open a case of beer, then put a couple of cans in his jacket. The captain walked over, pulled out his .45 and killed the man on the spot! We were shocked; you don't kill a man over a couple of cans of beer. As long as we were in that position we were never short another can of beer or anything else.

The absence of enemy aircraft allowed the division to move the 140th AAA with their M-16 half-tracks on line with the infantry. Mounting four .50 caliber machine guns, the M-16s' tremendous fire power could wipe out an enemy attack in a matter of seconds.

PRIVATE FIRST CLASS KENNETH ERCKENBRACK.
"B" BATTERY, 140TH AAA (AW) BATTALION.

As an artillery mechanic it was my job to check over the machine guns and traversing mechanisms on the M-16s. We had taken over the guns from the 24th and they were in bad shape. There were two M-16s in the valley and two on a ridge to the right. I believe we were supporting the 160th Infantry at that time. One gun in the valley wouldn't traverse and several of the machine guns wouldn't fire due to improper headspacing. The tracks on the ridge also had a few guns improperly headspaced. It took a while to get everything operating.

One night it was my watch and I was sitting on the hood of our M2-A1 half-track. The hood was warm as we had to start the engine every hour to keep it from freezing. I was intently peering ahead when seemingly from nowhere a hand tapped my shoulder. I nearly jumped out of my boots. It was a medic trying to locate an infantry outfit who had some wounded to attend to. I was grateful he was a friendly; he was lucky too, as I might have shot him. I never again stood my watch sitting on the hood of a vehicle.

One day we received a free half case of beer per man. A number of us young "Patriots" decided to sit down and chug the beer and have a good time of it. To add to the fun I proposed we all toast each State that we hailed from. That done, we toasted the states we didn't come from. Empty cans were strewn about and we still had much more to go. Then an uninvited guest arrived: Chinese mortars. I swear that they knew we were too young to be drinking and decided to set things straight.

I'm very grateful to the U.S. Air Force for taking control of the skies. If we had ever encountered jet fighter planes, we wouldn't have had a chance. We never would have been able to track them with the M-16s, they were just too fast. The M-16 was protected by only a $1/4$ inch of armor and carried two, forty-five gallon fuel tanks. We would have been rendered to burned meat in no time at all.[10]

CHAPTER 16

THERE'S 500 DEAD IN THE VALLEY

The rebuilding of the ROK Army, which had started in the fall of 1951, had now progressed to the point where ROK units were taking over more of the front. In March the ROK II Corps began replacing the 40th on the MLR and on March 30, 1952, the Koreans assumed control of the Kumsong sector. The Californians now moved about thirty miles to the west where they replaced the ROK 2nd Division in the Kumhwa Valley.[1]

CAPTAIN T. K. TURNAGE.
S-3, 1ST BATTALION, 223RD INFANTRY REGIMENT.

We were replaced by the ROK Capitol and 6th Infantry Divisions. Being the S-3, I was responsible for working with my ROK counterparts for the relief of our troops and their assumption of our positions. Key personnel came early for coordination and a reconnaissance so that we could show them where to go and who was where and so forth.

We kept trying to determine from them how many vehicles were going to be involved, the road patterns and priorities, and similar details normal to this type of operation. On the appointed day we awakened to find the main body had arrived. They had walked in.

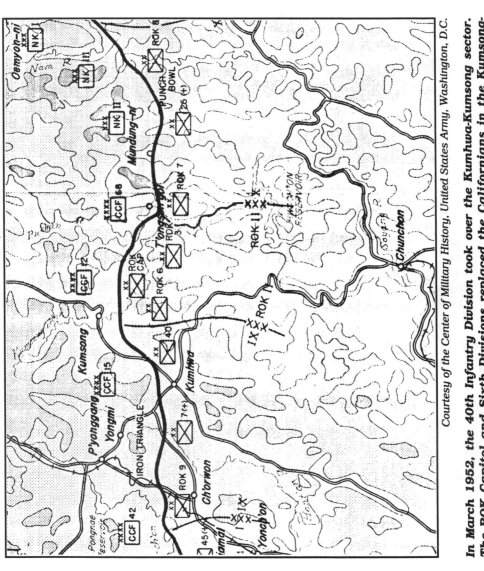

Courtesy of the Center of Military History, United States Army, Washington, D.C.

In March 1952, the 40th Infantry Division took over the Kumhwa-Kumsong sector. The ROK Capitol and Sixth Divisions replaced the Californians in the Kumsong-Chwapae-ri sector, and were then on the 40th's right flank.

There was a major enemy approach we were concerned about. It was a natural approach that came right up to the MLR. We had an attached platoon of the 140th AAA, covering it with their halftracks and quad .50 machine guns. We had our own organic .50 caliber machine guns and our .30 caliber machine guns.

We had that valley covered by something on the order of over twenty major automatic weapons. I recall when the ROKs came in and took over the area it diminished to something like three or four guns; they simply didn't have the firepower we did.

I was impressed with the professionalism of those people and their dedication. It was a tough, well disciplined division. They were just limited in the equipment they had available. They came in and relieved us, and we were sent over to the Kumhwa area.

As the men moved into their new positions several things became apparent. The recently departed ROKs had laid thousands of mines in the area and in many instances had left without leaving the plots to show the 40th where they were located. Another problem was that all of the bunkers and trenches were constructed for the smaller sized Koreans and would have to be enlarged to accommodate American troops. Also noted was that the ROKs' idea of field sanitation was a long way from U.S. Army standards.[2]

SECOND LIEUTENANT DONN STAFFORD.
"B" COMPANY, 578TH ENGINEER COMBAT BATTALION.

At the original position we just went ahead with road work that was under way by the 24th when we came in. That was our main job. Our first assignment at the new location was taking out a minefield that was near our company headquarters. It had been installed by the ROKs and was pretty tricky because they had put the minefield in at night, and the maps that the installers should have made up themselves were drawn up by their battalion headquarters. It was drawn by people who weren't even on the scene and they drew up a typical layout.

Well, the minefield we got into wasn't at all typical. My men were on their hands and knees with their bayonets looking for these mines. I'll never forget, we took it all out, then I went out to make sure it was clear. As I gingerly walked around I looked down and a trip wire was right off the toe of my boot. Here was one they had missed. So we had to go out again and make sure they got everything. I'll never forget that, I almost tripped one off after we had cleared the field.

Then we started doing a lot of minefield work that the infantry wanted done, both removing old mines and planting new minefields and trip flares out in no man's land. We had to go in front of the infantry to do this minefield work. Sometimes we were shelled by enemy mortars but it was never very accurate.

SERGEANT DAVID PRESSEY.
"F" COMPANY, 160TH INFANTRY REGIMENT.

Our second position was slightly to the rear and left of a ROK division; we could observe them from our higher hill. One day we saw a Korean soldier spread eagle on the ground and flogged. We were shocked to see our allies treat their soldiers in such a fashion.

This second position we occupied was covered with dead Chinese soldiers. They laid individually or in clumps where they had fallen. They had frozen, sometimes in grotesque positions. The bunker we occupied had been constructed so quickly that a dead Chinese soldier was half buried in the wall. His arm and hand stuck out into the bunker.

It was unpleasant, so we covered it with a poncho so we wouldn't have to look at it while we were eating. Finally one of my gunners decided to tear the bunker apart and remove the disgusting body. He climbed on the roof and began to dig in full view of the 160th Infantry, the ROKs and the Chinese. Of course this attracted the wrong kind of attention and we suffered through a fearsome artillery barrage. Pine trees came crashing down on our positions and scared us half to death as we huddled in our pits and trenches.[3]

The positions the 40th now occupied were much closer to the Chinese lines than in the Kumsong sector and the Chinese were much more aggressive. In the early hours of April 13, a small force hit the 223rd, killing ten GIs.

CORPORAL CLARK FINKS.
"L" COMPANY, 223RD INFANTRY REGIMENT.

We soldiered on the rest of the winter and then transferred down line to a position that was an island of small hills, separated from the Chinese MLR by a narrow valley. During the day we were connected by road to our MLR, but at night we buttoned up and the surrounding land belonged to the Chinese.

Due to someone's criminal oversight about 300 yards of perimeter on our back side, where the road came along a small
river to the point where our supply trucks unloaded, was
left completely open. There wasn't even a single strand of
barbed wire, and no one on watch except a single man in a
pup tent manning a telephone switchboard.

So, not too surprisingly, about 3 A.M. on a warm night in
April, the Chinese commandos came. One decapitated the
lone man on the switchboard and the rest then strolled
through the area of neatly aligned pup tents raking them
with their submachine guns. The few bunkers got grenades
tossed into them. This was the area where "M" Company,
the weapons company, had their 81mm mortars set up.

They had a huge pile of ammo neatly stacked out in the
open, just like the troops were. The Chinese had brought
with them a five gallon can filled with explosive. (I was told
the next day that it was nitroglycerin, but can't be sure.)
Fortunately, the "potato masher" grenade that the Chinese
tied to it turned out to be a dud.

I happened to be on duty manning our company's switchboard and had just stepped out of our bunker to get a breath
of air and shake off the sleep that was sneaking up on me,
when down at the base of the hill all hell broke loose. Our
.30 cal. machine gun that was just above the mortars (protecting our back door) was just going wild! Tracers everywhere! Seems like they were the only ones able to respond
to the Chinese.

I was told there were only five of them on the raid but don't
know for sure. The next morning I had a chance to go down
to the area. I followed the bloody footprints in the soft mud
under the bridge. One of the Chinese had tried to put on a
wound dressing, but it was so blood soaked that it came off
under the bridge where I found it.

They came in fast, inflicted a lot of casualties, almost blew
up our ammo dump, and most of them got away Scot-free.
The next day it looked like the entire Army Corps of Engineers was out there laying concertina barbed wire, digging
emplacements, trenches, etc.[4]

Later that month the Chinese again hit the 223rd, this time
with an estimated battalion size attack.

Courtesy of James Griffith

Captain James Griffith, 625th FAB, 40th Infantry Division, alongside the M-40 that blew up the Chinese ammo dump.

CAPTAIN JAMES GRIFFITH.
LIAISON OFFICER, 625TH FIELD ARTILLERY BATTALION.

I stayed up every night until one o'clock in the morning; nothing happened during the day or in the early evening hours. Most everything happened between ten and one. I was in my tent and my phone rang. It was eleven o'clock or just about. It was Colonel Blakey from Blue Battalion [2/223]. His was the outpost battalion, there was a lot of ground between his and the others. He said, "I can't get through to anybody else, yours is the only line that's still in. We've had 900 rounds of mortar fire in here and I've lost a lot of men and we're pinned down and can't do anything. Can you help us?"

I said, "I'll see," and that's the last I heard from him. I lost my line to him, too. I called the 625th FDC and got a hold of Captain Baumeister who was fire direction chief that night. I said, "Baumy, did you fire final protective fires at five o'clock?" He said, "Yes, we did." I said, "Good, then you should have good registration. Will you unload on Blue Battalion?"

Now we were just talking, not giving commands. I just wanted to know if we could put in accurate enough fire to do them some good and not kill all of our people. And he said, "Our firing was great," so he fired 3,500 rounds in there. Blakey came down off the hill in the morning. He grabbed me and said, "My God, you should have seen it, you hit 'em right on the wire. There's 500 dead in the valley, every shell was put right in."

I was tickled pink because I had been scared to death. Here I called for final protective fire which means firing right into their wire. I had thought, "Oh God, if that stuff is off I'm going to wipe out the whole damn battalion." But, as it turned out, it wiped out the whole Chinese unit that was down there. We were real happy about that.

Soon after this attack the 625th helped bag some high ranking Chinese officers.

Captain Griffith continues:

One of my forward observers was in an OP up on a high hill that looked down on this round top hill about a thousand yards out. He reported to me that there was an awful lot of activity around this hill, and that he had spotted some red and blue uniforms such as Chinese generals wore.

We cut a road up to the top of this ridge so corps artillery could bring up a 155mm "Long Tom" and take this hill under direct fire. We couldn't do much damage to it with our howitzers. We started in with fuse delay and after about ten rounds all we'd done was to blow a big hole in the side of the mountain. The C.O. of the 155 battery had come up with the gun to direct things, and he said, "There's nothing there, we're just digging a hole in the mountain and wasting ammunition." I said, "Let's try a couple more and see what happens." The gun fired again and through my glasses all I could see was a big hole in the side of the mountain. The gunner let another one go, and the 155 C.O. said, "See, nothing but a big hole." And just then I saw a tiny piece of concrete wall. I said, "Wait a minute, I think we've got something."

The gunner started to put concrete piercing in there, about four or five rounds, then he said, "I'm going to put a fuse delay in there and see what happens." So he put one in there. BOOM, the whole top of the damn mountain went. We'd hit an ammo dump; stuff was flying all over. One of the things sliding down the mountain was a bathtub, so we knew general officers had been in there.

The terrain in the Kumhwa Valley while not good tank country did allow the division armor elements some room to maneuver. During April and May, the 140th Tank Battalion and the regimental tank companies raided enemy positions three and four times a week.

SERGEANT GEORGE NITIS.
"C" COMPANY, 140TH TANK BATTALION.

We flew to Korea. We were taking over the tanks from the 24th Division and leaving the M-4s in Japan so we got to fly over. The 24th had the M-46 Patton with the 90mm gun. The Chinese bunkers were really tough. Bazookas couldn't put them out, mortars couldn't, bombs couldn't. The only thing that could knock out those emplacements was a tank 90mm high velocity armor piercing shell. We did a lot of bunker busting.

It was May 22nd, my birthday. Our mission that day was to go out into this valley and harass the enemy, just fire at any bunkers or movement we observed. They told the lieutenant in charge to just go to a certain position and harass the enemy. We took eight tanks and started out in a column formation; then after we entered the valley, three quarters of a mile or so, we went into a line formation. Our tank was on the far left.

My tank commander said, "Greek, veer to the left," and boom, I hit three land mines. It blew the track off on my side and thank God it did, because we didn't go any farther that day. Later I was told the way the bogie wheels were blown in, it may have been two mines tied together; normally a mine might blow a track off, but not damage the bogies.

Meanwhile the lieutenant continued on another quarter mile or more. He overshot the mark and went out too far and they got hit by everything: Chinese mountain guns, recoilless rifles, mortars, and bazookas.

By this time we were getting hit by mortar fire too. We called for the retriever and when it showed up someone had to crawl underneath the tank and hook up the tow cables. A new replacement on the tank was supposed to do this, but he froze. He was scared. He had never seen action before, so I went. All this time we were out in the open and mortar fire was coming in. A piece of shrapnel tore up my thumb, but I got us hooked up. They gave me the Bronze Star.

When we got back we found three tanks were shot out from under us that day, some of the ones that made it through the mine field. We lost three tanks and ten men killed or captured. The lieutenant was one of those captured. I just found that out last year [1991]; for forty years I thought he was dead.

FIRST SERGEANT DAVID HARRIS. "H" COMPANY, 160TH INFANTRY REGIMENT.

My cousin, Leon Cole, was a master sergeant with the 140th Tank Battalion. Our C.O. gave me a four day leave to visit him. Things were pretty quiet just then, this was in April. I got over there and Leon says, "How would you like to go on a turkey shoot?" I said, "What's a turkey shoot?" He said, "The tanks are going out in the valley and do some shooting. You can go as a BOG gunner [machine gunner that sits next to the tank driver]." I said, "OK."

We went out that morning, got into line and started moving right up on the Chinese lines firing away. There were thirty some tanks and all firing as fast as they could. Then the Chinese rounds started coming in, mostly mortars, the big ones, about the size of a 105mm shell. Most of the tanks were buttoned up, but some of the tank commanders left their hatches open. If the Chinese had had any proximity rounds like we had it would have killed them. We were out there about two hours. We were so close you could see their guns going off. I have no idea how much .30 cal. ammo I fired, but it was a lot. That was my day off.

As the 40th moved to the Kumhwa Valley, the first Guardsmen rotated home. In April and May, the pace accelerated and by the end of June only a few of the men who had made the trip from California remained in Korea.

CORPORAL CLARK FINKS.
"L" COMPANY, 223RD INFANTRY REGIMENT.

They moved us back into a rest area and decided it was time to pay the troops. What we would do with all that G.I. scrip on the front line was anyone's guess. When I went to sign and accept my pay, the lieutenant grabbed back $5.00 saying, "And this is for the Red Cross." I immediately stopped signing my name and got in a tug-of-war with him for my $5.00. I told him no way under the sun were they going to get my money! He said it was the captain's orders and that I would have to go to him. I did, and got my $5.00 back, but put myself at the top of the captain's "little list."

He had me pulling combat patrols right up to, and including, the night before I rotated out. That last night's patrol is the one I'll always remember. We went out at sunset, got missed by a Chinese sniper in the poor light, then went up the Chinese slope to set up an ambush position. The purpose was to protect our men in the valley who were laying more barbed wire.

It was almost uneventful. We went into position about an arm's length from each other and sat there in complete silence not daring to make a sound as the Chinese were about fifty yards above us. But a big black ant, the ubiquitous insect of Korea, got into my fatigues through a small rip. The ant posed no threat, I thought, until I realized that this one had come to dine.

There I was, trying to remain silent, all the while grappling madly with this roving ant that was taking large nips out of my behind. I eventually got him, but I'm sure it was a pro-Chinese ant. I had had a lot of ants crawl over me while on my "hill," but let me get on a Chinese "hill" for just one night and whamo, I'm attacked.[5]

As the troops left, General Hudelson made it a point to speak to them. He thanked them for a job well done and urged them to remain in the National Guard when they got home. Then it was his turn. On June 2, 1952, Major General Daniel H. Hudelson turned command of the 40th Infantry Division over to Brigadier General Joseph P. Cleland, Regular Army. And like his men, Hudelson headed home.

Arriving in Los Angeles, Hudelson spoke to the press. As always, the reporters got a good story. "The Chinese will overrun the country after the peace is signed. We simply don't have the manpower to stand up to the Communist hordes, even though our equipment is the best there is."

A formal inquiry into Hudelson's statement was convened at Sixth Army Headquarters in San Francisco. Hudelson didn't back down. "I may have been in error talking—when I thought I was a civilian—but I have not changed my opinion in the slightest." Sixth Army Commander, Lieutenant General Joe Swing, gave Hudelson a slap on the wrist, an administrative reprimand that went in his permanent service record.

Back on Capitol Hill, Army Secretary Frank Pace, Jr. and Chief of Staff General Joe Collins, were explaining Hudelson's latest remarks to Congress, assuring the law makers that Hudelson's comments did not reflect the Army's view of the situation in Korea. By now both Pace and Collins must have wished they had never heard of the 40th Infantry Division, Major General Daniel Hudelson, and the phrase "a better geographical spread." On June 16, Hudelson was released from active duty. He told reporters he planned on taking a long fishing trip.[6]

Meanwhile in Korea, Cleland, a paratrooper from the 82nd Airborne, set out to change the National Guard "image" of the 40th. If he couldn't outfit the unit with parachutes he would at least mold it into something more to his liking. What better place to start than with a new name and a new division insignia. And so was born the "Ball of Fire" division. Troops tore off the old "Sunburst" and sewed on the new red and yellow "Ball of Fire" patch, or, as it was more commonly called, the "Flaming Asshole."

Word of the unauthorized change soon got back to California where under the "One in One" plan (see chapter 18) the division had started to reorganize. Someone asked Hudelson, returned from his fishing trip and now retired, if there had been any kind of "gentlemen's agreement" about the change. Retirement had obviously not mellowed Hudelson, as he replied with a loud "NO." He further observed that the "Idea for a new insignia stinks."[7]

While Hudelson sounded off and Cleland remodeled the troops, the war dragged on. In late June, the division, with the exception of the 140th Tank Battalion and Division Artillery, went into IX Corps reserve. The tankers and artillerymen were attached to the 2nd ROK Division, providing fire support for the lightly armed Koreans. Back on line in mid-October and now attached to X Corps, the division would spend the remainder of the war in the Heartbreak Ridge-Punchbowl sector of the front. In the final year of the war, thousands of men would pass through the 40th. They would arrive, do their nine to twelve months and rotate home.[8]

PRIVATE TONY DeROSA.
"C" COMPANY, 160TH INFANTRY REGIMENT.

I enlisted in May of 1952. I wasn't doing much, just knocking around, so I decided to enlist. I got sent down to Fort Jackson, South Carolina, for sixteen weeks of infantry basic. It was good tough training, all the cadre were back from Korea and they knew their stuff. I got a leave, two weeks, I recall, and then flew out to San Francisco. From there it was by boat to Camp Drake near Yokohama.

At Camp Drake we were told our assignments. I was joining the 160th Infantry Regiment, 40th Infantry Division. After four or maybe five days at Camp Drake, we went to Korea. At Chunchon I got further assigned to Company "C". By this time all the Guardsmen were gone, as far as I know. The company was 100 percent replacements. I went on line October 23rd, 1952. At this time the regiment was on Heartbreak Ridge and "C" Company was holding the highest point, right at the center of the ridge.

During the next ten days or so I went out on three patrols, two ambush and one recon, but we didn't make any contact with the Chinese. Then on the night of November 3-4 we were attacked by a battalion size force. I recall very vividly the moments prior to the first shot being fired. The sounds of bugles were blasting in a very loud manner. Moments later floodlights came on from somewhere in back of us lighting up the entire front. I'd heard about these lights from the "old timers," but it was still a shock. You could see everything and everyone as if it was daylight. I never had a chance to think what was happening, I just started firing my M-1.

The Chinese came at us in "waves." Not everyone in the first wave had a weapon. They were cutting the wire in front of our positions, so the next wave who were fully armed had direct access to our positions. At one point they broke through our line and got in the trenches near the company headquarters. Hand to hand combat ensued. Our C.O., Captain Willard J. Hardy, personally led a counter attack that drove them out of our trenches. He later was awarded the Distinguished Service Cross for his actions.

I felt I got "baptized" pretty darn quick. I knew I'd be in for a long winter, which it eventually was.[9]

DeRosa made sergeant before rotating home and becoming a New York City fire fighter.

FIRST LIEUTENANT LEO CURTIN.
COMMANDING OFFICER, "D" COMPANY, 224TH INFANTRY REGIMENT.

I had been in the Merchant Marine during World War II out in the Pacific. When the Korean War broke out I went to the Military Sea Transport Service and got a job as a second mate navigator on the U.S.N.S. *Marine Phoenix*.

We took 3,500 Marines over to Yokohama, set out a hurricane, took on more troops, then went over and made the invasion at Inchon. When MacArthur pulled the Marines off line we took them around to the East Coast of Korea and made the invasion at Wonsan. It was supposedly the most heavily mined harbor in history to that time.

I had a discharge from the Maritime Service from World War II saying I was relieved from all future consideration under the Selective Service Act of 1940. Unfortunately for me, a new Selective Service Act was passed and I was drafted on January 2, 1951. I applied for Officer Candidate School, went to Fort Benning, and got commissioned in May of 1952.

I was with the 44th Infantry Division, an Illinois National Guard outfit training at Fort Lewis, when my orders for Korea came through. They flew us over to Japan and after a little orientation sent us by ship to Inchon. This was in early January of 1953. I got assigned to "D" Company of the 224th Infantry.

All the National Guardsmen were long gone except for one guy. I don't remember his name but he had been a school teacher somewhere in Southern California. He was the battalion S-2, had a good, fairly safe job, and was probably making more in the Army than teaching school.

We were on what was called "Sandbag Castle," on a ridge line, and the Chinks were on a ridge line opposite us and connecting the two was a saddle. The ridges were only forty yards apart. We were out there for over 120 days, forty yards from the Chinese. All of the machine guns and mortars were zeroed in on this little saddle, so when they attempted to charge us, which they would do every once in a while, you could fire right on them.

I was on the frontline the day the war ended. By this time I was Company C.O. All of the companies were way understrength. I had three officers and about a hundred men. It averaged about twenty white GIs, twenty black GIs, twenty Puerto Ricans, and forty Koreans. We were living in little bunkers on the reverse side of the hill. We slept during the day as all the enemy probes occurred at night.

About three in the afternoon we got word that the cease fire would go in effect at eleven that night. Then about five o'clock, right around chow time, I got a call from battalion. They said, "We're going to have a turkey shoot tonight at 10:30 for fifteen minutes and cease fire at 10:45. Fire everything you've got." I said, "Why the hell are we doing this?" The reason I said this is that things had been very quiet for a while, and the Chinese hadn't been firing at us unless we fired at them.

I called all my officers and NCOs in and said, "Here's what we'll do. Train your mortars to hit your registered concentrations, bring all the ammo you'll need into the firing position so you won't have to go out and resupply." I told the machine gunners, "Just reach up and pull the trigger. I don't give a damn where the rounds land." So everybody did just that for fifteen minutes, and naturally as soon as we started firing they started firing right back at us. But we were really dug in and didn't lose a man.

Then it was eleven o'clock. It was one of the most eerie silences I've ever heard in my life. Complete silence. That was it. The next day we started to pull back to Line MINNE-SOTA, about two and a half miles back.

Later joining the 49th Infantry Division in Northern California, Curtin played a key role in getting a new armory constructed in San Rafael, California.

On June 30, 1954, the 40th Infantry Division reverted to California state control. Forty-two years, and several reorganizations later, the division is now the 40th Infantry Division (Mechanized), with headquarters at Los Alamitos, California.

CHAPTER 17

LATE ARRIVALS

After the 40th and 45th Divisions went on line in December 1951, and January 1952, the shipment of National Guard units to Korea rapidly decreased. The slowdown had already started in the second half of 1951. In this six month period only four non-divisional Guard outfits joined the U.N. forces on the peninsula.

The 32nd Ordnance Battalion, Headquarters and Headquarters Detachment (Illinois), arrived at Pusan July 10. What actually arrived was not a unit, but a designation. Activated August 19, 1950, the unit was redesignated as Headquarters & Headquarters Detachment 32nd Ordnance Ammunition Battalion on December 1, and sailed for Japan the following month. On July 10, 1951, the unit was broken up and its personnel transferred to other units in Japan. That same day, now but a number on a sheet of paper, the Army assigned the 32nd to the 2nd Logistical Command at Pusan, where it was reconstituted. Why the unit was broken up is unknown.[1]

Another four months passed before the 213th AAA Battalion (Pennsylvania) landed in November. Activated in August of 1950, the Easton unit trained at Camp Stewart, Georgia. Alerted for Far East duty in November 1951, they arrived at Pusan that same month, the first of only two of the forty-one mobilized 90 and 120mm AAA gun battalions to serve in Korea.

Soon after landing, two batteries, "A" and "C," were detached from the battalion and sent to Inchon where they took up positions on two small islands in the harbor. Tides in the Inchon harbor are among the highest in the world, rising and falling as much as thirty-two feet. In order to get the large landing craft transporting the guns to the islands, the move had to be made at high tide and in the dark. The batteries, comprising four guns each, left Inchon at 2230 hours New Year's Eve and by 0230, January 1, 1952, were in firing positions.

The batteries were completely isolated on these small islands. All supplies and personnel had to be brought in by landing craft and a wait of two or three days was often necessary before the tide was right for these boats to land. Emergencies were taken care of by helicopter, and the only means of communication with the mainland was by radio. The rest of the 213th remained at Pusan as part of the air defense in that area.[2]

On December 5, the 145th Field Artillery Battalion (Utah) became the third artillery battalion from the Beehive State to serve in Korea. Armed with 155mm howitzers, the 145th joined X Corps in front of the Punchbowl. The next eighteen months would see the battalion firing in support of U.N. operations in the mountainous eastern sector of Korea, including the battles for Bloody Ridge, Luke the Gooks Castle, Sniper Ridge, and Christmas Hill.

The 623rd Field Artillery Battalion (Kentucky) celebrated the Christmas season by arriving in Korea December 23, 1951. Inducted January 23, in the fourteenth increment, the 155mm gunners were the last of the eleven National Guard non-divisional artillery battalions to serve in Korea. Assigned to X Corps in the Mungdung-ni Valley, the 623rd commenced firing their eighteen howitzers at the Chinese in early January 1952.

SECOND LIEUTENANT ARTHUR KELLY.
SERVICE BATTERY, 623RD FIELD ARTILLERY BATTALION (KENTUCKY).

When we got into our position we tried to pitch our tents. That snow covered ground was frozen so hard that a pointed wooden tent stake could not be driven into the ground. We got some of the steel rods that go through the ammo boxes and used them instead. Even then it took us almost all night to get a few of those things driven into the ground where we could get a tent set up.

I was the only officer in the unit who had not been to the basic officers' course at Fort Sill. My World War II service had been with the engineers, and being the ammo officer in Service Battery I didn't need any artillery skills. I felt bad about this and asked to be transferred to a firing battery.

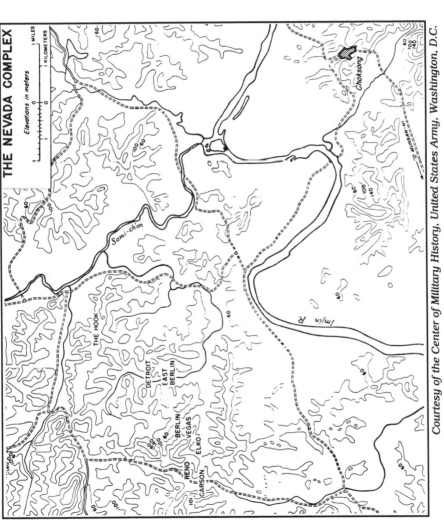

Courtesy of the Center of Military History, United States Army, Washington, D.C.

"The Hook" where Kentucky's 623rd FAB won the Navy Unit Commendation Medal supporting the 1st Marine Division.

I got assigned to "C" Battery. I knew absolutely nothing about artillery, nothing at all. So I went from one section to another and had the NCOs teach me. I started with the gun mechanics. I said, "I want you to teach me how to tear this howitzer apart." Then I went to the chief of the firing section and he taught me how to lay the battery. I went to each section until I'd learned it all. Then I went up to an observation post and learned how to adjust fire. My first mission was a combat mission.

In July, the 623rd relocated to Smoke Valley near the Punchbowl. Smoke generators operated during the day (hence the name) to hide the unit from enemy observation. Lieutenant Kelly continues:

In this location our forward observation post was near the top of a mountain peak. To get to the base of this mountain you had to walk through no-man's land for about three quarters of a mile. No-man's land was under enemy observation from their OPs which were on mountain peaks two to five thousand yards or so away. We crossed no-man's land during darkness and you had to be real careful or you could wander into enemy territory. Our observation post was manned by two men. We'd only been in this position two or three days when I heard we were having turkey for dinner that night. I didn't want to miss this so I got permission to come in early while it was still daylight.

I got down off the mountain and started walking in no-man's land down this little dirt road. I look over my shoulder and I can recognize a point out there where there's an enemy observation post, and I walk a little faster. I walk a little further and look back and see another enemy OP. I'm seeing more and more enemy territory pop up and I'm walking as fast as I can. About half-way in I say to myself, "You made a mistake, you should not have done this."

All of a sudden a machine gun opens up, I dive on the ground and just then a mortar round comes in. That damn thing hits no more than three or four feet from where I'm laying. Normally that would kill you, but there's a zone where if you're close enough the blast goes over you. I guess I was in this zone because I didn't get hit.

Needless to say my mind went to work and my heart started pumping. Being an observer I'm thinking, "Mercy, if he was that close with the first one, he'll probably hit me on top of the head with the next one." I'm waiting for the next round to hit, I know I'm going to be killed or wounded. Suddenly I realized nothing was going to happen. They must have thought they got me with the one round.

It was about two or three hundred yards to cover and I started crawling through the weeds. I wasn't making much headway, and I thought, "To hell with this." I decided to make a run for it. I jumped up and I'm zipping through this field, and I'm going ninety miles an hour. I finally get to some cover and I rest and drink some water and then walk on back to where the jeep is parked that takes the FOs back to the battery. The driver is sitting there and he looks at me and says, "Damn, Lieutenant, what happened to you?" And I said, "Nothing, let's go." We got in the jeep and headed back.[3]

Kelly, a World War II veteran remained in the Army. After commanding an artillery battalion in Vietnam he retired as a colonel in 1976.

October saw the 623rd moving again, this time to the I Corps area north of Seoul. Later that month the battalion received an urgent call for fire support from the 1st Marine Division in an area known as "The Hook." After the battle the Marines notified the 623rd that it was the best artillery support they had ever received and awarded the battalion the Navy Unit Commendation Medal. The 623rd also received the Republic of Korea Unit Citation Medal for supporting ROK divisions in the X Corps sector.[4]

1952 would see the arrival of the last four National Guard units to serve in Korea and the end of Army Guard mobilization in the United States. Landing February 17, the 32nd Quartermaster Group Headquarters and Headquarters Company (Pennsylvania) became the only National Guard quartermaster unit to serve in Korea. Activated in the seventh increment, the unit went to Fort Devens, Massachusetts, where they established a basic training school and supervised basic training for thousands of service troops. In Korea, the 32nd QM supervised over twenty companies—more than 2,500 troops—working at the largest Q.M. base depot in the Far East.[5]

The following month the 227th AAA Group Headquarters and Headquarters Battery (Florida) came ashore. Mobilized May 15, 1951, in the seventeenth increment, the 227th became the last activated Guard unit (by date) to serve in Korea. Only two more units would follow them.

MAJOR VERNON SIKES.
HEADQUARTERS, 227TH AAA GROUP (FLORIDA).

We left San Francisco in late February or early March. The sea was so rough that the port pilot could not get off the ship. He sailed to Japan with us. After seventeen days at sea we landed at Yokohama and then traveled by train to Sasebo, passing through Hiroshima which still looked devastated and desolate. We stayed at Sasebo a few days, getting winter clothing and other gear, then boarded a Japanese boat for the short trip to Korea.

Upon arriving at Pusan our unit was loaded like cattle on a large truck. It took about an hour to reach Tent City where we were bivouacked. The tents were in pretty bad shape; we had pot-bellied stoves, and froze at night.

About a week later we went by train to Taegu. We were quartered in Quonset huts about three blocks from Eighth Army headquarters. I will never forget Taegu. There were thousands of refugees from the north. At times we had to pick up starving and destitute people to clear the way for our vehicles to move about the city. It was there we had our first experience with the honey wagons which picked up human waste for fertilizing the farms.

After a couple of months we returned to Pusan to take over the air defense of that area. At this time I was the Group S-1 and later became the S-4. We had operational control of six AAA battalions at airfields in the southerly part of Korea. The battalions were located at Pusan, Taegu and Kunsan. We set up headquarters in an old school building overlooking the harbor and Pusan. During our time in Korea we never fired a shot or had a shot fired at us.

We were a southern outfit that loved grits for breakfast. Grits was not in the supply line, so we traded booze for grits that was available on supply ships in the harbor. My most vivid memory of Korea is getting diarrhea and going to an Army hospital. While I was there, train load after train load of wounded troops arrived. It was a frightening and pitiful sight to see so many seriously wounded men.

The diarrhea I acquired almost got me. I was very sick when I received my orders to return to the States. I bribed the replacement center personnel with booze to carry me aboard ship the night before we sailed. I was afraid when it was seen I couldn't walk the Army would send me to a hospital and not let me go home. After several days at sea I finally recovered and arrived at Seattle to see my wife waiting at the dock.[6]

Sikes, who had joined the Guard at the age of fourteen, commanded a number of units before being promoted to brigadier general and named assistant adjutant general of Florida in 1965.

It would be over six months before the next group of citizen soldiers saw the land of the Morning Calm. October 18, 1952, thirty-three days after climbing aboard the SS *Ballou*, in New York Harbor, the men of the 773rd AAA Gun Battalion (New York) were glad to put their feet on land anywhere, calm or not. The 773rd, headquartered in New York City, was another of the 90mm AAA battalions that comprised the majority of the non-divisional Guard units mobilized. Inducted May 1, 1951, as part of the sixteenth increment, the New Yorkers never dreamed they would see Korea.

After the usual processing it was off to Camp Stewart, where for nine long months they practiced and perfected their shooting. Then, just when they were sure they had found their home for the duration, it was back to the Bronx. There they joined four other battalions of the 16th AAA Group in providing ground-air defense for the New York-New Jersey metropolitan area. Their return to the Big Apple proved to be short lived. On August 12, they were alerted for duty in Korea, and on September 15, 1952, the *Ballou* started on its long voyage.

Among the men of the 773rd who staggered down the gang plank that fall morning at Pusan was First Lieutenant Emmett

Courtesy of Emmett Benjamin

Lieutenant Emmett Benjamin of New York's 773rd AAA learned a new meaning of the term "police brutality."

Benjamin. To this point Benjamin's military career had been varied, if not particularly notable; this trend would continue. A native
New Yorker transplanted to Florida at an early age, he had trained
in World War II as a bombardier and B-29 gunner. The war ended
before Benjamin saw combat. Returning home to Florida in 1946,
Benjamin followed the path of many returning GIs. He enrolled at
the University of Miami, got married and started a family.

Then, in 1948, Benjamin heard about a new Army program.
Short of company grade officers the Army offered Reserve commis-
sions in the combat arms to qualified ex-servicemen. He applied
and shortly thereafter Second Lieutenant Benjamin was on his way
to the AAA School, at Fort Bliss, Texas. From Bliss it was off to
Japan and the 865th AAA Automatic Weapons Battalion where he
served as a platoon leader.

In early 1950, released from active duty and home in Miami,
Benjamin joined Headquarters Battery, 712th AAA Battalion
(90mm), Florida Army National Guard. Since he was the only AAA
School trained officer in the unit, Benjamin's services were much
in demand and he bounced from one section to another, shaping
them up as he went along.

With the outbreak of war in Korea, the men of the 712th started
drilling with a new seriousness. But as the months passed and it
appeared the Army did not need the unit, training reverted to its
normal pace. By the spring of 1951, thoughts of mobilization and
Korea had long been forgotten. Then, one early April morning as he
drove to work, Benjamin heard over his car radio that the 712th
was being activated.

Going on active duty May 1, 1951, the 712th headed for Camp
Stewart where their neighbors were the New Yorkers of the 773rd.
The two units trained side by side for nine months before going to
New York to join the 16th AAA Group.

By now Benjamin had the duty he wanted. Promoted to first
lieutenant, he commanded "D" Battery with its four 90mm guns.
In August, Benjamin was suddenly transferred to 16th Group Headquarters, and after ten days transferred again to the 773rd. On
reporting to his new commander he was told, "You're now the battalion S-2, you're also the assistant S-3, and we're leaving for Korea in ten days." Benjamin, who had not a day of staff duty, got
hold of some manuals, started studying, and packed his bags.

In Korea the 773rd provided AAA defense for a new air base
under construction. Designated K-55, the base was located near
Osan where the men of Task Force Smith had first fought the North
Koreans over two years before. Three Air Force engineer aviation
battalions worked day and night on the field destined to be the

largest fighter strip in Korea. The men of the 773rd dug in, pointed their 90mm guns skyward, and waited for enemy planes.

There really wasn't much for the battalion S-2, assistant S-3 to do at K-55. Other than observing the South Korean police interrogate suspected spies (giving Benjamin a new definition to the term police brutality), things were pretty quiet. Several times he took patrols out looking for guerrillas who stuck in at night and shot up the Air Force equipment. The guerrillas melted into the civilian population and contact was never made.

The winter of 1953 finally turned to spring, and spring turned to summer, and then on July 27, 1953, it ended. The cease fire signed at Panmunjom left the war torn country still separated, almost in the same location it had been divided 37 months before. It remains so to this day.

By this time most of the Guardsmen of the 773rd were back in New York. The battalion reverted to state control in April, and the unit remaining in Korea, was redesignated as the 739th AAA. Benjamin stuck around for another three months and then in October rotated home.

He almost stayed. The Army liked him and he liked the Army. They offered him a Regular Army commission in the grade of captain, but there was a string attached. He would have to spend another six months in Korea followed by six months in Japan, before returning stateside. Benjamin thought about it long and hard, but back in Miami there was a wife and two kids waiting, and they wanted their man home.

Emmett Benjamin was not a hero and he would be the first to tell you that. He charged up no hills, wiped out no machine gun nests, suffered no wounds. He never fired a shot in anger and the only enemy he saw were prisoners. He went when he was called, did what he was told, and came home.

The years passed. Benjamin joined the VFW, the American Legion, and the AMVETS, dabbled in South Florida politics and raised a family. Then, in 1988, he read about an organization called the Korean War Veterans Association. The KWVA had been formed in 1985 with 39 charter members. Its primary purposes are three: 1. To seek out the truth about our 8,179 M.I.A. and 389 P.O.W. that didn't return from Korea. 2. To raise the awareness of the American people about the Korean War and those who served in it. 3. To raise and contribute funds for establishment of a National Memorial in Washington D.C. Emmett Benjamin had found a cause.

The KWVA was short of cash and the best remedy for that was new members, so Benjamin went to work. First he traveled the length and width of Florida; when he was done, the KWVA had three new chapters. Then someone from Colorado called and asked him how to go about setting up a chapter. He figured he was better at showing, than telling, so off he went. The result: a chapter in Colorado Springs. Then to Arizona, and another chapter formed.

Elected to the KWVA Board of Directors, Benjamin really got busy. Trips to Washington to lobby for the long awaited memorial were followed by chairing a fund raiser with six Medal of Honor recipients in attendance. Then a trip back to Korea that he describes as one of the most emotional experiences of his life, where he and other officers of the KWVA looked into the MIA/POW situation.

And then came a day that made it all worthwhile; June 14, 1992. In a moving ceremony on a hot Sunday afternoon, President George Bush broke the ground for the Korean War Memorial in Washington, D.C.

Emmett Benjamin has quietly said that he is devoting the rest of his life to the Korean War veteran. This man is truly representative of the National Guard and National Guardsmen. He has served his country, his state, and now he is serving his fellow man.

Perhaps he is a hero after all.

*   *   *   *   *   *

For every beginning an end. For every first a last. And so it came to pass on December 10, 1952, 709 days after the hard driving truckers of the 726th Transportation Truck Company first hit the frozen roads of Korea, the forty-third National Guard unit to serve in this forgotten war, landed at Inchon.

For the few, if any, National Guardsmen who remained in the 235th Field Artillery Observation Battalion (Pennsylvania), it was the last stop on an odyssey that had begun September 11, 1950, when they were inducted and shipped to Camp McCoy, Wisconsin. The 235th had barely commenced training when the Army began pulling men out of the unit and sending them to Korea as replacements.

The shortage of men and lack of equipment became so bad that two weeks after assuming command July 16, 1951, Lieutenant Colonel Salvo Rizza fired off a letter to the inspector general. Rizza requested that the unit, then in its twenty-ninth week of the training cycle, revert to the fifteenth week and start again from that point. Rizza also said that if the unit was not brought up to strength with both men and equipment it should be redesignated as a 105mm gun battalion. There is no record of the IGs response. Then, in January 1952, the unit was transferred to Fort Sill, where it began to fill up with draftees.[7]

CORPORAL MIKE PROSETTI.
"C" BATTERY, 235TH FIELD ARTILLERY OBSERVATION
BATTALION (PENNSYLVANIA).

I was drafted October 23, 1951, and sent to Fort Sill, Oklahoma, for basic. After basic I was assigned to "C" Battery, 235th Field Artillery Observation Battalion right there at Sill. When I joined the outfit the National Guardsmen were just starting to be discharged. As far as I know none of the original group went to Korea with us. I recall our first sergeant was a Guardsman, but he and a few other men had transferred in from the 187th Field Artillery Observation Battalion, a Brooklyn, New York, outfit.

We got to Korea the second week of December 1952, and stayed in the Inchon area for a while. The barracks there were built on stilts and the human waste from the latrines went right on to the ground where the Koreans scooped it up and hauled it away to use as fertilizer.

We moved to the front in a snowstorm and by the time we got there it was a blizzard. This area was about ten miles north of the 38th Parallel and called the Kumsong Bulge. It was defended by ROK troops with some American artillery support. I was computer chief for the survey section. The surveys would come in about five P.M. and I would compute them. We did all kinds of survey work like putting in OPs, checking battery centers and surveying in radar sets.

We were surveying in one of our radar sets one day. Frank Pollauf and Art Voland were working at the top of a hill taking and recording angles. The rest of us were at the bottom of the hill just joking around as there wasn't anything for us to do right then. The Chinese spotted Frank and Art and started firing mortars at them, but the rounds were going over the hill and dropping in on us. From then on just the recorder and instrument man went out to survey. The rest of us stayed at the CP.

I was picked to teach surveying to fourteen ROK soldiers for three months. The first two days were a disaster, only three of them spoke any English. On the third day I picked one of them to interpret for me and from then on things went much more smoothly. When I got home I received a letter from my interpreter. I was glad to hear they had all come through the last Chinese push safely.

I volunteered to go up to the FLASH base to put a cement floor in their bunker. This was the supply point for our OPs and about half a mile in back of the MLR. When that was done they wanted a new bunker built on the foundation of an old farm house. A couple of PFCs, Rennie and Lund, along with ten chogies (Korean laborers) helped me. The first day the chogies gave me a bad time saying, "moola moola" (I don't understand). I started cursing their ancestors in the Korean I had picked up from the ROKs I'd trained. They went hysterical with laughter wanting to know where I had learned to speak number ten (bad language).

We were working on the roof of the bunker when we started to be shelled. I leaped off the rear of the bunker along with Rennie; Lund jumped off the front, tripped, and broke his leg. Rennie and I helped him across the road to a bunker. We were sitting there waiting for the shelling to stop when one hit right in front of the bunker. The door blew in and I felt something hit my foot. When the dust settled I looked down to see what had hit me. I picked up a piece of shrapnel the size of a golf ball; it was still hot. All it did was scar my boot.

After breakfast on May 27, 1953, we were told that the Chinese had broken through and that we were pulling out. We loaded up the trucks and just when I thought we were done, the first sergeant, Joe Pineau, asked me how much beer we had. John Lang and I were in charge of the PX and beer ration and I had completely forgotten about the beer. I told him I had 250 cases, but no trucks to put them in. He pointed to two trucks and said, "Empty them, they just have extra tents in them."

The men who were at the FLASH base told me what had happened to the OPs. We had two OPs on Hill 949, five men in each one. When the word came to pull out, the men in the right flank bunker booby trapped their bunker and left. The men in the left flank bunker were radioing for help; they had taken a hit and the entrance to their bunker was blocked.

The men from the right bunker could see soldiers digging at the bunker entrance and radioed that everything was OK, ROKs were digging them out. It turned out it was Chinese wearing American helmets. A shot was heard and then four men came out with their hands up. When the truce was finally signed, these four were among the first men released.[8]

For the past fourteen years, Prosetti has been employed at the Nassau Inn, in Princeton, New Jersey.

CHAPTER 18

STACK ARMS

"On 31 December 1951, the unit was informally notified that it had amassed nine months of Class 'A' combat credit. This was worth 45 points for rotation purposes. Evidently three months of service was considered Class 'B' combat credit and was worth nine points. Nevertheless, 80 members of the unit were immediately eligible for rotation."

So wrote Major General Robert Appleby in a history of the 131st Transportation Truck Company (Pennsylvania). On February 1, 1952, exactly thirteen months to the day after their arrival, Appleby and his fellow National Guardsmen left Korea and started home.[1]*

The war in Korea would be the first time since the Civil War that large numbers of men would be discharged while fighting continued at the front. At the time of the Inchon landing in September 1950, the Army had already started to plan a rotation system. Implemented in April of 1951, the plan would rotate over 152,000 men in the next nine months. Depending on how much time remained on their enlistment, these men were sent home for discharge, or transferred to other units in the Far East or elsewhere.[2]

---

* The five National Guard truck companies that served on the Korean mainland were credited with four points per month for much of their service. Testament to how often—and how close—these "rear echelon" units were to the front.

This policy lifted morale in that it let every man know the time he would serve in Korea. However, to some extent the policy had a detrimental effect on unit performance. Understandably a soldier might be overly cautious if he thought his replacement would be waiting when he returned from a patrol. To prevent this, units would at times send "short-timers" back to the rear area when they had a week or so remaining in Korea.[3]

The rotation plan, or the "Big R" as the troops called it, had a number of clauses and conditions and went through several revisions before reaching its final form. The final plan stated that every man would serve thirty-six months in the Far East; for every month in close combat a soldier was credited with four months Far East service.

The soldiers in Korea converted the months to "points"; therefore, for a front line infantryman, nine months at the front converted to thirty-six points and you were on your way home. A man serving in a support unit would receive credit for only three, or two points, depending on how far from the front his unit operated. Troops in Japan received one point. The awarding of points was handled by GHQ in Tokyo. The first men started home April 22, 1951; ironically, that night the biggest battle of the Korean War commenced.[4]

As the war dragged on, budget and manpower requirements forced several changes in the plan. These changes, the last occurring in April of 1952, were of a minor nature redefining who was to receive three points and who would receive two. Officially, three points went to "Troops who are not often exposed to extreme combat hazards, but must live under comparatively rigorous conditions." If you weren't living rigorously, you only got two.[5]

To make the rotation plan work, an endless line of trained, qualified replacements were needed. The Army planned to use draftees as its principal source of manpower. This seemed fine until it was remembered that NCOs and officers also needed to be replaced. A man with six months training cannot replace a platoon sergeant or a company commander.

Once again the Army turned to the only source of trained personnel: the reserve components and in particular the National Guard. As the 28th and 43rd Infantry Divisions had been drained in the fall of 1950, the summer of 1951 saw the 31st (Mississippi-Alabama) and the 47th (Minnesota-North Dakota) Infantry Divisions ripped apart to supply trained men for the units of Eighth Army. The 31st, stationed at Fort Jackson, South Carolina, was hit time after time that summer.

SERGEANT GEORGE ELLIS.
"A" BATTERY, 104TH AAA (AW) BATTALION, 31ST INFANTRY DIVISION (MISSISSIPPI-ALABAMA).

On December 18th 1950, we got the word that the 31st was being mobilized and that Fort Jackson, South Carolina, would be our new home. We got there in January and lived in squad tents heated by two small coal burning stoves. With inclement weather and the smoke from the stoves it wasn't long before everybody came down with a cold or influenza. I was lucky, only had a mild case. In February almost six hundred men were hospitalized; March and April were about the same. Then we had a meningitis outbreak and got inoculated for that. Sick call was about the only reason for falling in every morning.

I was a squad leader on the 40mm guns. We were supposed to have the M-19 full tracked twin 40s, but we still had the single barreled towed gun. All of the M-19s were needed in Korea and the only time we saw one was when we were given a demonstration of its firepower. In April the fillers began to arrive, we gave them a combined basic designed for the AAA. By June they had completed the basic cycle. June also saw the first men from our unit shipped to the Far East.

My turn came in July. I wasn't surprised, in fact, I kind of looked forward to it. They took about thirty men from "A" Battery. I got a two week leave and then reported to Camp Stoneman, California, and shipped out. We landed at Sasebo and were taken by bus to Camp Drake.

Two days later we left for Inchon and a replacement depot. I was sure I'd be going to an AAA outfit; that's what I'd been training with for the past three years. Instead I got assigned to "C" Battery, 780th Field Artillery Battalion, an Army Reserve outfit from Virginia (see chapter 4).

The 780th was armed with 8 inch howitzers, four guns to each of the three firing batteries. These were the biggest artillery pieces in Korea at that time and there were only two battalions, us and the 17th FAB, that had them. I later found out that only four 8 inch artillery battalions served in Korea.

Anyway, here I was, a squad leader in a light AAA unit, assigned to the FDC of an eight inch howitzer outfit, about which I knew nothing. Lucky for me the operations sergeant, Gene Calaway, and the executive officer, Lieutenant Parsons, were patient teachers and soon I was proficient in plotting and working fire missions.

Three weeks later I got my first taste of real combat. Our battery got separated from the rest of the battalion and put in support of the Marines near the Punchbowl. The Marines were trying to take Heartbreak Ridge. Lieutenant Parsons and I were on duty in the FDC with a corporal on the radio in our $^3/_4$ ton truck. We were about seventy-five yards from the guns.

All of a sudden, about 1300, we started to get incoming fire. A 76mm shell impacted about twenty feet from our position; shrapnel tore through the tent wounding Lieutenant Parsons in the neck. A shard was sticking part way through his helmet and at first I didn't think I could get the helmet off his head. I got it off and got a compress against the wound which was bleeding pretty bad, but we were soon able to continue the mission. The shelling continued for four or five hours, and we had seven men wounded.

The next time we were shelled we lost three men killed, one of whom was Sergeant Jonnie Hutchins, who had been in "C" Battery of the 104th and was from Russelville, Alabama. I eventually became operations sergeant and was about to become chief of a gun section when my enlistment was up. I bade the 780th FAB and Korea good-bye after eight months and twenty-one days of combat.

In 1990 the Army Reserve honored the 780th by selecting it to represent all Reservists and Reserve units that served in the Korean War by a U.S. Army Reserve historical painting. As the years go by I grow more proud of my service in the National Guard and the Regular Army during the Korean War.[6]

Returning to Alabama, Ellis went to work for Reynolds Metal Company from which he retired after thirty-nine years.

Many of the Regular Army personnel assigned to Guard units had only a short time remaining on their enlistments, this meant that Guard units began losing men almost upon arriving in Korea. A sampling of excerpts from unit monthly command reports attest to the problem.

196th FAB. (TENNESSEE).

July 1951. "Replacement problems, unit now $^1/_6$ short of authorized personnel."

213th AFAB. (UTAH).

March 1951. TO&E shortages: 1 Officer, 4 WO, 65 EM.

April 1951. TO&E shortages: 4 WO, 40 EM.

987th AFAB. (OHIO).

March 1951. "A requisition was submitted to EUSAK for the personnel shortages in the battalion but no replacements were received."

June 1951. "Lost 24 EM under the Phased Release of Enlisted Reservist Plan. Replacements hard to come by."

July 1951. "The present replacement picture is not good, particularly for Officers and Warrant Officers. Shortages at the end of July were 5 Officers, 1 Warrant Officer, 46 Enlisted Men.[7]

While it did not alleviate the manpower shortage, the integration of the Army made better use of the men available. General Ridgway had advocated integration ever since he took command of Eighth Army in December 1950, but high ranking officers both in the Pentagon and in Korea fought this ground breaking move, and it was not implemented until late in 1951. It would be mid 1952 before Eighth Army completely integrated.

MAJOR VERNON SIKES.
HEADQUARTERS, 227TH AAA GROUP (FLORIDA).

The Army integrated while we were in Pusan. I was the co-ordinating and assignment officer for all the units in our command. Although a Southern born officer, I had complete confidence that integration would work and believed it would actually improve our overall operation.

We had a few problems—the black troops wanted separate quarters and all black gun crews. Our Southern colonel, Colonel Percy L. Wall, said absolutely not—that the order was to integrate, and we did. It was a wise decision to completely mix up everyone. It worked out exceptionally well and actually was very beneficial. I was pleased with the results.

In 1965, as an aide to Governor Haydon Burns, I became Florida's first Civil Rights Coordinator.[8]

FIRST LIEUTENANT JOSEPH BRACY.
COMMANDING OFFICER, 715TH TRANSPORTATION TRUCK COMPANY (DISTRICT OF COLUMBIA).

One thing I experienced over there, I saw the Army integrated while I was in Korea. I was commanding the 715th Transportation Truck Company out of Washington, D.C.

when it happened. I'd left the 726th TTC and taken over the 715th around the 1st of February 1952, when their C.O. rotated home.

I had been with the unit about a month when the integration began. There was no advance notice or fanfare. If you needed x number of truck drivers or maintenance personnel you sent a request in and they sent you a qualified replacement. I saw my unit go from 100 percent black to about 60 percent white, 40 percent black inside of four months.

In many of the units they did it overnight. You went to bed 100 percent black or white and the next day people transferred in and out, and that night your unit might be only 70 percent black or white. For some reason my outfit was integrated gradually as new people were needed. I think this was probably a better way to do it; over a few months' time.

I got a new first sergeant and a new mess sergeant, both Regular Army and both white. They were very good people, tremendously efficient. Not many people realize how vital a good mess sergeant is to a unit.

We had not one racial difficulty. The only problem I had was when the MPs were ticketing the truck drivers. The MPs were very tough on speeding; with the poor roads and the possibility of accidents this was understandable. At times the white fellows said the MPs were picking on the black drivers and wanted to protect them, and I had to calm them down. When I left in May 1952, I was the only black officer in the company. We had no problems at all.

FIRST LIEUTENANT CHARLES RICE.
EXECUTIVE OFFICER, 45TH RECONNAISSANCE COMPANY,
45TH INFANTRY DIVISION (OKLAHOMA).

In March 1952, we got seven black troops in the unit, the first time we had ever received any black troops. I got them together, and I told them—and this was kind of an awkward situation for me—I told them regardless of what they'd heard about the Oklahoma National Guard, they would be treated fairly. I put two of them in each platoon and one in headquarters.

Soon after this we made a two platoon raid across this valley about 3,000 yards in front of the MLR. The Chinese were set up along a river bed; we could see the smoke from their fires. We hit them right at dawn and caught them cooking breakfast and shot them up pretty good. Then our men crossed the river and started up a hill on the other side. I was up on an OP directing the smoke and fire from the 180th Infantry's Heavy Mortar Company.

After the raid, Ozell Johnson, one of the NCOs told me, "I started up the hill on the other side of that river. They were shooting at us and I jumped down behind a rock. Here I saw Tarvin (this was one of the black replacements). Man, he left me way behind; he was going up that hill. It shamed me into action. I went up there and I finally caught him and I said, 'Tarvin, I think this is as far as we'll go.'" The black replacements performed very well and we had no trouble at all.

As the stalemate at the front and at the peace talks continued, still more men were needed, and two more National Guard infantry divisions were mobilized. In January 1952, the 37th (Ohio) and the 44th (Illinois) became the last National Guard units activated during the Korean War. The 37th went to Fort Riley, Kansas, the 44th to Camp Cooke, and then to Fort Lewis. Both of the divisions' stated mission was to train recruits. But like the six National Guard Divisions before them, they would send thousands of men to Korea.

Another Korean War innovation, and the best morale booster the Army ever came up with, was the R & R (Rest and Recuperation) program. Each month a few men from each company or battery would be selected to spend five days in Japan. Upon arrival the lucky soldier would be paid, fed a steak dinner, and given a new uniform if needed. After being assigned a bed at an Army run hotel, or nearby military base, the soldier then hit the streets of Japan, where he would relax and partake in the local customs before returning to Korea a new man. Before the war ended, 800,000 men would make these morale boosting trips.[9]

Because of the Army's policy of replacing men individually instead of replacing entire units, another new plan affecting the National Guard emerged from the depths of the Pentagon. This was the "G3 Plan" or, as it came to be known, the "One-in-One Plan."

The plan went like this: after two years of active duty the mobilized Guardsmen would be home and once again civilians. However, their unit and colors would remain in Korea, or wherever else it happened to be stationed, continually receiving and rotating out replacements. After the unit had been under Federal control for two years, the state the unit originated from could request the Army to form a new Guard outfit bearing the same designation.

These units would be held to a strength of 50 percent officers and 25 percent enlisted personnel and have the suffix NGUS (National Guard United States) added to their designation. The men would be issued individual arms and equipment, but the new outfits would receive only a limited amount of organizational equipment.[10]

For example: in mid August of 1953, the combat veteran National Guardsmen of the 40th Infantry Division NGUS (California) spent two weeks climbing the hills of Hunter Liggett Military Reservation on the central California coast. Meanwhile, in Korea, the men of the 40th Infantry Division, who two weeks earlier had been dodging incoming artillery fire at the Punchbowl, were praying that the recently signed peace agreement would hold.

By 1954 there would be units stationed across the country and around the world, their identity separated by those four letters, NGUS. Anyone who has served a week in the Army can picture the potential problems lurking in this scheme. It would be May of 1956, almost three years after the cease fire, before the last mobilized National Guard unit returned to state control.[11]

When a man completed his Korean tour, he said good-bye to his buddies, turned in his gear and left. A few days in Japan, then home, discharged, and it was over. Some had hardly been missed. They tell of being greeted on a street corner with "Where've you been? I haven't seen you around." Other Guardsmen were more fortunate in that sometimes a large group would be discharged together and upon arriving home, particularly if they came from a small town, the men would be feted to a welcome home dinner.[12]

PRIVATE FIRST CLASS RONALD RANSOM.
"B" BATTERY, 204TH FIELD ARTILLERY BATTALION (UTAH).

I don't know how many points we got, but I was in the last damn group to rotate home; except for a few senior officers in the battalion. I was young, I was single, and they kept me right up to the bitter end.

I didn't rotate out of there until February of '52, and that was the last group. There were only a few of us left from the original group and I kept bitching, "When am I going home? When am I getting out of here?" They never did give me an answer until about two or three days before it happened. I think the first sergeant finally told me.

We didn't turn in all of our equipment; I don't think we turned in our rifles till we got to the air base at Inchon, and maybe not till we got to Japan. We were in Japan about a week and they took everything, everything we had that was not our personal property like our wallet and watch. We had to turn in our souvenirs. I had a violin I'd picked up; I used to play the violin and I wanted it bad, but they took it.

They didn't allow us to go into Tokyo or Yokohama at all. That didn't stop a lot of us because there were people there who knew where the holes in the fence were, so we were able to go in and get a beer and do a little something. We were in Japan about a week, then boarded a troop ship.

We landed in San Francisco and from there went by troop train over to Camp Stoneman on the other side of the Bay. We were there about a week, maybe less. Then they sent us to Camp Carson, Colorado. I got a thirty day leave, went home and got married. I believe there were seven of us left from "B" Battery when we reported back to Carson. By then they had decided to discharge us and that was it.

For the returning Guard officers the trip home was very simi lar to PFC Ransom's, with one notable exception. After landing at San Francisco, or Seattle, many of the company grade officers were put in charge of troop trains carrying soldiers to their separation points. The shepherding of these recently returned combat veterans was an experience never forgotten.

FIRST LIEUTENANT CARL STEVENS.
45TH INFANTRY DIVISION (OKLAHOMA).

The first night I got back in the States, I got thrown in jail. I was walking down the street in San Francisco and I was proud. I mean, here I am, I'm back in the holy land and wearing my Thunderbird. And this guy looked at it and said, "Oh, the ruptured duck," or something like that. I hit the son of a bitch and knocked him down and the Shore Patrol got me and put me in the brig.[13]

They wrote me up and turned me out the next morning and I went back to Camp Stoneman. They put me in charge of a seven car troop train going to Fort Sill, Oklahoma, full of men back from Korea, going to be discharged. I went through the train and appointed a sergeant in each car to be car commander, mainly to keep the men from jumping out the windows and tearing things up.

So they started drinking, of course, and I mean they were drunker than hoot owls. The next morning a master sergeant came through and said, "Lieutenant, we're out of whiskey, out there." I said, "You drank mine, I don't have any left." And he says, "Well, can we stop this train?" I said, "I can't stop this train unless it's an emergency."

Between the cars there was a little rope of some sort and it's a brake. Well, they must have got together and someone must have known what that was because about 1000 hours that morning, that train started screeching to a halt. Well, I started back through there and those guys had got between those cars and stopped that damn train right almost in front of the one liquor store in this little old town. They were just like ants getting off that train. They either bought or stole every bottle in that store.

Late that afternoon some of them came through. They said, "Come here, Lieutenant, we want to show you something." I said, "What in the hell have you guys done now?" They took me to the last car at the end of the train. They had tied blankets and sheets together and tied them around a ladder, and all you could see for about half a mile were blankets and sheets popping like a big shirttail back there.

They had a civilian who was actually in charge of the train; I was in charge of military personnel. When we got to Fort Sill, this civilian said to me, "Lieutenant, I've been doing this for two years, and I've never been so glad to see you bastards leave in all my life."

EPILOGUE

It ended July 27, 1953. At least the shooting stopped. The next day U.N. forces pulled back two and a half miles to Line MINNESOTA, creating the Demilitarized Zone (DMZ) separating the two Koreas. Now, over forty years later, the 2nd Infantry Division, that so many National Guard units supported in 1951, stands watch on the DMZ, waiting for the North Koreans to again invade their brothers to the south.

Was it worth the price? 54,246 American dead, 103,284 wounded, and another 8,177 still listed as missing. Did Harry Truman make the right decision when he committed American troops to that far off corner of the world in June of 1950? Today a rebuilt South Korea stands as our strongest ally in Asia, and a major trading partner. South Korea would be the only nation in the world to send a full division to Vietnam to assist the United States in the next fight to stop Communist aggression.

But again the question, was it worth the terrible price? The National Guardsmen and the men who served with Guard units in Korea, agree, almost to a man, that Truman had no choice. If we didn't stop them in Korea it would have been somewhere else. A Utah artilleryman sums it up as well as anyone.

MR. ERIC HANSEN.
204TH FIELD ARTILLERY BATTALION (UTAH).

It was the forgotten war; you never hear about it. But you remember. You remember looking through a scope and seeing the infantry trying to take a hill, and you can see men being shot and falling. And when they came back off

259

the hill for relief you could see in their eyes what they'd been through. You remember all that and you think what did we gain? Well, we didn't gain anything so to speak, but we helped the Korean people gain something, and that's what America is all about.

On the other big question of the war, Truman's firing of MacArthur, there is no such consensus. Two fine gentlemen, both veterans of two wars, living but a few miles apart in Oklahoma City, have differing points of view on the subject.

MR. WELDON JACKSON.
45TH INFANTRY DIVISION (OKLAHOMA).

Truman screwed up when he fired MacArthur. I had a lot of respect for MacArthur, and I think he was done wrong. He was an egotistical bastard, but a good man.

MR. CHARLES RICE.
45TH INFANTRY DIVISION (OKLAHOMA).

You're damn right Truman did the right thing in firing MacArthur. I think he did the right thing, I really do. I think MacArthur was arrogant, granted he was a great general, but he was so arrogant. I think he deserved to be let go, and I admire Truman for doing that.

For the men you have met in these pages much of what they endured would fade over the years; much, but not all. They would never forget their comrades, especially the ones that didn't come home.

MR. DAVID PRESSEY.
40TH INFANTRY DIVISION (CALIFORNIA).

I never again would experience the closeness and comradeship of those that endured Korea with me. I will never forget my Episcopal Chaplain, Father Crane, killed on the front line ministering to us, or Maupin, the best point man who ever went on a patrol and who died with a burp gun bullet in his throat, or Wyklanski, our faithful Polish gunner, wounded as he left the front for the safer rear areas.

For those that survived, we still share the comradeship cemented by a common fear and equal suffering. There was nothing spectacular about us except we did our duty as good soldiers without recognition or reward except from our comrades.

*   *   *   *   *   *

The four decades after Korea would see both Army and Air National Guard units mobilized many times. In fact, one or more Air Guard units were on active duty for a large part of these forty years. In most of these mobilizations, only a few units were involved and other than their families and friends, few knew that the Guard had been called up. In many instances individual Guardsmen, and at times full units would voluntarily go on active duty.

First it was Cuba where four Alabama Air Guard pilots were killed flying ground support missions for the Cuban exiles over the Bay of Pigs. Later that summer of 1961, the Soviets precipitated the Berlin crisis. Eleven Air Guard fighter squadrons (two hundred sixty planes) flew to Europe to reinforce NATO air units. On the Army side, the 32nd Infantry (Wisconsin) and the 49th Armored (Texas) Divisions, along with hundreds of smaller units, mobilized. A total of 65,000 Guardsmen went on active duty.[1]

The debate over mobilizing the National Guard during the Vietnam War made Army Chief of Staff, General Joe Collins' hesitation to mobilize Guard divisions in 1950 seem like a snap decision. The first mention of a possible Guard call-up was in a Defense Department memorandum to President John Kennedy, dated November 11, 1961. At this time, American Army troops in Vietnam numbered under a thousand men![2]

For six years the debate dragged on. Then, after the North Koreans seized the Navy intelligence ship *Pueblo*, in January 1968, the Air Force activated fourteen Air Guard units.

Later that year the Army activated a limited number of ground units. National Guard outfits from Alabama, Idaho, Illinois, Indiana, Kentucky, New Hampshire, Rhode Island and Vermont served in Vietnam. As in the Korean War eighteen years earlier Guardsmen would be pulled from their units and sent to the front as replacements. Four thousand three hundred eleven men fell into this category. The 69th Infantry Brigade, comprised mainly of Kansas Guardsmen, sent 2,397 officers and men to Vietnam. Forty of these men were killed in action.[3]

Even though they were over in a matter of hours, both the Grenada intervention in October 1983, and the overthrow of Panamanian dictator Manuel Noriega, in December 1989, saw Guard units going on active duty.

On August 2, 1990, Iraqi troops invaded the Sheikdom of Kuwait. Five days later American troops began deploying to Saudi Arabia. On that day Air Guardsmen volunteers from Mississippi's 172nd Military Airlift Group flew one of the first airlift missions into the theater of operations. Thus began OPERATION DESERT SHIELD-DESERT STORM, the largest American military operation since Vietnam. Two weeks later President George Bush authorized the call up of Guard and Reserve forces, and on August 28, the first of the 398 Army Guard units to be mobilized reported for duty.

The Allied Coalition's air war against Iraq opened on January 16, 1991. South Carolina's 169th Tactical Fighter Group and New York's 174th Tactical Fighter Group were there. In the weeks to come they would fly 3,645 missions.

When Desert Shield turned to Desert Storm, February 23, Guard artillerymen from Arkansas, Kentucky, Oklahoma, Tennessee, and West Virginia fired in support of Coalition forces. While some of these outfits had traded their howitzers in for rockets, many of the unit designations remained the same as forty years before.

Once again the 196th from Tennessee (now a brigade), the 158th from Oklahoma, and Kentucky's 623rd were in action. Meanwhile, Guard engineers breached Iraqi minefields, and Guard support units kept the supplies flowing, and cared for the wounded. A total of 37,848 Army Guard men and women served on the Arabian Peninsula.[4]

When eighteen American servicemen were killed, and nearly a hundred wounded in Mogadishu, Somalia, October 3–5, 1993, the Guard was there. Led by Major Sylvia J. Johnson, 118th Aeromedical Evacuation Squadron, Tennessee Air Guard, Guard men and women from six states treated the wounded. Operating as a battalion aid station the unit continued their life saving work while mortar fire fell within twenty-five meters of their position.[5]

Bosnia-Herzegovina 1993, and again the National Guard is called upon. As of February 1, 1994, Air National Guard and Air Force Reserve volunteers had airlifted more than 34,423 tons of supplies, food and equipment into Sarajevo, and air-dropped another 15,040 tons into Eastern Bosnia-Herzegovina. This humanitarian mission is not without its perils. On January 19, 1994, Kentucky Guardsmen from the 123rd Airlift Wing came under mortar fire while unloading a C-130 cargo plane on a Sarajevo runway. No one was hit, but the plane was holed in four places.[6]

1993 also saw Maryland's 175th Fighter Group, Iowa's 185th Fighter Group and Idaho's 124th Fighter Group in action. The 175th took part in OPERATION DENY FLIGHT, prohibiting flights by belligerent forces over Bosnia-Herzegovina. While the 185th took part in OPERATION PROVIDE COMFORT, providing protection for the Kurds in Northern Iraq, the 124th flew 636 air combat missions as part of OPERATION SOUTHERN WATCH, enforcing the Iraq no fly zone. On two occasions Iraqi radar locked on to Guard pilots who quickly responded with HARM anti-radar missiles, and Saddam Hussein was short two radar sites.[7]

Many centuries ago the Greek philosopher Plato wrote that "Only the dead have seen the end of war." The ensuing years have proved Plato correct. Yet, as we near the end of the twentieth century the present administration is once more cutting our nation's military forces to the bone.

The Regular Army is being scaled back to ten divisions, the same number as at the outbreak of the Korean War. Plans call for an Army National Guard of 367,000 men and women by 1999, about forty thousand more than in the summer of 1950. At present the National Guard is an integral part of the Total Force concept, but even now some in Washington and the Pentagon are calling for drastic reductions in the Guard, including the breakup of all National Guard divisions.

When the call comes again, as it surely will, how will the Guard stand?

Will it be as in the summer of 1950, with units at half strength, training with obsolete, worn out equipment? Will Guardsmen be sent into combat without unit training as was Pennsylvania's 176th AFAB? Will Guardsmen land in freezing temperatures wearing summer uniforms as did Alabama's 107th TTC in January 1951?

Or will the Guard be "Healthy and strong, ready to take its place in the first line of defense in the first weeks of an emergency," as General George Marshall said back in 1945.

I wonder.

APPENDIX A

One of the first mobilization orders. Note that it supersedes an earlier order and that the listed units are reporting for duty on four different dates. The order shows two units reporting for duty, but seven days after the date of the order. However other documents show that the 1437th Engineer Treadway Bridge Company was first alerted on 22 July 1950, and the 216th AAA Group Headquarters and Headquarters Battery on the 23rd. It was obviously a time of confusion. Of the fifteen units on this order five would serve in Korea (see Appendix B).
Courtesy of Ernest J. Perron.

GO 119

General Orders
Number   119

HEADQUARTERS FIFTH ARMY
Chicago 15, Illinois, *7 August 1950*

INDUCTION OF NATIONAL GUARD UNITS

1. General Orders Number 113, this headquarters, 28 July 1950, is rescinded.

2. By direction of the President and the Secretary of Defense under authority conferred by the Selective Service Extension Act of 1950 *(Public Law 599, 81 Congress)*, the following units and members thereof of the National Guard of the United States are ordered into the active military service of the United States to serve therein for a period of twenty-one *(21)* consecutive months, or such other period as may be authorized by law, unless sooner relieved. Locations and dates of entries into active military service are listed below.

UNIT	T/O&E NUMBER	DATE	HOME STATION	EFFECTIVE DATE
216th AAA Group, Headquarters & Headquarters Battery	44-12	8 Oct 48	St Paul, Minnesota	14 August 1950
1437th Engineer Treadway Bridge Company	5-627	7 Sep 45	Sault Ste Marie, Michigan	14 August 1950
32d Ordnance Battalion, Headquarters & Headquarters Detachment	9-76	30 Nov 48	Springfield, Illinois	19 August 1950
*1279th Engineer Combat Battalion	5-35	15 Sep 48	**Detroit, Michigan	19 August 1950
107th Ordnance Medium Maintenance Company	9-7	13 Sep 48	Pontiac, Michigan	19 August 1950
1438th Engineer Treadway Bridge Company	5-627	7 Sep 45	Rolla, Missouri	19 August 1950
106th Ordnance Heavy Maintenance Company	9-9	17 Mar 49	Springfield Missouri	19 August 1950

GO 119

2

UNIT	T/O&E NUMBER	DATE	HOME STATION	EFFECTIVE DATE
300th Armored Field Artillery Battalion	6-165N	5 Aug 48	**Sheridan, Wyoming	19 August 1950
196th Infantry	7-11N	21 Apr 48	**Aberdeen, South Dakota	1 September 1950
147th Field Artillery Battalion	6-25N	21 Apr 48	**Sioux Falls, South Dakota	1 September 1950
200th Engineer Combat Company	5-17N	4 Feb 48	Custer, South Dakota	1 September 1950
193d Heavy Tank Battalion	17-35N-20	Jul 50	**Colorado Springs, Colorado	3 September
915th Medical Ambulance Company	8-317-20	25 May 50	Indianapolis, Indiana	12 September 1950
231st Engineer Combat Battalion (Army)	5-35	15 Sep 48	**Grand Forks, North Dakota	3 September 1950
109th Engineer Combat Battalion	5-35	15 Sep 48	**Rapid City, South Dakota	3 September 1950

*Negro personnel

**Indicates home station of unit headquarters. The home station of each subordinate company size unit is its unit rendezvous.

2. All persons so ordered into the active military service of the United States are, from the effective dates indicated above, relieved from duty with National Guard of their respective states, territories, and the District of Columbia, so long as they shall remain in the active military service of the United States, and during such time shall be subject to such laws and regulations for the government of the Army of the United States as may be applicable to members of the Army whose permanent retention in the active military service is not contemplated by law.

3

4. By direction of the President each officer and warrant officer of the National Guard, appointed in the National Guard, who shall have been federally recognized or examined and found qualified for Federal Recognition by a duly constituted board of officers, and shall have been assigned to a position vacancy for a commissioned officer or warrant officer in a unit ordered to active duty under this order prior to the effective date of entry into the active military service, who does not hold an appointment in the National Guard of the United States in the same grade and arm or service in which he has been most recently examined and found qualified for Federal Recognition by a duly constituted board of officers, is tendered appointment in the National Guard of the United States in same grade and arm or service in which he shall have been most recently federally recognized or examined and found qualified for Federal Recognition. Each person so appointed will forward oath of office with individual report prescribed by paragraph 10, Army Regulations 130-10. Service numbers will be assigned by the Adjutant General upon receipt of report of entry into the active military service of the United States; except that if the individual is a former officer of the Army, the service number previously assigned to him will be used and entered on all records.

5. Department of the Army will issue reorganization directives for units concerned at earliest practicable dates after arrival at training station.

6. Individual and organizational supplies and equipment now on hand will accompany the units upon entry into the active military service.

7. The provisions of Army Regulations 130-10, as amended, and current directives in connection therewith, will be complied with.

BY COMMAND OF LIEUTENANT GENERAL CHAMPERLIN:

OFFICIAL:

R. L. ANDERSON
Colonel, AGD
Adjutant General

H. E. EASTWOOD
Brigadier General, GSC
Chief of Staff

APPENDIX B

ARMY NATIONAL GUARD UNITS THAT SERVED IN KOREA 1950–1953.

IN NUMERICAL ORDER	STATE	INCREMENT MOBILIZED	KOREAN SERVICE FROM
30th Ordnance Bn. Hq & Hq Det.	NJ	1	21 Mar 51
32nd Ordnance Bn. Hq & Hq Det.	IL	3	10 Jul 51
32nd QM Group Hq & Hq Company	PA	7	17 Feb 52
40th Infantry Division	CA	4	11 Jan 52*
45th Infantry Division	OK	4	5 Dec 51*
101st Signal Battalion	NY	3	7 Apr 51
106th Ordnance (H) Maint. Company	MO	3	26 Mar 51
107th Ordnance (M) Maint. Company	MI	3	9 Mar 51
107th Transportation Truck Co.	AL	3	8 Jan 51
116th Engineer Combat Battalion	ID	5	28 Feb 51
121st Transportation Truck Co.	PA	3	4 Jan 51
131st Transportation Truck Co.	PA	3	1 Jan 51
138th Engineer Pontoon Bridge Co.	MS	1	16 Feb 51
145th Field Artillery Battalion	UT	5	5 Dec 51
151st Engineer Combat Battalion	AL	2	9 Feb 51
167th Trans Truck Bn Hq & Hq Det.	PA	3	1 Jan 51
176th Armored Field Artillery Bn.	PA	3	17 Feb 51
194th Engineer Combat Battalion	TN	3	16 Feb 51
196th Field Artillery Battalion	TN	3	9 Feb 51

204th Field Artillery Battalion	UT	3	2 Feb 51
213th AAA Gun Battalion	PA	2	11 Nov 51
213th Armored Field Artillery Bn.	UT	3	16 Feb 51
217th Medical Collecting Company	AR	3	4 May 51
227th AAA Group Hq & Hq Battery	FL	17	21 Mar 52
231st Trans Truck Bn Hq & Hq Det.	MD	3	1 Jan 51
235th FA Observation Battalion	PA	7	10 Dec 52
252nd Transportation Truck Co.	AL	3	1 Jan 51
300th Armored Field Artillery Bn.	WY	3	16 Feb 51
378th Engineer Combat Battalion	NC	1	24 Feb 51
568th Ordnance (H) Maint. Company	TN	1	19 Mar 51
623rd Field Artillery Battalion	KY	4	23 Dec 51
715th Transportation Truck Co.	DC	1	5 Jan 51
726th Transportation Truck Co.	MD	3	31 Dec 50
773rd AAA Gun Battalion	NY	16	18 Oct 52
936th Field Artillery Battalion	AR	3	10 Feb 51
937th Field Artillery Battalion	AR	3	10 Feb 51
955th Field Artillery Battalion	NY	3	2 Feb 51
987th Armored Field Artillery Bn.	OH	1	16 Feb 51
1092nd Engineer Combat Battalion	WV	3	3 Mar 51
1169th Engineer Group Hq & Hq Co.	AL	1	28 Feb 51
1343rd Engineer Combat Battalion	AL	2	9 Feb 51
1437th Engineer Treadway Bridge Co.	MI	1	2 Mar 51
2998th Engineer Treadway Bridge Co.	TN	3	27 Feb 51

* First division elements credited with Korean service.

All dates for Korean service are from Department of the Army, General Order No. 80. 22 November 1954.

ABBREVIATIONS

AAA	Antiaircraft Artillery
ADC	Assistant Division Commander
AFAB	Armored Field Artillery Battalion
AIT	Advanced Individual Training
AW	Automatic Weapons
AWOL	Absent without Leave
BAR	Browning Automatic Rifle
BSMO	Break Station-March Order
CCF	Chinese Communist Forces
C.O.	Commanding Officer
CONARC	Continental Army Command
COS	Chief of Staff
CP	Command Post
CSMO	Close Station-March Order
DA	Detached Assignment
DMZ	Demilitarized Zone
EUSAK	Eighth United States Army Korea
FAB	Field Artillery Battalion
FDC	Fire Direction Center
FECOM	Far East Command
FO	Forward Observer
GHQ	General Headquarters
H&I	Harassing & Interdiction
JCS	Joint Chiefs of Staff
KMAG	Korean Military Advisory Group
MLR	Main Line of Resistance
MP	Military Police

MSR	Main Supply Road
NATO	North Atlantic Treaty Organization
NCO	Non-Commissioned Officer
NKPA	North Korean People's Army
OD	Officer of the Day
OP	Outpost
PX	Post Exchange
RA	Regular Army
RCT	Regimental Combat Team
ROK	Republic of Korea
R&R	Rest & Recuperation
SP	Self Propelled
TDY	Temporary Duty
U.N.	United Nations
X.O.	Executive Officer

NOTES

INTRODUCTION

1. Clay Blair, *The Forgotten War* (New York: Times Books, a division of Random House, Inc. 1987), pp. 84, 471, 567, hereafter *The Forgotten War*.
2. Ibid., pp. 78, 124, 522–523.
3. David Rees, *Korea: The Limited War* (New York: St. Martins Press, 1964), p. 223.

CHAPTER 1: CALL TO ARMS

1. Washington time is thirteen hours behind Korean time. All ranks, assignments, and units are as at time of narrative.
2. *The Forgotten War*, pp. 74–77.
3. Ibid., pp. 77–85.
4. William Day IV, *The Running Wounded* (Riverton, Wyo.: Big Bend Press, 1990), p. 6, hereafter *The Running Wounded*.
5. *National Guardsman* Magazine, Washington, D.C. November 1950, inside front cover, pp. 6, 28–29, inside back cover; December 1950, p. 5.; January 1951, p. 2.; February 1951, p. 6.; April 1951, p. 2.; June 1952, p. 2.; December 1953, p. 4, hereafter *National Guardsman* Magazine.
6. Jim Dan Hill, *The Minute Man in Peace and War* (Harrisburg, Pa.: The Stackpole Company, 1964), pp. 373– 380, hereafter *Minute Man*.
7. *National Guardsman* Magazine, December 1950, p.14.; *The Forgotten War*, p. 391.
8. *National Guardsman* Magazine, April 1951, p. 16.; August 1951, p. 5; *The Forgotten War*, pp. 122–123.
9. Induction & Release of Army National Guard Units 1950–1956. (Washington, D.C.: National Guard Bureau, Department of the Army, hereafter Induction & Release; John Mahon, *History of the Militia and the National Guard* (New York: Macmillan Publishing, a Division of Macmillan, 1983), p. 209; *National Guardsman* Magazine, March 1952, pp. 2–6.
10. Induction & Release.
11. James F. Schnabel, *Policy and Direction: The First Year* (Washington, D.C.: Office of the Chief of Military History, United States Army, 1972), pp. 122–123, hereafter *Policy and Direction*; *The Forgotten War*, p. 78.
12. *Policy and Direction*, pp. 122–123.
13. Ibid., pp. 123–125.

14. *The Pennsylvania Guardsman*, Harrisburg, Pa.: Fall issue, 1950, p. 2, hereafter *Pennsylvania Guardsman*.
15. Letter, Cacciola to author, May 2, 1994.
16. Command report: 107th TTC, 19 August 1950–31 March 1951. Command reports are slightly edited.
17. Letter, Fuqua to author, June 11, 1994.
18. Letter, Cowper to author, May 10, 1993, phone interview May 15, 1993.
19. *National Guardsman* Magazine, November 1951, p. 18.

CHAPTER 2: WE'RE GETTING READY TO GO TO KOREA

1. *National Guardsman* Magazine, May 1955, p. 6.
2. Ibid.
3. *Policy and Direction*, p. 122.
4. Letter, Finks to author, May 17, 1993.
5. Tillman P. Witt, *Moving On. The story of the 279th Infantry Regiment* (Oklahoma City: Monograph Number 2 in a series published by the 45th Infantry Division Museum, 1980), pp. 17–18, 25. Guy Nelson, *Thunderbird* (Oklahoma City: 45th Infantry Division Association 1970), p. 35. Hereafter *Thunderbird*.
6. Phone Interviews, March 12, and April 10, 1993.
7. Phone interviews, March 11, and March 29, 1993. Letter, Mueller to author, April 23, 1993.
8. Thomas S. Grodeci, "From Powder River to Ooyang. The 300th Armored Field Artillery in Korea" (Washington D.C.: Center of Military History, n.d.), pp. 23–24, hereafter "Powder River."

CHAPTER 3: KEEP ON TRUCKIN'

1. All dates for Korean service are from Department of the Army, General Order No. 80, November 22, 1954.
2. Charles Johnson, Jr., *African American Soldiers in the National Guard* (Westport, Conn.: Greenwood Press, 1992) pp. 177–179.
3. *The Forgotten War*, pp. 578–580, 592–604.
4. Ibid., p. 501.
5. *National Guardsman* Magazine, October 1951, p. 18.
6. 107th TTC unit history. Provided by Mr. H. C. Fortenberry, Haleyville, Ala..

CHAPTER 4: DISPLACE FORWARD THE GUNS

1. *The Forgotten War*, pp. 576–577 n.
2. Command reports: 176th AFAB, February; March, April 1951; *Pennsylvania Guardsman*, December 1951, p. 15.
3. Letter, Steffy to author, June 28, 1993.
4. *The Running Wounded*, p. 64.
5. Colonel Jack F. Diggs, U.S. Army (ret.) "The 142d Field Artillery 1889–1976." A history which includes: 2nd Arkansas Infantry; 936th Field Artillery Battalion; 937th Field Artillery Battalion (Fayetteville, Ark.: unpublished manuscript, 1976), p. 174, hereafter "142d Field Artillery."
6. Letter, Stinson to author, June 10, 1993.
7. *The Forgotten War*, pp. 789–790; Command report: 937th FAB, April 1951; 142d Field Artillery, pp. 221–222; *National Guardsman* Magazine, April 1988, article by Major General Bruce Jacobs (ret.), p. 50, hereafter Jacobs article.
8. Letter, Gatliff to author, May 5, 1993.
9. *The Forgotten War*, pp. 787–788, 799–800; 142d Field Artillery, p. 222; Command report: 937th FAB, April 1951; Jacobs article.
10. Colonel Joe Whitesides (ret.), *204th Field Artillery Battalion in Korea* (Bountiful, Utah: privately printed, n.d.), pp. 39–41, hereafter *204th Field Artillery*.

11. Letter, Kercheval to author, February 12, 1994.
12. Command report: 213th AFAB, April 1951.

CHAPTER 5: WE GOT THE FLOCK OUT OF THERE

1. Billy C. Mossman, *Ebb and Flow: November 1950–July 1951* (Washington, D.C.: Center of Military History, United States Army, 1990), p. 384, hereafter *Ebb and Flow*.
2. Letter, Cacciola to author, June 27, 1994.
3. Command report: 176th AFAB, April 1951; *The Forgotten War*, p. 827.
4. Command report: 936th FAB, April 1951; "142d Field Artillery," p. 177.
5. Command report: 937th FAB, April 1951; "142d Field Artillery," p. 223.
6. Letter, Gatliff to author, May 5, 1993.
7. 204th Field Artillery, pp. 43–46.
8. *The Forgotten War*, p. 828.
9. Letter, Steffy to author, October 4, 1993.
10. *The Forgotten War*, pp. 831–832.
11. Command report: 213th AFAB, April 1951; *Ebb and Flow*, p. 402.
12. Letter, Christensen to author, June 11, 1994.
13. Command report: 196th FAB, April 1951; *The Forgotten War*, pp. 832–833.
14. *Ebb and Flow*, pp. 436–437.

CHAPTER 6: THEY'LL NEVER GET OVER THAT HILL

1. *Ebb and Flow*, pp. 441–442.
2. Command report: 300th AFAB, May 1951; *The Running Wounded*, pp. 66–82; "Powder River," pp. 44–51.
3. *The Running Wounded*, p. 87.
4. Ibid., pp. 3, 87.
5. Command report: 196th FAB, May 1951.
6. *The Forgotten War*, pp. 883–886.
7. "Powder River,"p. 75.
8. *The Forgotten War*, pp. 893–899.
9. "Powder River," p. 77.
10. Ibid., pp. 79–82.
11. Command report: 213th AFAB, May 1951; Presidential Unit Citation. EUSAK General Orders Number 1014. 23 December 1951; *Richfield Reaper* newspaper, Richfield, Utah, August 15, 1990. A special 15 page section commemorating "A" Battery's mobilization. Not only informative it demonstrates the pride small towns have in their National Guard units. Several former members of the 213th sent copies of this paper to the author.
12. *The Forgotten War*, pp. 912–917.
13. Ibid., pp. 941–946, 950–955.
14. Letter, Kercheval to author, February 12, 1994.
15. Letter, Gatliff to author, May 5, 1993.
16. Letter, Cacciola to author, May 2, 1994.
17. Colonel Harry G. Summers (ret.), *Korean War Almanac* (New York: Facts on File, 1990), pp. 160–161, hereafter *Korean War Almanac*.
18. Letter, Kercheval to author, February 12, 1994.
19. *The Running Wounded*, p. 216; *Korean War Almanac*, p. 114.

CHAPTER 7: BRIDGES & ROADS

1. Kerry L. Diminyatz, "The 40th Infantry Division in the Korean Conflict: The Employment of the California National Guard in an Undeclared War." (A thesis Diminyatz wrote in 1990 while obtaining his master's degree, hereafter "40th Division in the Korean Conflict"), p.48.
2. Letter, Sheffield to author, June 3, 1993, p. 48.

 3. Letters, Fuqua to author, June 11, and July 9, 1994.
 4. Command report: 151st ECB, April 1951.
 5. Letter, Matteson to author, September 22, 1993.
 6. 116th ECB unit history. Provided by Colonel Richard Oliver (ret.), Tiburon, Calif.
 7. *National Guardsman* Magazine, August 1951, p. 15.
 8. Command report: 1092nd ECB, April 1951.
 9. 194th ECB unit history. Provided by Mr. George Warne, Oak Ridge, Tenn.
10. Letter, Warne to author, May 31, 1994.
11. *National Guardsman* Magazine, July 1951, p. 20.
12. Letter, Perron to author, February 7, 1994.
13. Letter, Sheffield to author, June 3, 1993.
14. *National Guardsman* Magazine, September 1951, p. 19.
15. Letter, McKee to author, August 3, 1994.
16. Letter, Vinson to author, July 15, 1994.
17. Letter, Matteson to author, April 14, 1994.

CHAPTER 8: FOR WANT OF A NAIL

 1. Russell F. Weigley, *History of the United States Army* (New York: The Macmillan Company, 1967), pp. 510–511.
 2. 106th Ordnance Company unit history. Provided by Mr. Harold L. Baker, Springfield, Mo.
 3. Letters, Bushart to author, April 28, and September 26, 1993.
 4. *National Guardsman* Magazine, April 1952, p. 17.
 5. 30th Ordnance Battalion Headquarters Detachment unit history. Provided by the New Jersey Department of Military and Veterans Affairs, Trenton, N.J.
 6. Letters, Cowper to author, October 1, and October 18, 1993.
 7. *National Guardsman* Magazine, September 1951, p. 18; John G. Westover, ed. *Combat Support in Korea* (Washington, D.C.: Combat Forces Press, 1955), pp. 93, 218.
 8. Induction and Release.

CHAPTER 9: THE THUNDERBIRDS

 1. Shelby Stanton, *Order of Battle U.S. Army, World War II* (Novato, Calif.: Presidio Press, 1984), pp. 112–113.
    The name "Thunderbirds" refers to the division shoulder insignia, a yellow bird of Indian design sewn on a red diamond shaped patch.
 2. *Thunderbird*, pp. 35, 105, 132.
 3. Ibid., p. 105.
 4. *Thunderbird*, pp. 105–106; *The Army Lineage Book*. Volume II, Infantry. (Washington, D.C.: Department of the Army, 1953), pp. 583–585.
 5. *45th Division News*. September 6, 1950, and April 1991, hereafter *45th News*.
 6. *Annual History Army Field Forces* 1950. Volume II. (Washington, D.C.: Department of the Army, page number illegible), hereafter *Army Field Forces*; *Thunderbird*, p. 107.
 7. Ibid.; various interviews.
 8. *Fort Polk*. Unofficial guide and directory. (San Diego: MARCOA Publishing, 1993).
 9. *45th News*, July 5, 1951, and September 20, 1951.
10. *The Forgotten War*, pp. 550, 623, 625, 639.
11. *Policy and Direction*, pp. 344–345.

CHAPTER 10: LIFE WAS GOOD ON HOKKAIDO

 1. *Army Field Forces*, page number illegible; *Thunderbird*, p. 108.
 2. Colonel James H. Weaver (ret.), *45th Division Training Regiment* (Oklahoma City: Monograph number 12, in a series published by the 45th Infantry Division Museum, 1989) pp. 2–5.
 3. *45th News*, May 31, 1951, and July 12, 1951.

4. Ibid., August 16, 1951.
5. Letter, Ray to author, February 16, 1994.
6. "40th Division in the Korean Conflict," pp. 50, 59.
7. *The Forgotten War*, pp. 941–946, 960.
8. Ibid., p. 960.
9. Phone interview with Brigadier General Rex Wilson (ret.), February 22, 1994.
10. Walter Hermes, *Truce Tent and Fighting Front* (Washington, D.C.: Office of the Chief of Military History, United States, Army, 1966), p. 202, hereafter *Truce Tent*.
11. Ibid., pp. 202–203. Some former Thunderbirds feel that Ridgway's reluctance to use them in Korea stemmed from an incident that occurred on Sicily during World War II. On the night of July 11, 1943, elements of Ridgway's 82nd Airborne Division parachuted on to Farello airfield. Due to a communications foul up they were taken under fire by Navy ships off shore, and troops on the island including the 45th. 318 aircrew and paratroopers were killed in the tragedy. Various interviews. Leroy Thompson, *The All Americans: The 82nd Airborne* (New York: Sterling Publishing Company, 1988) p. 38.
12. *Truce Tent*, pp. 202–203.
13. The use of the words "Up Front," here, and in the following two chapters are from the book of the same name by World War II Thunderbird Bill Mauldin. A New Mexico Guardsman, Mauldin received a Purple Heart in 1943, and a Pulitzer Prize in 1945. His classic cartoon characters Willie and Joe portray the life of the frontline infantryman better than any writer could ever hope to. Both *Up Front*, and *The Brass Ring*, Mauldin's story of his days with the 45th, are highly recommended.
14. "Order of Battle 45th US Infantry Division." (Washington, D.C.: Office of the Chief of Military History, United States Army, n.d.), p. 1. Hereafter "45th Order of Battle."

CHAPTER 11: UP FRONT AGAIN

1. "45th Order of Battle," p. 1.
2. From an article in the February 1956 issue of *Saga* Magazine, by Bruce Jacobs. At this time Jacobs was a free lance writer and a 2nd lieutenant in the 50th Armored Division (New Jersey). Today, Major General Bruce Jacobs (ret.) is Historian Emeritus of the National Guard Association.
3. "45th Order of Battle," p. 1.
4. Ibid.
5. Ibid., pp. 1–2.
6. Ibid., p. 2.

CHAPTER 12: OUTPOST EERIE

1. Omer L. Manley, *Hands Up* (New York: Carlton Press Inc., 1978), pp. 7–11, hereafter *Hands Up*; Russell A. Gugeler, *Combat Actions in Korea* (Washington, D.C.: Center of Military History, United States Army, 1987), pp. 222–235.
2. Letter from Major General Fred Daugherty (ret.) to General Edwin H. Burba, Jr., November 27, 1990, describing the Outpost Eerie battle. Copy given author by General Daugherty, November 14, 1993.
3. Ibid.; phone conversation with General Daugherty, February 26, 1994; *Hands Up*, pp. 12–13.
4. Stevens neglects to mention that he received the Silver Star for his actions that night.
5. *National Guardsman* Magazine, June 1952, p. 14.
6. "45th Order of Battle," p. 2.
7. Ibid. p. 3., *45th News*, April 1991.

8. First Lieutenant Bernard F. Brown, *The Thunderbird*. A 45th Division History, 2nd ed. A history prepared by the division in 1954. p. 15.
9. Ibid., pp. 16–17.
10. "45th Order of Battle," pp. 3–5.
11. Ibid., p. 9.
12. *U.S. Army 45th Infantry Division*. Author and date unknown. (Found at Carlisle Barracks, PA), p. 8.

CHAPTER 13: KOREA REVISITED

1. *The History Team, the 40th Infantry Division*. 40th Infantry Division the Years of World War II (Baton Rouge, La.: Army and Navy Publishing Company, 1947), p. 144.
2. Ibid., pp. 151–156.
3. Ibid., pp. 171–176.; Charlie Maher and Bill Paterson, *Fortieth in Review* (Tokyo, 40th Signal Company, 1952). A yearbook style publication telling the division's history from mobilization through the day the division left Japan for Korea, p. 2, hereafter *Review*.
4. Ibid., pp.3–4.; "40th Division in the Korean Conflict," pp. 31–33.
5. *Policy and Direction*, p. 124.
6. Unit Strength figures for all mobilized Guard Units vary greatly from source to source. In the case of the 40th Infantry Division, four different sources have a variation of over 600 men. The number cited is from page "a" of a pamphlet put out by the division June 15, 1951, hereafter Pamphlet.
7. *National Guardsman* Magazine, February 1951, p. 2.
8. Vandenberg AFB fact sheet, 1992; "40th Division in the Korean Conflict," pp. 36–37; *Review*, p. 8; *Los Angeles Examiner*, September 8, 1950, hereafter *Examiner*.
9. Pamphlet, page "a".
10. *The Forgotten War*, pp. 250–251.
11. Pamphlet, page "a"; *National Guardsman* Magazine, January 1985, p. 40.
12. Pamphlet, pp. "a" and "b", McClanahan, Parker, Samples, Stafford, interviews.
13. *Review*, foreword to book, no p.n.
14. "40th Division in the Korean Conflict," pp. 38–39; McClanahan interview.
15. "40th Division in the Korean Conflict," p. 40.
16. *National Guardsman* Magazine, March 1951, p. 12.

CHAPTER 14: NO, WE'RE FROM CALIFORNIA

1. Pamphlet, pp. 11–12.
2. *Examiner*, February 28, 1951; *Army Field Forces*, page number illegible.
3. *Review*, p. 54.
4. Pamphlet, pp. "b" and 3.
5. Ibid., pp. 5–6.
6. Ibid., pp. 5 and 16–20; "40th Division in the Korean Conflict," pp. 43–44.
7. *National Guardsman* Magazine, May 1951, p. 19.
8. "40th Division in the Korean Conflict," pp. 46–47; *Review*, pp. 88–97.
9. Letter, Erckenbrack to author, April 26, 1993. Phone interview April 26, 1993.
10. Letter, McClanahan to author, May 6, 1993.
11. Phone interview, May 15, 1993.
12. *Examiner*, April 20, 1951; *Review*, p. 172.
13. "40th Division in the Korean Conflict," pp. 49–50.
14. Ibid., pp. 50–52; *Examiner*, July 12, and July 14, 1951. Phone interview with Major General Donald N. Moore (ret.), May 5, 1993. General Moore commanded the 1st and 3rd Battalions, 160th Infantry Regiment, during the Korean War.
15. "40th Division in the Korean Conflict," pp. 52–53. *Examiner*, August 25, and 28, 1951.
16. *Review*, pp. 133–162.

CHAPTER 15: WE GO NEXT

1. *Review*, p. 214.
2. Ibid., pp. 214–215.
3. "Order of Battle 40th U.S. Infantry Division" (Washington, D.C.: Office of the Chief of Military History, United States Army, n.d.), p.2, hereafter "40th Order of Battle."
4. *Pacific Stars and Stripes*. The *Stars and Stripes* articles used as references were found in an old scrapbook. The dates had been cut off when the articles were clipped out, hereafter *Stars and Stripes*.
5. Letter, Pressey to Mr. Dale Reilley. Copy furnished by Mr. Reilley and used with Mr. Pressey's permission, hereafter Pressey letter.
6. *Stars and Stripes*.
7. Ibid.
8. Letter, Finks to author, May 17, 1993.
9. *National Guardsman* Magazine, August 1952, p. 11.
10. Letter, Erckenbrack to author, May 27, 1994.

CHAPTER 16: THERE'S 500 DEAD IN THE VALLEY

1. "40th Order of Battle," p.2.
2. Various interviews.
3. Pressey letter.
4. Letter, Finks to author, May 17, 1993.
5. Ibid.
6. "40th Division in the Korean Conflict," pp. 110–112.
7. *National Guardsman* Magazine, August 1953, p. 5.
8. "40th Order of Battle," pp. 3–8.
9. Letter, DeRosa to author, May 9,1994.

CHAPTER 17: LATE ARRIVALS

1. 32nd Ordnance Battalion Headquarters and Headquarters Detachment unit history. Provided by the Illinois Nation Guard, Springfield, Ill.
2. *Pennsylvania Guardsman*, June 1952, p. 7.
3. From a tape provided by Colonel Kelly, February 1, 1994. Phone interview March 4, 1994. Colonel Arthur L. Kelly USA (ret.), *Washington County, Kentucky, Bicentennial History 1792–1992* (Paducah, Ky.: Turner Publishing Company, 1994), pp. 110–112. Provided by the Kentucky National Guard, Frankfort, Ky.
4. Ibid.
5. *Pennsylvania Guardsman*, September 1952, p. 32.
6. Letter, Sikes to author, March 7, 1994.
7. Command reports, 235th FAOB, 1951–1952.
8. Letter, Prosetti to author, June 21, 1994.

CHAPTER 18: STACK ARMS

1. Major General Robert H. Appleby (ret.), *The 131st Transportation Truck Company* "From Mobilization thru Korea" (Mechanicsburg, Pa.: privately printed, 1990) pp. 13–14.
2. *National Guardsman Magazine*, March 1952, p. 2.
3. Various interviews.
4. *Ebb and Flow*, p. 365; *National Guardsman* Magazine, March 1952, p. 2.
5. *45th News*, April 4, 1952.
6. Letters, Ellis to author, April 4, and April 16, 1994.
7. Designated unit command reports.
8. Letter, Sikes to author, March 7, 1994.
9. *Korean War Almanac*, p. 229.

10. *National Guardsman* Magazine, June 1952, p. 2.
11. Induction and Release.
12. Various interviews.
13. The "Ruptured Duck" refers to the Honorable Service Badge given to discharged veterans at the end of World War II.

EPILOGUE

1. Kenneth Anderson, *U.S. Military Operations 1945–1985* (New York: The Military Press, 1984), p. 96; *The Minute Man*, p. 548; *National Guardsman* Magazine January 1963, p. 10.; May 1964, p. 22.
2. Ibid., August 1985, p. 40.
3. Provided by the National Guard Bureau, Historical Services, Falls Church, Va.
4. Annual Review of the Chief, National Guard Bureau, 1991.
5. *National Guardsman* Magazine, February 1994, p. 10.
6. Ibid., April 1994, p. 73.
7. Ibid., January 1994, p. 8, and March 1994, p. 12.

BIBLIOGRAPHY

PRIMARY SOURCES

The primary sources of this book are the sixty-six personal interviews, and the twenty-six written narratives. Without these there would be no book. The dates of the written narratives are listed in the endnotes. The dates and locations of the interviews are listed below. In many instances the interviews and narratives were followed up by one or more letters and/or phone calls.

INTERVIEWS

Date	Name	Location
07/25/92	GEORGE NITIS	SPARKS, NEV.
07/25/92	EMMETT BENJAMIN	SPARKS, NEV.
09/09/92	MIKE GALLEGOS	STOCKTON, CALIF.
09/11/92	ROLFE GLASHAN	SACRAMENTO, CALIF.
10/02/92	AMON BAUMGARTEN	OAKLAND, CALIF.
11/12/92	ERIC HANSEN	SACRAMENTO, CALIF.
11/16/92	DONN STAFFORD	SACRAMENTO, CALIF.
11/27/92	ED STROM	SACRAMENTO, CALIF.
12/03/92	WARREN ZIMMERMAN	MODESTO, CALIF.
12/05/92	HESTER PARKER	SACRAMENTO, CALIF.
12/17/92	ROBERT APPLEBY	CARLISLE, PA.
12/17/92	CARL BOHR, SR.	PINE GROVE, PA.
12/17/92	HARRY SHOLLENBERGER	PINE GROVE, PA.
12/17/92	THOMAS TOBIAS	PINE GROVE, PA.
12/17/92	EUGENE WOLFE	PINE GROVE, PA.
12/17/92	BERT YODER	PINE GROVE, PA.

12/22/92	BEDFORD BENTLEY	BALTIMORE, MD.
12/22/92	JOSEPH BRACY	BALTIMORE, MD.
12/22/92	GEORGE BROOKS	BALTIMORE, MD.
12/22/92	JOHN HOLT, SR.	BALTIMORE, MD.
12/22/92	LESTER HUDGINS	BALTIMORE, MD.
12/22/92	SIMON PORTER	BALTIMORE, MD.
01/27/93	CALVIN SAMPLES	VALLEJO, CALIF.
02/05/93	NORMAN KING	LODI, CALIF.
02/22/93	LEO CURTIN	NOVATO, CALIF.
02/22/93	DON McCLANAHAN	NOVATO, CALIF.
03/16/93	DARCE EMERSON	MANTECA, CALIF.
03/24/93	RALPH STOCKWELL	PASO ROBLES, CALIF.
03/25/93	DAVE MATTESON	GREENBRAE, CALIF.
04/03/93	EARL HUMMELL	SACRAMENTO, CALIF.
04/08/93	RAYMOND KOMMEL	PASO ROBLES, CALIF.
04/08/93	FLOYD MOODY	CANBRIA, CALIF.
04/19/93	RICHARD OLIVER	TIBURON, CALIF.
06/11/93	ROBERT HOLTBY	RESEDA, CALIF.
06/11/93	CLAUDE ALLISON	MARINA DEL REY, CALIF.
06/12/93	TOM BRINKLEY	HAWTHORNE, CALIF.
06/12/93	FRANK SARIÑANA	AZUSA, CALIF.
06/13/93	THOMAS TILLMAN	COVINA, CALIF.
06/14/93	T. K. TURNAGE	RANCHO MIRAGE, CALIF.
06/14/93	JAMES GRIFFITH	TEMPLE CITY, CALIF.
06/15/93	JESS CARRANZA, JR.	LOS ALIMITOS, CALIF.
06/15/93	BUDDY HALL	SANTA BARBARA, CALIF.
10/06/93	RONALD RANSOM	SACRAMENTO, CALIF.
10/30/93	REX WILSON	OKLAHOMA CITY, OKLA.
10/31/93	WOODY HARRIS	STILLWATER, OKLA.
11/01/93	EDDIE COPE	OKLAHOMA CITY, OKLA.
11/01/93	VERNON RIBERA	EDMOND, OKLA.
11/02/93	JODY MCLAIN	OKLAHOMA CITY, OKLA.
11/02/93	CHARLES RICE	OKLAHOMA CITY, OKLA.
11/03/93	JERRY HARBERT	OKLAHOMA CITY, OKLA.
11/03/93	TOMMY HAWKINS	EDMOND, OKLA.
11/03/93	WELDON JACKSON	OKLAHOMA CITY, OKLA.
11/04/93	FRANK BOYER	OKLAHOMA CITY, OKLA.
11/04/93	JIMMY TERRY	NORMAN, OKLA.
11/05/93	GEORGE BEWLEY	OKLAHOMA CITY, OKLA.
11/05/93	ROBERT FAKEN	OKLAHOMA CITY, OKLA.
11/06/93	GUY WILKERSON	BENTONVILLE, ARK.
11/06/93	BILL CATLETT	BONNEVILLE, ARK.
11/07/93	FRED DAUGHERTY	OKLAHOMA CITY, OKLA.
11/08/93	EMMETT STEEDS	OKLAHOMA CITY, OKLA.
11/09/93	BILL MARTIN	OKLAHOMA CITY, OKLA.
11/09/93	CARL STEVENS	OKLAHOMA CITY, OKLA.
11/09/93	CHARLES BROWN	OKLAHOMA CITY, OKLA.
11/10/93	JOHN PETERS	OKLAHOMA CITY, OKLA.

05/23/94   HARRY NELSON   LANCASTER, CALIF.
05/24/94   DAVID HARRIS   SANTA MARIA, CALIF.

ARCHIVAL SOURCES

The Citizen-Soldier Museum Archives, Sacramento, Calif. A scrapbook of
    newspaper clippings from the *Los Angeles Examiner*, and *Pacific Stars
    & Stripes*, telling of the 40th Infantry Division from mobilization through
    their first month of Korean combat. A collection of *National Guardsman*
    Magazines published 1950-1995. The Army Lineage Book. Volume II,
    Infantry.
U.S. Army Center of Military History, Washington, D.C. A copy of General
    Order No. 80.
The National Archives depository at the Federal Records Center, Suitland,
    Md. The unit command reports are located here.
The 45th Infantry Division Museum Archives, Oklahoma City, Okla. Infor-
    mation on the 45th Infantry Division, and the Oklahoma Guardsmen
    who were mobilized in 1950.
The U.S. Army Military History Institute at Carlisle Barracks, Pa. Order of
    Battle 40th and 45th Infantry Divisions. Annual History Army Field
    Forces 1950. Miscellaneous Information.
Some of the State National Guard Public Information Offices were very
    helpful in supplying mobilization records or the names of men that
    might be of assistance. Unfortunately some did not respond at all, or
    said that requested information was classified. Of particular help were
    the PIOs of Alabama, Illinois, Kentucky, Mississippi, New Jersey, and
    Tennessee.

UNPUBLISHED OR PRIVATELY PRINTED SOURCES

Appleby, Major General Robert (ret.) *The 131st Transportation Truck Com-
    pany "From Mobilization Thru Korea."* 1990.
Brown, Bernard F. *The Thunderbird.* A 45th Division History, 2nd ed.1954.
Diggs, Colonel Jack F. U.S. Army (ret.) "The 142d Field Artillery 1889–
    1976." A history which includes: 2nd Arkansas Infantry; 936th Field
    Artillery Battalion; 937th Field Artillery Battalion. 1976.
Diminyatz, Kerry L. "The 40th Infantry Division in the Korean Conflict:
    The Employment of the California National Guard in an Undeclared
    War. 1990.
Grodeci, Thomas S. "From Powder River to Soyang: The 300th Armored
    Field Artillery in Korea." n.d.
Whitesides, Colonel Joe (ret.) *204th Field Artillery Battalion in Korea.* n.d.
30th Ordnance Battalion Headquarters and Headquarters Detachment
    unit history. Provided by the New Jersey Department of Military and
    Veterans affairs.
32nd Ordnance Battalion Headquarters and Headquarters Detachment
    unit history. Provided by the Illinois National Guard.
106th Ordnance Company unit history. Provided by Mr. Harold L. Baker.
107th Transportation Truck Company unit history and unit command
    report. Provided by Mr. H. C. Fortenberry.

116th Engineer Combat Battalion unit history. Provided by Colonel Richard Oliver (ret.)

194th Engineer Combat Battalion unit history. Provided by Mr. George Warne.

OTHER SOURCES NOT MENTIONED ELSEWHERE

Mr. Bob Faken, Ponca City, Okla. A collection of the 45th Infantry News, newspapers, 1950–1952.

Major General Bruce Jacobs (ret.) Copies of articles he had written, a set of the 45th Infantry Division monographs, and a number of names of people to contact.

Lieutenant Colonel Ralph Mueller (ret.) A collection of *Pennsylvania Guardsman* Magazines, 1949–1954.

BOOKS

Compared to the immense volume of books on World War II, and on Vietnam, the number of published works on the Korean War are minuscule. For any study of the Korean War two books are indispensable. They are:

Blair, Clay. *The Forgotten War*. New York: Times Books a Division of Random House, 1987.

Summers, Colonel Harry G., Jr. (ret.) *Korean War Almanac*. New York: Facts on File, Inc., 1990.

Two books written by National Guardsmen on their Korean experiences are:

Day, William W. IV. *The Running Wounded*. 4019 Prestwick Place, Riverton Wyo. 82501. 1990.

Manley, Omer L. *Hands Up*. New York: Carlton Press Inc., 1978.

Other works that were referred to:

Anderson, Kenneth. *U.S. Military Operation 1945–1985*. New York: The Military Press, 1984.

Gugeler, Russell A. *Combat Actions in Korea*. Washington, D.C.: Center of Military History, United States Army, 1987.

Hermes, Walter G. *U.S. Army in the Korean War: Truce Tent and Fighting Front*. Washington, D.C.: General Printing Office, 1966.

Hill, Jim Dan. *The Minute Man in Peace and War*. Harrisburg, Pa.: The Stackpole Company, 1964.

Johnson, Charles, Jr. *African American Soldiers in the National Guard*. Westport, Conn.: Greenwood Press, 1992.

Maher, Charlie and Bill Peterson. *Fortieth in Review*. Tokyo: 40th Signal Company, 1952.

Mahon, John. *History of the Militia and the National Guard*. New York: Macmillan Publishing, A division of Macmillan, 1983.

Mesko, Jim. *Armor in Korea - A Pictorial History*. Carrollton, Texas: Squadron/Signal Publications, 1984.

Mossman, Billy C. *U.S. Army in the Korean War: Ebb and Flow*. November 1950–July 1951. Washington, D.C.: General Printing Office, 1990.

Nelson, Guy. *Thunderbird: A History of the 45th Infantry Division*. Oklahoma City: 45th Infantry Division Association, 1970.

Rees, David. *Korea: The Limited War*. New York: St. Martins Press, 1964.

Schnabel, James F. *U.S. Army in the Korean War: Policy and Direction*: The First *Year*. Washington, D.C.: General Printing Office, 1972.

Stanton, Shelby. Order of Battle U.S. Army, World War II. Novato, Calif.: Presidio Press, 1984.

———. *U.S. Army Uniform of the Korean War*. Harrisburg, Pa.: Stackpole Books, 1992.

The History Team, The 40th Infantry Division. 40th Infantry Division the Years of World War II. Baton Rouge, La.: Army and Navy Publishing Company, 1947.

Thompson, Leroy. *The All Americans, The 82nd Airborne*. New York: Sterling Publishing, 1988.

Weigley, Russell F. *History of the United States Army*. New York: The Macmillan Company, 1967.

Westover, John G., ed. *Combat Support in Korea*. Washington, D.C.: Combat Forces Press, 1955.

INDEXES

GENERAL INDEX

This is a general subject and name index. Indexes of National Guardsmen and men assigned to National Guard units, and a unit index follow.

285

THE NATIONAL GUARDSMEN AND THE MEN ASSIGNED TO NATIONAL GUARD UNITS

An extensive search was made by the author to determine the first names of the men listed below. Twelve names could not be found.

INDEX OF MILITARY UNITS

British
British Brigade, 51
Gloucester Battalion, 51
45th British Field Artillery Regiment, 51

British Commonwealth
27th Commonwealth Brigade, 66
16th New Zealand Artillery Regiment, 52, 66

Korea, Republic of (ROK)
II Corps, 223
Capitol Division, 223
1st Division, 80
2nd Division, 233
5th Division, 68,73
6th Division, 61-62, 66, 223
7th Division, 73
9th Division, 83, 144-45, 152
19th Regiment, 67
27th FAB, 52
30th FAB, 83

Philippines
20th Infantry BCT, 168, 171

Turkey
Turkish Brigade, 38, 57, 152

United States
AIR NATIONAL GUARD

AEROMEDICAL EVACUATION SQUADRONS
118th, 262

AIRLIFT WINGS
123rd, 262

FIGHTER GROUPS
124th, 262
169th, 262
174th, 262
175th, 262
185th, 262

MILITARY AIRLIFT GROUPS
172nd, 261

ARMY UNITS
(NATIONAL GUARD, REGULAR, RESERVE)

ANTIAIRCRAFT BATTALIONS
104th, 251-52
140th, 181, 191-92, 197-98, 211, 222, 225
145th, 136
213th, 237-38
712th, 2, 244
739th, 245
773rd, 3, 243-45
865th, 244

ARMIES
Sixth, 71, 194, 232
Eighth, x, 22, 26n, 36, 40, 50, 52, 74, 79-80, 145, 172, 253
    and National Guard replacements, xi, 250

BRIGADES
Constabulary, 5
69th Infantry, 261
196th Artillery, 262

COMMANDS
Far East Command (FECOM), 19, 135
2nd Logistical, 237

CORPS
I, 21, 29, 43, 58, 66, 71, 79-80, 91, 165
    N.G. units assigned to, or by, 27, 40-41, 46, 52, 54, 84-85, 95-96, 108, 241
IX, 29, 69, 79, 108
    N.G. units assigned to, or by, 27, 41, 52, 61, 66, 84-85, 92, 95, 104, 211, 233
X, 29, 69, 72, 75, 79, 91
    N.G. units assigned to, or by, 37, 40-41, 52, 68, 71, 84-85, 90, 172, 233, 238, 241
DIVISIONS
82nd Airborne, 6-7, 111, 232
2nd Armored, 6
49th Armored, 261
1st Cavalry, 2, 20, 32, 135-40, 166
1st Infantry, 5, 19, 111
2nd Infantry, xii, 5, 36-37, 40, 71, 74-75, 90, 259
3rd Infantry, 29, 37, 46-47, 51, 57-60, 74-75, 122, 145
7th Infantry, x, xii, 7, 29, 68, 74
24th Infantry, 2, 32, 66, 132, 186, 225, 229-30